To Alice, Katie,
Jake.

Go Blue!

# THE BIG HOUSE

## Fielding H. Yost and the Building of Michigan Stadium

### Robert M. Soderstrom

HURON
RIVER
PRESS

Campus map by Bruce Worden

10 9 8 7 6 5 4 3 2

Printed in the United States of America.

Huron River Press
308½ South State Street
Suite 30
HURON
RIVER
PRESS
Ann Arbor, MI 48104
www.huronriverpress.com

LIBRARY OF CONGRESS CATALOGING-IN-PUBLICATION DATA

Soderstrom, Robert M., 1947-
  The Big House : Fielding H. Yost and the building of Michigan
Stadium / Robert M. Soderstrom.
     p. cm.
  ISBN 1-932399-11-9
  1. Michigan Stadium (Ann Arbor. Mich.)--History. 2. Michi-
gan Wolverines (Football team)--History. I. Title.
  GV416.M53S63 2005
  796.332'63'0977435--dc22
                                        2005019690

*To my children*

*Sara, Paul, and Lance*

*True Blue, every one*

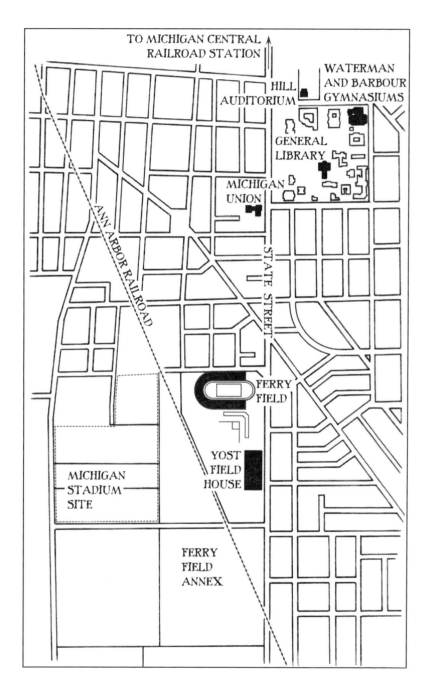

**Campus Map 1922**

# Contents

# Acknowledgements

A completed book of this magnitude, written not as a full-time project, but rather as time permitted, owes much to many. First and foremost, I am perpetually indebted to my brother, William R. Soderstrom of Milwaukee, who, with much patience and intelligence, served as my primary editor. This book is much better for his gentle, but important suggestions.

The staff at the University's Bentley Historical Library was very helpful and supportive from the first day I appeared there. The library is a great university asset and well served by the professionals who work there. In particular, I would like to express my gratitude to Karen Jania and Malgosia Myc who were invariably able to answer every reference question I could conceive. I am also appreciative of the help provided by Nancy Holler, Danville Public Library, Susan Richter, Vermilion County Library, and Hershall E. Lee, historian of the Curtis G. Redden American Legion Post 210, all of Danville, Illinois.

Bruce Madej, assistant athletic director at the University of Michigan, provided critical support when this project was in the formative stages. His encouragement and assistance was crucial to making this effort a reality.

Many friends provided important suggestions as the chapters unfolded. I am particularly indebted to Dr. Jim and Darlene

Christner, Peter Levine, Phil Olson, Dr. Wayne Swart, and Dr. Charlie and Kathy Wessels.

Finally, my greatest cheering section has been my family. My father, an inveterate Illini, nonetheless read every line with verve. My children, Sara, Paul and Lance, and son-in-law, Tom, endured innumerable Yost stories whenever I emerged from the library. My wife, Susan, perhaps deserves most credit for bringing this book to reality. Whenever the project seemed overwhelming, the sources too difficult to find, or the effort beyond the time available, Susan would gently but firmly put me back to work.

The greatest debt of all, of course, is owed to the incomparable University of Michigan community of which I have been so privileged to be a member since 1968.

Robert M. Soderstrom, M.D.
Grand Blanc, Michigan
May, 2005

# Foreword

As the twentieth century came to a close, spectator sport had seen more than its share of legends and visionaries. Yet, when the plethora of names are bandied about, few would argue with the genius of "Meeshegan's" Fielding H. Yost. Broadcaster Bob Ufer immortalized the linguistic turn in the Michigan pronunciation, but that was the way Yost would refer to our university.

Whatever Yost did, it would be of epic and legendary status.

As a football coach, he was magnificent. He was heralded for being the first football coach to use the forward pass as a legitimate offensive weapon. He initiated the "quick-start" offense, earning for himself the nickname of "Hurry-up," but also he used the first linebacker and was the first to use a fake kick. From 1901 to 1905, Yost's Wolverine football teams went 55-1-1 and scored 2,821 points, giving up only 42.

In 1904, the Wolverines defeated West Virginia 130-0. When the West Virginians returned home, *The Daily New Dominion* of Morgantown interviewed them and reported: "It was declared that every player on Yost's team weighed eight tons and had an average speed of 96 miles an hour…One player said he was plucked up in the air and thrown over the head of a creature which was at least 100 feet high and had eight pairs of arms."

But that was just the start of the legend.

While Yost had no football players who could run 96 miles an hour, possessed eight pairs of arms, or grew to 100 feet, his expectations were enormous for himself, his football team and his university.

As an athletic director, he was truly visionary.

Forty years after he came to Michigan from Stanford, Yost retired from his epic career as athletic director, having built a magnificent athletic plan that would set the tone for over a century of sports in Ann Arbor.

He built the first field house of its kind in the country and then the first intramural building. Yost enticed the legendary Scottish golf architect, Alister Mackenzie, to design the university's golf course. And, of course, he designed a legendary football stadium —one that could seat 75,000, but with footings in place to eventually double the capacity of Michigan Stadium.

No one could envision the incredible crowds Yost believed would come to a Wolverine football game. Yost conceived Michigan Stadium when there were few automobiles, freeways were non-existent and there was little travel. But he knew fans would find a way to attend football games—and especially to watch his beloved Michigan Wolverines.

Michigan can proudly claim four athletic icons, a mark very few universities can match. Fielding H. Yost, Fritz Crisler, Don Canham and Bo Schembechler were giants on the national sports scene decade after decade, but without a visionary like Yost, Michigan as we now know it would not be the same. This book relates in great and wonderful detail a critical period in Yost's career at Michigan, a time when many of his dreams for the university became reality.

He started the great athletic tradition that 'Meeshegan' men and women of today know and love. He was the first true Michigan Man.

Bruce Madej
Assistant Athletic Director
University of Michigan
Ann Arbor, MI
May, 2005

# Chapter 1

# The Prologue

Perfectly nestled in the hills of Ann Arbor, Michigan, lies the 111,000 seat University of Michigan football stadium. Known throughout the college football world as "The Big House," it is the largest university owned stadium in America, loved and revered by Wolverines everywhere. The place is an awesome edifice, whether filled to capacity with ardent football fans or completely empty at dusk on a summer evening. There may not be a more ideally arranged football field anywhere.

The stadium is the common ground upon which the whole university comes together. Students from all the colleges, alumni from all walks of life, and faculty and administrators all share a common experience at this place. Often it is one they talk about for weeks, sometimes one they talk about for years, and it is a shared happening that binds the university community like no other.

Of course, such events occur at universities all across the country, but it is not just the games played that make Michigan Stadium so unique. It is, too, ever so much, the place. The amphitheater is itself a memorable event. Many a Michigan fan can describe in detail the first time their eyes beheld the massive arena that celebrates maize and blue football.

There are memorial stadiums, double-decked ones and horseshoes, but no structure supersedes the simple yet beautiful symmetry of Michigan Stadium. It is a place worth knowing, a place worth contemplating, either with 100,000 others or by oneself. Every Wolverine knows this. Others know it, too. Michigan Stadium is one of the major tourist attractions in southeast Michigan; it is the number one attraction in Ann Arbor.

Most importantly, it is the legendary home of the Michigan Wolverines, the winningest football program in America. For a quarter of a century, every home appearance of the famed maize and blue squad has packed Michigan Stadium with more than 100,000 fans, a record equaled nowhere else.

But how did the stadium come about? What is the story behind the building of this honored place? Many a legend has been told and re-told by Michigan adherents, but to learn the full story one must begin with 1922, that most memorable year in Michigan football history.

At that time, Michigan's football fortunes were still in the hands of a remarkable and forceful innovator, Fielding H. Yost. By 1922, Yost had coached the Michigan football team for over 20 years. Virtually from the day of his arrival in Ann Arbor, Yost was a Wolverine legend. His first team in 1901 scored 550 points to none for the opponents. In 1901, 1902, 1903, 1904 and 1905, Michigan teams completely dominated opponents, earning the moniker of point-a-minute teams for the number of times they scored more than 60 points in a game. This was when Yost became known by the nickname, "Hurry-up." There was no huddle in those days, and Yost urged his teams on offense to jump up after every down, hurry to the line of scrimmage, and put the ball in play before defenses could adjust. Yost, only 30 years old in 1901, was quickly recognized as one of the great innovators of the game.

But a coach is only as good as his last game, and by 1922 the Yost legend had become somewhat tarnished. For a variety of reasons, many having to do with Yost's incredible successes, the Western Conference (the forerunner of the Big Ten) laid down a series of new rules in 1906. Many of them seemed to be aimed at

Michigan and her coach. As a result, and following considerable debate, Michigan elected to leave the conference in 1907. The Western Conference then passed a rule that no team in the conference could play against a team that had once been in the conference and left. Of course, since the rule applied only to Michigan, the Wolverines had to look elsewhere for competition. For 10 years, Michigan played mostly against eastern teams, trying to cultivate rivalries with schools like Penn, Syracuse, and Cornell.

Finally, in 1918, Michigan elected to re-join the Western Conference. That football season was abruptly discontinued because of the terrible influenza epidemic that swept the country. Public health authorities put a stop to the gathering of large crowds for fear of spreading the disease. As a result, Michigan played only five games that year, but was undefeated, beating two Big Ten teams, Chicago and Ohio State.

However, the 1919 season was the source of much distress in Ann Arbor. Yost had coached 18 seasons at Michigan and never had a losing season until 1919, but that record didn't protect him from those who always expected to be victors. Not only did Michigan go 3 and 4, but the Wolverines lost nearly every Big Ten game. Beating only Northwestern, Michigan lost to Ohio State, Chicago,

*Fielding H. Yost*

Photo courtesy of Bentley Historical Library, The University of Michigan

Illinois and Minnesota. The last game, against the Gophers, was an embarrassing 34-7 loss on Michigan's home field. No one could remember such a season.

Rumors circulated that Yost might leave coaching. Doubts were expressed about his ability to coach the modern game of "open" football. His critics acknowledged that Yost was a master of the old rugby-like football where players advanced the ball by running and kicking it down the field. In 1901, the game had no forward pass and football was dominated by runs into the line. The forward pass clearly made the game more "open" by providing the offense a variety of options for moving the ball. Teams began to design running plays that moved left or right about the ends and took advantage of the ability to fake a pass. These changes greatly challenged defensive strategists. Detractors claimed Yost didn't seem to understand this new game. Criticism became more specific. Yost didn't substitute enough. He favored fraternity men too much. He could beat the little teams, but couldn't consistently win against real competition. Critics pointed out that his record against perennial powers Penn was 4-6-2 and Cornell, 3-4. Against the major eastern teams, he only had a winning record of 5-4-1 against Syracuse during the time Michigan was out of the Western Conference.

Fielding Yost's response to this debacle was to rededicate himself to Michigan and to the program. Interviewed by the *Michigan Daily* in 1919, he said,

> The spirit here at the University must be renovated. We have got to have the spirit of service…We must have the willingness upon the part of the men who make up the football team to work, not for one year, but for three years to get a place on the squad. A winning team is not composed of men who are novices at the game…We're lacking in the spirit that sends 75 men out for football every afternoon all during the season…Out of the 6000 men on the campus this fall only 37 men eligible for the Varsity reported on Ferry Field…I hope that we can develop a

better spirit before next year, one that is substantial. Too many men think that when they attend a mass meeting or a game and cheer for the team that they are doing their duty towards the University. Yelling does not win an athletic contest…What we need now is more material support in the form of men down on the field in moleskins. Every Michigan man owes his University a duty of service.[1]

Yost made a plea to the inter-fraternity council to get the best men out for football and to keep them academically eligible. He redoubled his efforts with alumni organizations to find promising athletes and bring them to campus. His assertion that "every Michigan man owes his University a duty of service" became a fervent motto for both students and alumni.

Modest improvement was seen in 1920 when Michigan went 2-2 in the Big Ten. In 1921, Michigan was expected to introduce a strong team, but all hopes were shattered in the first Big Ten game of the season. Before 45,000 fans in Ann Arbor, at that time the largest crowd ever to see a game in the Midwest, Michigan fell to Ohio State, 14-0. The Buckeyes were already considered Michigan's "dearest enemy"[2] and this was their third victory in a row over the Wolverines. Prior to 1919, Ohio State had never beaten Michigan in 15 attempts, but the Buckeyes won in 1919, 1920, and now in 1921. Despair engulfed the Ann Arbor campus. A letter to the *Daily* proclaimed, "Yost is no longer capable of directing the active training of our football squad. He has been a great coach. We lift our hats to his past achievements and glory in his success. But his day is done. Someone else must take his place."[3]

The Grand Rapids Alumni Association could tolerate the situation no longer. Following the 1921 season, they passed a resolution calling for Yost's replacement. In response, a Michigan newspaper editor was moved to write:

---

[1] *Michigan Daily*, 11/23/19, p 1
[2] *Michigan Daily*, 10/4/22, p 6
[3] *Michigan Daily*, 10/26/21, p 3

It is difficult to see just what Michigan alumni want.

The criticism that the Michigan coach plays favorites is too foolish to deny. Anyone with the slightest acquaintance with Fielding H. Yost knows that he is too big a man to let personal feelings influence his picking a team. No alumnus wants a winning team any worse than the big coach. He wouldn't give any more than his right eye for a real championship. To accuse him of deliberately keeping a man on the side-lines when a poorer man is playing on the team is to accuse him of being an imbecile.

The football public, from undergraduates to the public in general, fail to take into account the greatest factor of football—the boys on the team. They forget the teams are made up of mere boys of an average age between 18 and 20. A coach may have his team in the pink of condition, thoroughly grounded in knowledge of the game and perfect in its execution of his particular offensive plays, yet once the boys are on the field of play, he has no control over their actions. They are boys and they make mistakes; mistakes mean lost games and when games are lost the coach is blamed…

Coach Yost ranks as one of the big coaches of the country. It is extremely doubtful if any other coach could have made more of a team out of his material this fall than he did. With a little football luck Michigan would have won from Ohio State, and to a coach "football luck" means that the nineteen year old boys he is working with shall function like a machine. It is to their credit and the coach's if they do work like a machine even in one game.[4]

In fact, Yost retained significant support. Hundreds of petitions and letters denounced the Grand Rapids resolution. Yost was compelled to say, "I ought to erect a monument to those Grand Rapids

[4] *Albion Evening Recorder*, 11/26/21

alumni. If it hadn't been for them, I might never have known how many friends I had and how loyal they are, both to myself and to Michigan."[5]

The *Michigan Daily* editorialized at the end of the 1921 season,

> The trouble is that we have become too much accustomed to victory in the past. When the conference was small and when Michigan's opponents were young and weak, we won everything. But now we are bucking the best there is, and we find ourselves suddenly confronted with the inevitable losses which must come periodically among strong contenders. Probably, after all, the mishaps of this year's schedule have been a good lesson; let us hope, at least, that they have taught us how to lose gracefully and without calamity, howling pessimism, and the customary critical complaints.[6]

The University of Michigan had already made its position clear. On July 1, 1921, Yost had been named Director of Intercollegiate Athletics and was employed directly by the Board of Regents. His salary was paid by the Regents, and he was also given the responsibility of "establishing, conducting, or supervising additional courses in the training of coaches and playground instructors and similar matters."[7] The understanding was that Yost would make Ann Arbor his home all year. Prior to 1921, he had spent the football season in Ann Arbor, but he had lived the rest of the year in Nashville, Tennessee, the hometown of his wife, Eunice. While Yost loved football and working with athletes, he had a law degree from West Virginia University and in the off-season he worked on various business and legal interests. Because of the coach's new appointment, the whole Yost family would now make Ann Arbor their home. Eunice Yost enjoyed the atmosphere that existed around her renowned husband and often traveled with the team to away

---

[5] Falls, et al, **A Legacy of Champions**, 1996, p 50
[6] *Michigan Daily*, 11/20/21, p 2
[7] Yost papers, Box 7, Yost, 40 Years at Michigan

games. The Yosts had one son, Fielding Jr., who they fondly called Buck. Buck would spend much of the 1920s at a preparatory school in New York State, but the family was quite close and he would eventually enroll at the University of Michigan and play on the varsity football squad in 1931.

Yost was very pleased to accept the full-time position and stated that he would continue to coach the football team, but on a voluntary basis and for no salary, accepting only the income paid to him as Director of Intercollegiate Athletics. In January 1922, University of Michigan President M. L. Burton wrote Yost a warm letter, in which he related,

> I am tremendously interested in the splendid work which you are doing about the state and country in the interest not only of the Intercollegiate Department of Athletics but also of the University as a whole…You are doing exactly the kind of work the University had needed for a long time and I congratulate you upon it.[8]

Despite this praise, Yost had to know going into the 1922 season that his efforts were under scrutiny like never before. The Grand Rapids resolution represented a viewpoint held by many students and alumni. Yost was 51 years old in 1922. He had been head football coach at Michigan since 1901. Was he a coach whose best teams were in the past? Could he win under the rules of modern football? Was Michigan under his tutelage destined for mediocrity, or were there still some championships to be won?

---

[8] Yost papers, Box 7, Yost, 40 Years at Michigan

# Chapter 2

# 1922: The Season That Laid the Cornerstone

Invitations were sent out in mid-August 1922 to 47 men asking them to return to Ann Arbor for early fall practice, which would begin on Friday, September 15. Michigan had several returning candidates from the 1921 team, but numerous replacements would be needed on the line. The *Michigan Daily* put it this way: "The 1922 Varsity has a fine backfield, capable ends with plenty of substitutes for these positions and one tackle, but three other regulars must be found for the center of the line and several good substitutes for these positions must be on the squad."[9] When asked about the outlook, Yost said, "The prospects can hardly be called rosy...The success of the team will depend on how the new men develop to fill the line positions left vacant...The success or failure of a football team is largely determined by the strength of the line."[10]

In late September, the *Daily* noted that hundreds of undergraduates were viewing the football drills on Ferry Field. Yost had cut the varsity to a roster of 35 after two scrimmages, but the major problem for team development was that there weren't enough players on the reserves. On the 29th of September, Yost couldn't hold a scrimmage because there were too few men on the reserve squad to play the Varsity. Yost made an appeal to the student body for more players.

---

[9] *Michigan Daily*, 8/13/22, p 1
[10] *Michigan Daily*, 8/13/22, p 1

Just now our glaring weakness is in the reserves. Out of a student body of over eight thousand only a handful are reporting for the reserve team—hardly enough to line up, let alone enough to make a good team. And right here is where Michigan spirit meets its real test. If Michigan spirit means anything it surely means that the University is worth working for. Can it be interpreted in terms of work? What are you doing? Are you making a man of yourself and building for Michigan on the gridiron, or are you 'letting George do it?' Today is the time for action. There is no better way for you to serve Michigan athletics than to report…at once…Talk accomplishes nothing—work beats Ohio State. Which do you choose for your motto?[11]

Yost reinforced that the reserves were not just fodder to be beaten up by the Varsity. He promoted four men from the reserves to the Varsity and stated that any others showing ability would also be advanced. Yost's letter was circulated to fraternities and independent organizations on campus and published in the *Daily*. All those who had any football experience at all were asked to report.

The response was immediate. By October 5, Yost reported that he had the biggest reserve squad in years and that its effort was helping to whip the Varsity into shape. That day, 2000 fans showed up on Ferry Field to watch the Varsity beat the reserves, 21-7.

Michigan's first game of the 1922 season was two days later in Ann Arbor against the Case Scientific School of Cleveland. Michigan had beaten Case 24 of 27 previous contests, and Coach Yost was clearly not worried. In fact, he left the game in the hands of his assistants and took the train on Friday to Columbus, Ohio, to scout the Ohio State game against Ohio Wesleyan. Accompanying Yost were Irwin Uteritz, his starting quarterback, and the Michigan captain, Paul Goebel.

The players left in Ann Arbor rewarded Yost's confidence in

---

them by blasting Case, 48-0, before 8000 fans in a rainstorm. The individual star of the game was Harry Kipke, the brilliant halfback from Lansing, who would one day be Michigan's head football coach. Kipke inaugurated his junior year of football by breaking free on several occasions for substantial gains. The Michigan crowd was encouraged by the appearance of Eddie Johns back at guard. Johns had starred for two previous years on the Varsity, but had run into academic trouble and was thought to be ineligible for the season. Miraculously, his problems were ironed out just before the opening of the season, resulting in markedly improved line play with Johns in his usual place. If there was a concern among fans from the performance, it was that Case completed five passes of from five to 25 yards while Michigan didn't even attempt any. The next game on the schedule promised to provide more of a contest.

## The Vanderbilt Game

Automobiles with which to take the members of the football team to the Michigan Central station today are being sought by William Lichtenberg, '23, football manager. The team is to leave the Michigan Central station for Nashville, Tenn., at 12:50 o'clock this afternoon. Consequently, it will be necessary for the students who are willing to volunteer their machines to be at the Union by 12 o'clock. Since 28 men are included in the party which will make the trip to Vanderbilt, at least seven machines will be needed.[12]

With this plea for help on the front page of the *Michigan Daily*, October 12, 1922, the Michigan football program unknowingly embarked on the remarkable journey that was to lead to the building of the greatest and most beloved stadium in America. The game against the Vanderbilt Commodores would renew a series that last saw the teams meet in 1914, but no ordinary game would be played that day. Michigan was honored to be the invited team to participate

---

[12] *Michigan Daily*, 10/12/22, p 1

in the dedication game for Vanderbilt's new 25,000-seat Dudley Stadium, named after Dr. William L. Dudley, father of Vanderbilt's athletic system and long president of the Southern Athletic Association. The U-shaped stadium of steel and concrete was billed as the greatest facility of its kind in the South. The Commodores saw the day as the most important in their athletic history.

Elaborate dedication ceremonies were held before the game, including a parade of Vanderbilt students and Nashville citizens through the city to the stadium. An airplane delivered the game ball by flying low over the stadium and dropping it from the cockpit. The Governor of Tennessee made the dedication speech and welcomed the Michigan squad to Nashville. Coach Yost responded,

> Michigan appreciates the honor of being here on the occasion of the dedication of this wonderful stadium which through the years will do so much to develop the strength, loyalty, and the ideals of generous service in the young manhood of the South. Michigan congratulates Vanderbilt, Nashville, and the state of Tennessee on the completion of this magnificent structure which will mean so much for their mutual good. I might add that I have a great personal interest in all that this is and means. Michigan gave McGugin, one of her former football stars, to Vanderbilt as her coach. My home is in Nashville and it was here that Dan and I found the two women that united us in bonds of kinship. May the better team win this opening game.[13]

Indeed, Dan McGugin, the Vanderbilt coach, was a Michigan graduate and letterman. He and Yost shared a great and enduring friendship. They first met in 1899 when Yost was coaching the football team at Kansas. Kansas defeated Drake that year, but Yost was very impressed by a tenacious Drake guard by the name of McGugin. When Yost began his legendary career at Michigan

---

in 1901, he brought McGugin to Ann Arbor to play two years at guard. McGugin then enrolled in the Michigan Law School and assisted Yost with the football team. When Vanderbilt sought a new coach in 1904, Yost helped McGugin secure the job. McGugin, then only 24 years old, brought immediate respect and national eminence to Vanderbilt football. In fact, in his first four years at the Vanderbilt helm, McGugin's teams so dominated the South that no southern club even crossed the Commodore goal line. He coached there for 30 years, from 1904 to 1934, and achieved a record of 193 wins, 52 losses and 19 ties.

The connection between Yost and McGugin, however, ran even deeper. When McGugin was married shortly after arriving in Nashville, Yost was best man at the wedding. He was immediately smitten by the sister of the bride and married her in 1906. Thus the clash in Vanderbilt's new stadium pitted brother-in-law against brother-in-law, two coaching geniuses who were genuine friends.

Vanderbilt had 21 lettermen back and had already beaten Middle Tennessee Normal and Henderson-Brown College. Theirs was an experienced team. While the Commodores were bound to be fired up over their stadium dedication game, Michigan was nonetheless heavily favored. In fact, Yost and McGugin had played each other seven times since McGugin arrived at Vanderbilt and Michigan had won every encounter. It proved to be a sweltering southern day, however, and perhaps the weather played a role in sapping Michigan's strength.

The game ended in a 0-0 tie. Michigan gained much more ground than Vanderbilt and was once stopped on downs at the Commodore 1-yard line. Vanderbilt made only one first down in the whole game, but their defensive play was flawless and held Michigan scoreless.

Back in Ann Arbor, thousands of Michigan students followed the game at Hill Auditorium. The alumni association helped to secure an immense electronic football scoreboard that had first been used in Columbus during the previous year's game between

Ohio State and Chicago. The grid was 11 feet tall and 15 feet wide, controlled entirely by electricity and operated by one man. The gridiron was marked off in five-yard lines by lights with other lights indicating the position of the teams and different players. Thus, when a play was made, the ball was moved down the field the corresponding distance and different lights were lit, relaying the amount of yardage gained and the man carrying the ball. A special telegraph wire was leased running directly from Vanderbilt's stadium to the board operator at Hill Auditorium so the game could be followed almost as it happened. The event was a huge success, and plans were immediately made to use the electronic grid-graph for other away games.

So the Wolverines left Nashville with a 0-0 tie, but this was not to be the only stadium dedication game in which they played during the 1922 season. There was another one scheduled the following week, and this game was in Columbus.

## The Ohio State Game

The post-war decade of the 1920s was one of great prosperity, and college football began attracting larger and larger crowds. Athletic departments began to realize extraordinary revenue from football. Stadiums around the Midwest were filling with spectators in a way that no one had ever seen before. In a comment on ticket sales in 1922, Yost said,

> The demand for football tickets is larger this year than ever before in Michigan's football history. This is true of the Illinois and Wisconsin games as well as the Ohio State game. There will be no question about there being a capacity crowd at all three of these games.[14]

The national football story of the 1922 season was the opening of the phenomenal new stadium at Ohio State University. Built at a cost of $1,500,000 (the equivalent of $16,867,000 in 2005), the

---

[14] *Michigan Daily*, 10/10/22, p 1

double-decked concrete and steel structure, seating 75,000, would rival the Yale Bowl in seating capacity. Many stadium experts of the day considered the open horseshoe model to be a major improvement over the solid "bowl" type of stadium. It was thought that air circulation through the open end of the stadium would be a great relief for both players and spectators. Ohio State's endeavor would be one of the first of many great stadiums to be built on campuses across America during the 1920s.

If the new Buckeye stadium filled to capacity for the dedication game with Michigan, it would represent the largest crowd to ever witness a football game in the Midwest. It would eclipse by far the previous record crowd of nearly 45,000 that watched the Michigan-OSU match-up in Ann Arbor in 1921.

Soon, there was no question that the stadium would fill to capacity. The excitement over the contest had been at a fever pitch in both Ann Arbor and Columbus for months before kick-off. As far back as June 1922, Yost had sent a request to Ohio State for Michigan's allotment to the game to be increased from 10,000 to 15,000 tickets.

Yost got his first view of the stadium when he skipped the Michigan game with Case and went to Columbus to scout the Ohio State-Ohio Wesleyan game. One can only wonder what he must have thought when he entered the place. When Yost had arrived in Ann Arbor in 1901, bleacher seats around Regents Field, Michigan's original home field, seated about 300. In 20 years, he had witnessed a most remarkable evolution of his beloved game.

While Yost had characterized Michigan's Ferry Field as the best facility in the Midwest as late as 1921, the field certainly didn't qualify for such accolades any longer. Everywhere, stadium building was on the drawing boards. Iowa had just expanded its facility to 42,000 seats and the University of Illinois had announced plans for an impressive memorial stadium on their campus. Minnesota was studying the option and even the University of Chicago was discussing a new facility.

An editorial in the *Daily* wondered where it would all end.

Along with competition in countless other lines among the colleges of the country now comes the stadium race, each trying to outdo the other in size and beauty of football grandstands. Not only are colleges attempting to out-do each other, but also to out-boast each other by impressing on their competitors that they are superior as an institution at least by the criterion of football stadiums…

One sometimes wonders just when the limit of larger stadiums will be reached, indeed one wonders if it will ever be reached. Not many years ago a crowd of 16,000 at any athletic contest was a thing to be heralded; today even the minor events attract an attendance of 30,000; and no football game can be called great unless a 50,000 capacity stadium is taxed to overflowing and ticket scalpers are busy on the outside.

Although Ohio State has not yet dedicated her new stadium holding 63,000, Illinois comes forth with the announcement that hers will have a capacity of 92,000 when completed. Who will be the next bidder to raise the others a few thousand seats?[15]

Clearly, college football had evolved into an immensely popular spectator sport. The clamor for tickets was forcing athletic departments all over the country to reassess their facilities.

The frenzied meeting between Michigan and Ohio State in the great new stadium in Columbus would further highlight the attraction this game held for thousands of fans. In 1922, Michigan had a student body of just over 11,000 students. More than 6000 of them were planning to make the trek to Columbus for the game. To this day, it might be the greatest percentage of Michigan students ever to see an away football game. Most were traveling by train, and several overnight excursions were leaving from Ann

---

[15] *Michigan Daily*, 10/19/22, p 4

Arbor Friday night, with more on the rails early Saturday morning. The Michigan student body included 1700 women, and those who planned to go not only had to sign up at the Dean of Women's office, they were also required to come up with 10 cents extra to pay the fees for chaperones.

No such obstacle was placed in the path of male students, but one can infer that there must have been some past experiences the University was hoping to avoid repeating. The *Daily* editorialized three days before the game,

> By far the majority of the rooters will be conveyed in special trains provided for the purpose…the students who take the train to Columbus should have a most enjoyable time in the course of the trip…It has been made clear by the railroad companies, however, that no damaging of the cars or furnishings in the trains will be tolerated. In the past these companies have at certain times been the victims of rowdyism which has demolished their property and they have announced that should any such occurrence be repeated during the coming week end Michigan students will never be able to charter special trains again…"Respect for the property of the railroads" must be the slogan of those embarking on the trains Friday and Saturday if they are to maintain their own self-respect. The stakes are too great to disregard this warning.[16]

The next day's editorial was again aimed at Michigan's men:

> Yesterday the *Daily* issued a warning to students making the trip to Columbus this weekend to watch their behavior, particularly on the special trains which have been provided for the journey.

> But there is something even more fundamental than that in the request that Michigan men be especially careful of their actions this Friday and Saturday. When so large a

[16] *Michigan Daily*, 10/18/22, p 4

group of students go from one university to another, it is quite natural that upon the conduct of this body rests the formation of opinions regarding their university.

Columbus this weekend will be a melting pot for immense masses of people from all over the central west. They will be constantly in contact with the men who go down from Michigan to support their team. In the short time of their acquaintance they will make judgments, snap judgments; that is only human nature.

Every Michigan man, then, owes a moral duty to his university to see that he conducts himself in a manner which casts no reflection on the character of his university…They seldom judge by the behavior of the great majority, but rather by the misbehavior of the small minority…This fact must be kept in mind by the men who travel to Ohio State. They are carrying with them not irresponsibility, but on the other hand a genuine responsibility, namely, the upholding of the name of Michigan…Upon the actions of the men who go to Columbus this Saturday depends the reputation of Michigan in the middle west. Let's fight hard, and root hard, but don't let's be un-Michigan.[17]

There were some other worries about the game and the behavior of Michigan men. President Burton issued this warning during game week:

There is no occasion for discussing the morals of betting. It is an attempt to get something for nothing and, in the long run, the world is not made up that way. There is occasion for pointing out from an intensely practical point of view that betting is a short-sighted and vicious attack upon intercollegiate athletics. The student who bets on his team, thinking that he is thereby giving

---

genuine evidence of his loyalty to his university, is deceiving himself. Betting breeds unjust criticism of the team, tends to shatter student morals and substitutes commercialism for sportsmanship. Let us play the game for the game's sake.[18]

Coach Yost had his say,

Most students, alumni, or townspeople who bet on their teams have sort of a vague idea that by doing so they are demonstrating their loyalty. As a matter of fact, they are in nearly every case sowing the seed of actual disloyalty. The time when a team needs and appreciates support is when it is losing. And right then is the time when the one who bets usually forgets all about loyalty. If they lose money…before they know it they are finding all kinds of fault with the team, the coaches, and everything from the water boy to the President. And all this because they lost a few dollars which they had no business betting.[19]

The Michigan Band had only 45 members in 1922, and they paraded in uniforms that were old and tattered. In early October, the *Daily* reported the band might be forced to take the field in civilian clothes. The last time the band had new uniforms was 1913, so its attire had been patched and repatched for many years. Worse yet, Ohio State's band had marched sprightly onto Ferry Field the previous year with brand new scarlet and gray outfits.

The Michigan Band wanted to expand from 45 to 75 members, but to provide new uniforms for that number they needed $3000. Without new outfits, according to the *Daily*, they wouldn't go to Columbus at all. A quick survey of marching bands at other conference schools showed that they had all received new uniforms within the previous four years. The *Daily* editorialized that the university "should feel much the same concern as if the football team had not

[18] *Michigan Daily*, 10/17/22, p 1
[19] *Michigan Daily*, 10/17/22, p 1

had a new suit of clothes for an equally long period of time."[20]

The problem was quickly remedied. The Regents of the university came up with $1500, and the Board in Control of Athletics immediately matched that sum. There must have been some new uniforms in a warehouse somewhere, for the Michigan Band was in its new outfits within days, just in time for the trip to Columbus. The uniforms were fashioned from dark blue broadcloth, and the large overcoats worn by their predecessors were replaced with shorter suitcoats. A striking trio of maize silk braids swept across the front of the uniform, and a gold stripe for each year of service in the band was fastened to the left arm. The cape was lined with maize silk. The editor of the *Daily* was rhapsodic: "Michigan is going to Columbus in gorgeous attire."[21] Michigan's band would be in appropriate dress for this stadium dedication.

The Michigan alumni were planning to have the Wolverine fans form a block "M" in the stands at Ohio Stadium. Each participant would hold up a maize or blue banner at the appropriate time. A yellow M surrounded by a field of blue was a routine symbol at Ferry Field home games, but the block M had never been organized before on a foreign field. Much planning went into the effort. The idea that a golden M would adorn the stands of Ohio's new stadium on dedication day warmed many a Wolverine heart.

The Michigan cheerleaders were all male, as were the members of the band. They were focused on the school's songs and making sure everyone knew the words. The freshmen, especially, were expected to get up to speed. The *Daily* printed "The Yellow and Blue" in three stanzas so it could be memorized by new students. (This would be a major challenge today for those thousands of Wolverines who know the song primarily by, "Hail!") The *Daily* editorialized about proper song etiquette.

> A custom that has sprung into vogue during the course
> of the last year or two is that of standing up while "The

---

[20] *Michigan Daily*, 10/6/22, p 4
[21] *Michigan Daily*, 10/16/22, p 4

Victors" is being played. There is nothing particularly objectionable in honoring so splendid a composition as "The Victors" through this courtesy, except that the impression's likely to be given outsiders or students new to the University that this is the University of Michigan song—the one which should be sung standing and with heads bared, at all times.

In the past Michigan has reserved this respect for "The Yellow and Blue." The other songs such as "Varsity" and "The Victors" should be sung earnestly and with all due enthusiasm, but the highest respect in the way of standing with heads bared should be reserved for "The Yellow and Blue."[22]

Down on Ferry Field, the team had been through long practices all week in preparation for this historic encounter. Yost announced secret sessions, but complained that practices couldn't really be secret on Ferry Field. Tennis courts were adjacent to the field, and all kinds of other intramural activities took place there. Students and others were constantly coming and going. To limit bystanders, Yost locked the gates to the field and tried to have intramural participants use the far south end of the athletic facility, away from the football field.

Sometime during the week, Dan McGugin, the Vanderbilt coach and former Wolverine player, wrote a remarkable letter to Paul Goebel, Michigan's football captain.

I wish I could make you and your teammates understand just how the wearers of the "M" feel towards your team. You cannot know just now but as the years go by and you all get scattered, you will understand. Every man who ever wore the "M" will think of the Ohio State game this week a thousand times; men who battled with the "M" on their breast, before you and your teammates were born, will think of every one of the members of the team

---

[22] *Michigan Daily*, 10/14/22, p 4

this week; they will try to know how you look, how you
will come on the field and most of all they seek to know
what is in your hearts.

You have an enormous responsibility next Saturday. We
can't bear to lose the game. Two years ago when Michigan
had such a weak team, alumni everywhere began rallying
to Michigan. Many of you are at Ann Arbor, consciously
or unconsciously, due to the loyal interest of some Michigan man. You are the fruit, in a sense, of the loyalty and
affection of these men…You have the high honor of
bearing the colors; they must be planted high. No man
should give less than all he has. You must uphold the old
tradition—"The Fighting Men of Michigan."[23]

Ohio State held its last practice in preparation on Thursday
afternoon. Witnesses said it was the best exhibition of the year.
Every imaginable pass play was used with success, and all kinds of
shifts and trick plays were utilized. It was clear to observers that
the Buckeyes would hold nothing in reserve against Michigan. The
*Daily* ran this assessment of the coming clash:

The general feeling in Columbus seems to be that
Michigan on paper is stronger than the Buckeye aggregation…However, the Scarlet and Grey adherents are
counting on some unknown force to come to their aid
at the last moment and change a hopeless cause into sure
victory…Michigan supporters are not at all confident of
victory. The setback received at Nashville…has served to
kill any overconfidence that might have been evident in
the Wolverine camp…A general reliance on Yost and the
traditional fighting spirit of the Varsity is about the main
hope that is being carried to Columbus…Nothing in the
way of press reports coming from the enemy camp has
served to rouse as much feeling locally as the statements

[23] Board in Control, Box 5, September 1922

from Columbus that Ohio State was expected to win by outfighting and outguessing the Wolverines.

The general feeling on the campus is that a Michigan team outfought is something unknown in a big game and that whatever the outcome of the game this afternoon, the Varsity will be fighting until the last play is finished…The whole proposition narrows down to the single query, can the Wolverines stop the Scarlet and Gray overhead offense?[24]

Michigan's questionable ability to defend against the passing game was not the only problem it faced. Ohio State's line was also bigger, averaging 199 pounds per man, while Michigan's weighed in at 183. In fact, the Wolverines had only one lineman who weighed over 200 pounds. On the other hand, Butch Pixley, the Buckeye captain and guard, was rumored to weigh almost 300 pounds.

All this preparation culminated in what was billed as the greatest pep rally in university history, held the Thursday night prior to the game at Hill Auditorium. The *Daily* set the tone.

Tonight in Hill Auditorium Michigan men will participate in a pep meeting which should reveal a fighting spirit the equal of which has never before been known at Michigan. The object of the meeting is not mere pastime. The assembly has for its purpose the uniting of thousands of students in a determined effort to beat Ohio if it is humanly possible.

Three years in succession Michigan has met defeat at the hands of the scarlet and gray. The desire for revenge is burning in every true Michigan man. It is not necessary to fan the flames of this desire. But the meeting tonight will help us pull together—to give the team everything conceivable in the way of moral support.[25]

---

[24] *Michigan Daily*, 10/21/22, p 1
[25] *Michigan Daily*, 10/19/22, p 4

At the appointed hour, thousands of students showed up at Hill. The Band appeared in its spanking new uniforms. The cheerleaders led the crowd in the M-I-C-H-I-G-A-N locomotive cheer and several renditions of all the college songs. The team and coaches were also scheduled to appear, and the whole assemblage would then embark for the train station at the foot of State Street (now the Gandy Dancer restaurant).

However, the team didn't arrive for the excited capacity crowd at Hill Auditorium. They were ensconced at the Union, going through a last minute review of a movie of the previous year's loss to the Buckeyes. Coach Yost reviewed the game play by play, focusing on the costly errors and lack of execution that had resulted in another Buckeye victory. Once the film review was complete, the team left for the train station where they were met by the massive throng following the band from Hill Auditorium. It was said to be the largest crowd ever to gather at the station to send off the team.

Michigan had 32 players on the travel squad that embarked to dedicate Ohio's great stadium. Football squads were much smaller 80 years ago because 11 starters were expected to play both ways, on offense and defense. Substitutions could be made, but this was long before the advent of modern football in which teams play with one offensive squad and a completely different defensive one.

On Friday before the game, a constant parade of cars traveled down Ann Arbor's Main Street as students exited town for Columbus. The *Daily* described the procession,

> Led by a vanguard of some 20 jalopies gaily bedecked in maize and blue and large block "M's," this strange parade made its way throughout the town. Many bore glaring quotations such as "We'll dedicate your damned stadium," "From and for Michigan," and "Crush the Buckeyes."[26]

Drivers were reminded that the speed laws in Ohio were strictly enforced and were 30 mph on highways, 15 in the business sections.

---

[26] *Michigan Daily*, 10/21/22, p 1

Special sleeper trains were brought to Ann Arbor and departed at midnight for a nonstop route to Columbus, with three cars reserved for women. Four coach trains were scheduled to leave at 15-minute intervals beginning at 6:00 A.M. Saturday, with one whole train reserved for the female fans. All the preparations were in place for this great contest, but, with fan enthusiasm peaking, some uneasiness still prevailed in the President's office. On the Friday before the game, the front page of the *Daily* carried this plea from President Burton.

> The most severe test of the University of Michigan this weekend will not take place in the new stadium. I have no fear whatever about our team taking its tests courageously and successfully. They will honor Michigan. Never forget that.
>
> But candidly, will the University in every respect be honored by those who bear her name and go as spectators to support the team and to cheer the players on to victory? I know no Michigan student would deliberately harm Michigan. I know this minute that not one of you intend to bring shame and disgrace on your Alma Mater. The practical situations which are liable to develop on the trip, however, may test you to the breaking point. One step will lead to another and before you realize it the damage is done. So the wise method will be eternal vigilance. Positively refuse to take one step on the wrong path. A clear cut determination now will see you through. A failure to comply with railroad regulations, the use of illegal beverages, general conduct not becoming an intelligent man or a self-respecting woman will bring serious discredit upon Michigan, will rob your successors of privileges which you crave, and might seriously effect the welfare of the University.
>
> I believe in you unreservedly. I ask you earnestly and loy-

ally to be fine, vigorous, manly and womanly representatives of the University which I regard as second to none in America. May you have a trip which in the years to come will be one of the proud and cherished memories of your college days.[27]

The stage was set.

Hundreds of Michigan fans poured out of the Columbus rail station about a mile from the new stadium. Ohio State, at the last minute, had erected wooden bleachers in the open end of the stadium to seat another 10,000 fans, bringing capacity that day to 72,000. Even so, thousands of fans milled about outside the stadium without tickets.

The stadium dedication ceremonies included a procession led by "The Stadium Girl," a co-ed selected from the Ohio State student body. The Michigan Band played "The Yellow and Blue," followed by the Ohio State band, which played the songs of the other Big Ten colleges while their respective flags were raised on the poles around the top of the stadium (the famed "script Ohio" was nowhere to be seen in those days; it was performed for the first time in Ohio Stadium by the Michigan Band in 1932).

President Thompson of Ohio State formally dedicated the stadium in a brief address. The Michigan and Ohio State bands joined and played "The Star Spangled Banner" as the nation's flag was raised on the pole at the open end of the stadium. The university cadets fired a 21-gun salute with three-inch field pieces. The procession then filed to their reserved boxes, while the Michigan band played "The Victors" as it marched down the field. The Michigan alumni were proudly sporting their maize and blue colors in the huge block "M" they created in their section of the stands, the fans were cheering back and forth, and the teams took the field.

So what happened? Here's how it started: Michigan was downed receiving the opening kick-off on their 16-yard line. On first down, they punted. Yes, that's right, they punted. It was common football strategy in those days and one to which Yost greatly adhered. The idea was that when deep in one's territory turnovers could occur on offense, so the best approach was to get the ball out of there. In rugby, the ball is commonly advanced by kicking. American football at the turn of the century closely resembled rugby much more than today's game does, and, even into the 1920s, the punting game remained a primary offensive weapon.

Yost always developed great punters and this team was no exception. Harry Kipke had a phenomenal day against the Buckeyes, punting 11 times for an average of nearly 50 yards. Any coach today would be thrilled to have such a kicker. In fact, Michigan's whole offense revolved around the utility of the punting game. Yost liked to have the team line up in "punt formation" so the other team wouldn't know whether they planned to pass, run or punt. If the punting game could be won, then slowly but surely the opponent would be backed further into their own end of the field. Then, if they made a mistake, the Yost machine would jump all over them. One of his former players described Yost's philosophy this way,

> How often have we heard him say: "Pass, punt and pray."
> What's the easiest way to gain ground? Pass or punt
> your way down the field. Then hold 'em and pray for
> a break. If they fumble, fall on it. If they pass, grab it.
> Hold 'em. Take the ball away from them deep in their
> own territory.[28]

So on first down in the game everyone recognized as the greatest the Midwest had ever seen, Michigan punted.

However, the overall strategy worked this time. Michigan's captain, Paul Goebel, hit a field goal in the first quarter to take a 3-0 lead. Then, in perfect accordance with Yost's offensive strategy, the Buckeyes fumbled in their own territory, and Kipke scored on a quick run around end to make it 10-0 at the half.

In 1922, the team that was scored against could elect either

---

[28] Fitzgerald, F.J., **Hail to the Victors**, 1995, p 52

to receive the kick-off or to kick off to the other team. Again, the strategy was to keep the other team deep in their own territory. Once or twice in this game, Ohio State did elect to kick off after Michigan had scored.

Michigan continued to dominate the game in the second half. In the third quarter, the ever-present Kipke intercepted an OSU pass and returned it 45 yards for a touchdown, making the score 16-0. The extra point was missed. Kipke then finished off the Buckeyes with a perfect drop-kick field goal in the fourth quarter to make the final score 19-0. (Many years later, Kipke would say that winning this game was his greatest thrill as an athlete.) The Buckeyes never even got points on the board in their own dedication game.

There may never have been a more wonderful Michigan afternoon. Wolverines were ecstatic. Fans poured out of the stadium and

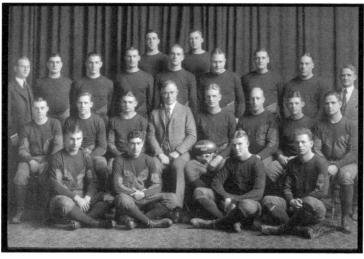

*Photo courtesy of Bentley Historical Library*

***The University of Michigan Football Team of 1922:***
***This team won Michigan's first Big Ten title since 1904***

*Row 4: Curran, Steele*

*Row 3: Lichtenburg (student manager), Slaughter, Blott, Neisch, Garfield, Vandervoort, White, Van Orden, Hahn (trainer)*

*Row 2: Uteritz, Muirhead, Kipke, Coach Yost, Captain Goebel, Cappon, Kirk, Roby*

*Row 1: Steger, Keffer, Dunleavy, Knode*

followed the band in a delirious march to the heart of Columbus. The *Daily* was euphoric. Front page articles pointed out that both Yale and Harvard had lost their stadium dedication games and now so had OSU. Michigan escaped the Buckeye "aerial attack," which was 8 of 17 for the day with one critical interception. An editorial proclaimed,

> All other clashes faded into insignificance while the country turned its eyes on Columbus…was a reincarnation of the days of old, of the days when Yost's point-a-minute-elevens were the talk of the country. Such a game has seldom before been played in football history. Eighteen thousand Michigan students and alumni journeyed to Columbus to witness the victory—18,000 hurling defiances at 50,000 Ohio supporters—18,000 who cheered louder and sang longer than the 50,000—18,000 who took home with them the prize 50,000 so greatly coveted—Victory.[29]

Yost issued the following statement.

> The only thing I have to say is that I want to thank the coaches for their great assistance in the preparation of our men for the game. Their loyalty and cooperation have been wonderful. Michigan never had greater reasons to be proud of what her football men did than on this last Saturday. Every man gave to his utmost.[30]

Privately, he wrote to a relative, "It was a glorious day and a very wonderful victory and it is needless for me to write you how much we are pleased with the outcome."[31] A few days later, to Dan McGugin at Vanderbilt, Yost elaborated,

> The team played a remarkable game at Ohio State. Both teams were keyed to the highest peak. I have never

---

[29] *Michigan Daily*, 10/24/22, p 4
[30] *Michigan Daily*, 10/24/22, p 6
[31] Board in Control, Box 5, October 1922 (1)

seen a football team in the same high mental attitude as Michigan was at Columbus. Ohio had worked just as hard and had the same extreme desire to win this game as Michigan had. It was a fierce and hard battle from whistle to whistle and it was an exceedingly well played game from the Michigan standpoint.[32]

While Yost's close relationship with McGugin was unique, perhaps his greatest confidant was Charles Baird. Baird was a successful banker in Kansas City in 1922, the same man who eventually donated the carillon for Burton Tower. But back in 1901, he was the University of Michigan athletic representative who actually hired Yost. The two remained dear friends, and following this great victory Yost wrote him,

> The winning of the Ohio State game meant more to me than anything else in my career. A year ago I set my heart on winning this game and since that time we made every preparation possible to win so the outcome was very gratifying. I really think it meant more to Michigan than any athletic victory in her history.[33]

However, even in 1922, the pressure on a coach was intense. Yost confided to Baird in the same letter, "I have been sick more or less the past two weeks…a little nervous indigestion due to intense interest and more or less worry in preparation for the Ohio State game."

Clearly, Fielding Yost was very pleased with this historic triumph over the team that was already Michigan's greatest rival. On October 24, he received a most wonderful letter from University President Burton that must have been very gratifying.

> My Dear Mr. Yost: I do not want you to get the impression that I think that in the slightest degree your success as a member of this University depends upon winning all

[32] Yost papers, Box 2, folder (2)
[33] Board in Control, Box 5, November 1922 (1)

of the games which you play. I cannot, however, refrain from expressing to you very earnestly my heartiest congratulations upon the evidence of your splendid work. The game Saturday was the finest game that I have seen a Michigan team play. I say it without any qualifications. I watched every inch of the game with the keenest interest and it seemed to me that you have developed a team which ranks among the very best of the country; at any rate please accept my hearty congratulations and best wishes for the rest of the season.[34]

The euphoria on campus was complete.

However, Wolverine fans began to wonder, once the dust had settled, about the adequacy of their own football facility. Yost regularly described Michigan's athletic plant as the finest in the Midwest, particularly the newly expanded football stadium on Ferry Field which, officially seating nearly 40,000, had previously had the largest capacity of any university west of Philadelphia. But those who had traveled to Columbus had experienced an awakening. The *Daily* writers were in awe of Ohio State's creation:

It is difficult to describe to anyone who was not in the vast stadium Saturday afternoon just what the effect of the immense horseshoe, filled to the overflowing, was. The first sight of the stands was sufficient to take one's breath away, with row after row of human beings rising to unbelievable heights…[35] Many persons having seats in the top tier suffered nervous spasms when they reached the top of the deck and realized its sheer steepness of angle.[36]

Clearly, Michigan had been challenged by more than just football at Ohio State.

[34] Board in Control, Box 5, October 1922 (1)
[35] *Michigan Daily*, 10/24/22, p 6
[36] *Michigan Daily*, 10/24/22, p 5

## The Illinois Game

The team was finally back in Ann Arbor for their next contest, a critical showdown with the Fighting Illini of Illinois. What was the old stadium like?

Two statues have stood guard above the entrance to the Michigan Union since it opened in 1919. A dignified, robed figure is on the right, and represents a scholar looking toward central campus. On the left, however, a more jaunty figure, representing the Michigan athlete, stares confidently down State Street toward the old playing field. To follow that gaze, one travels south on State Street from the Union, down the hill and across Packard to the corner of Hoover and State. This is where the stadium known as Ferry Field once stood. Named after D. M. Ferry, who donated the land, it was Michigan's home field from 1906 to 1926.

Looking west on Hoover, one sees the intramural building today, but in 1922 the north stands of Ferry Field occupied this site. These were wooden stands. Proceeding further south on State Street, just past the athletic offices on the corner, one immediately comes upon the old main gate to Ferry Field, the very gate Yost used to lock when he wanted to conduct secret practices. Adjacent to the old gate is the current Ticket Office. This building was opened in 1912 and served as the Michigan team's clubhouse. It was here the team dressed for games and it was to this building they would retreat at halftime. No doubt many a Yost pep talk reverberated from these walls.

Now walk past the new academic building for athletes and turn right into the parking lot. Proceed to the field that lies within the track, adjacent to the intramural building. If one stands in the heart of that field, facing west, the concrete south stands would have been on the left, the wooden north stands on the right, and a movable set of wood stands would have closed the west end of the stadium. This was Ferry Field, and it was on this hallowed ground that Yost's great teams of the 1920s laid the foundation for Michigan Stadium, visible on the hill to the southwest.

What did the football uniforms look like in 1922? First of all, the famous winged helmet was nowhere to be seen. It didn't show up until Coach Fritz Crisler arrived in 1938. Michigan wore leather helmets in those days, all black. The jerseys were blue with maize numbers only on the back. Some of the players wore protective leather patches on the sides of the chest and over the extensor surfaces of the arms. Maize pants completed the outfit. There was no white jersey for road games. In those days, teams wore the same uniform, home or away.

With the advent of the passing game, the football itself had been modified. It was much narrower than the egg-shaped ball that was used at the turn of the century, but it still had a mid-circumference that was an inch and a half wider than the missile that is used today. The playing field had the same dimensions as today, but there were no hash marks, and no numerical yardmarkers on the field, just white lines every five yards. The yardmarkers were placed on the sidelines. A major difference was that the goal posts were on the goal line instead of at the end of the endzone.

In a 1927 letter, Yost described the pre-game ceremonies:

> At all of our home games, it has been customary for the Michigan Band to appear on the football field about twenty minutes before the time of the game. The Flag Pole is located at the east end of the field. The band enters the field from the east side, parades to the west end, and back to the flag pole. The National Anthem is played and the flag raised. If the visiting school band is here, they are invited to join in this ceremony and the playing of the National Anthem.
>
> The Michigan Flag Pole is a memorial to Michigan men who were killed or died during the World War. A Memorial Tablet…has been placed on the flag pole, so after the Flag has been hoisted to the top, it is lowered to half mast and remains at half mast the entire time it

is displayed...After the football game, the flag is raised to the top of the pole and then lowered immediately and put away.[37]

The flag pole and memorial plaque still stand at the east end of Ferry Field.

What kind of shape were the Wolverines in for the Illini? One event occurred in the Ohio State game that would amaze the modern football fan. Remember that Yost issued a plea for more student involvement on the reserve team in late September. From off the campus, with virtually no football experience, came one L.S. White of Reed City. White so impressed Yost that after just two weeks he was promoted to the varsity. In the second quarter of the Ohio State game, one of the starting linemen went down with a broken arm. Incredibly, the replacement inserted into the Michigan line was White, a player who three short weeks before was just another student on campus. Nonetheless, the loss of the starter on the Michigan line was of great concern. On the very same play that the lineman broke his arm, Michigan's tough running back, Douglas Roby, broke his leg. So the Wolverines had some starters to replace for the coming game on Ferry Field.

The Illini, however, were not having one of their better years, having lost their first two games to Butler and Iowa. Nonetheless, coached by famed Robert Zuppke, they were always unpredictable and dangerous. Yost was taking no chances and closed all practices for the week. Through the athletic department, he issued the following statement on Tuesday,

> The first battle is won, but now we must face the future and realize that General Zuppke is invading Ann Arbor next Saturday with a very strong team...No football game can be won by the efforts that are past. The results of next Saturday's game will depend on what Michigan does this week in preparation for it and in the game

---

[37] Board in Control, Box 9, January 1927 (3)

itself. The fighting spirit must be the same as was shown in Ohio Stadium…[38]

Two days before the game, the *Daily* ran a huge banner entitled, "Pep Meeting Tonight! Let's Greet the Stadium Dedicators!" The team would be present and so would the band, but the following day the *Daily* made clear who the hero was:

> "Michigan's Grand Old Man," Fielding H. Yost, received the greatest ovation of his career last night when he came upon the stage in Hill Auditorium, faced an audience of over 5000 shouting Michigan men and women, and holding up the football won in the Ohio State game, announced, "I've brought home the bacon." From the first notes of "The Victors" to the last echoes of "The Yellow and Blue," the huge throng was in a state of wildest excitement…Yost spoke first of the spirit shown by the team at Ohio State where they were "absolutely unbeatable. Never in my 30 years experience have I seen a football team keyed up to such a high pitch of enthusiasm"…He asserted his belief that the Ohio State battle was one of the greatest games in the history of Michigan football. "We have now removed the Ohio State hoodoo!"[39]

At the end of the rally, however, Yost felt compelled to remind the student body that only a few seats were located on the 50-yard line and that complaining about one's seat assignment at football games showed poor spirit. Seats at Ferry Field were becoming tough to get. Around the conference, schools were astounded at the demand for football tickets. The *Daily* reported,

> Football in the Midwest rapidly is assuming the proportions of a very successful industry and causing Western Conference officials to scratch their heads in perplexity over the problem of seating between 2,000,000 and

---

3,000,000 persons this season in bleachers designed in the days when football was "just another piece of college foolishness." Between 1,500,000 and 2,000,000 spectators will get the thrill of Big Ten games this season and judging from the experiences in former years, Conference officials believe that from one-third to one-half that many will be turned away...At Ohio State University, where a new $1,500,000 stadium seating 63,000 persons was dedicated Saturday, 72,000 persons jammed their way into the enclosure and thousands were turned away. The demand for tickets to the big intersectional clash between Chicago and Princeton...was so brisk that all of the seats were sold nearly three weeks before the game...Stagg Field has a seating capacity of only 31,000, but more than 100,000 applications...were received. Extraordinary crowds have turned out at all of the Conference games thus far this season. The Iowa-Illinois game at Urbana last Saturday drew 23,000 while the Wisconsin-Indiana game at Madison drew another capacity crowd, 26,000.[40]

Michigan's game against Illinois was played on Ferry Field before 41,000 fans. Harry Kipke didn't even play because he'd been sick with the flu most of the week, hospitalized in the health service for three days. Nonetheless, the Wolverines smothered the Illini, 24-0. Michigan scored in the second period following an Illinois fumble at their own 25-yard line, returned the opening kick-off of the second half for a touchdown, and scored in the fourth quarter on a pass play. The Illini never seriously threatened the goal line. The *Daily* continued its worship:

> It is Yost who instilled in the hearts of those Michigan players who smothered the men of Zuppke, a fighting spirit that no Michigan team has ever borne. It is Yost whose agile brain conceived the attack that shattered the

---

[40] *Michigan Daily*, 10/24/22, p 7

vaunted defense of Illinois. It is Yost who put on Ferry Field what is probably the greatest eleven that has worn the Maize and Blue since the "point-a-minute" days of 1901 and '02. Michigan defeated Illinois. Michigan out gamed her, outsmarted her, rubbed her nose in the sod of Ferry Field in a way that will make Illinois hearts ache for the sweetness of revenge.[41]

That revenge would come the next time the two teams would meet, in 1924, but that story will be told in due course. In 1922, at this point in the season, Michigan fans were beginning to anticipate a Big Ten title, which would be the first for Michigan since 1904. Two teams stood in the way of an undefeated Big Ten championship: Wisconsin, 4-0 at this point, and Minnesota, the team against which Michigan traditionally ended the season.

## The Michigan Agricultural College Game

However, there was a minor diversion on the way to the last two contests. The Michigan Agricultural College, located in East Lansing, was on the schedule. In 1922, the school was not a member of the Big Ten conference and therefore represented a non-league game for the Wolverines. It had an enrollment of 1700, 300 of whom were female. MAC, as it was known, was not usually a threat to Michigan football prowess.

Michigan had won 13 of the 16 meetings. However, two legendary victories over the Wolverines in 1913 and 1915 and a tie in 1908 made it clear the Aggies could not be completely overlooked. In 1919 and 1921, Michigan had played MAC the week before the Ohio State game and, in 1920, Michigan played them before Illinois. In all three Big Ten contests played after the MAC game in those years, Michigan lost. It all came to a sharper focus in 1921 when Michigan suffered several key injuries in the MAC game and then lost to Ohio State the following week.

---

[41] *Michigan Daily*, 10/29/22, p 1

A sportswriter for the *Detroit News* put it this way,

> Michigan and MAC play their annual game of football next Saturday. This game has for years caused much discussion and comment, not because of the result in points, but on account of the consequences of injuries. Michigan supporters have been opposed to playing MAC and the East Lansing eleven would undoubtedly have been off Michigan's schedule years ago but for political pressure. Most of the Michigan-MAC games have resulted in serious injuries to one or more of Michigan's star players and because of these accidents Michigan was badly handicapped in her big games.

> There have been open arguments that games between Michigan and MAC are not the best thing for football. It is pointed out that sportsmanship is lacking and that these games are simply "blood battles." The injuries suffered by Michigan players in MAC games may have all been unavoidable accidents, but Michigan supporters refuse to believe that. MAC is charged with playing on the well-known policy of "We may not be able to beat you, but we'll fix you so that others will"…Some good football elevens have come out of East Lansing…The Aggies have twice beaten Michigan decisively. Several other times the Wolverines were more or less fortunate to win. MAC has suffered, however, in football prestige because of the impression created in the games at Ann Arbor. She may not be deserving of the blame, but still it exists.

> Michigan is a large state. Michigan is capable of supporting two major elevens. With good sportsmanship Michigan and MAC could both ride to gridiron glory in the West.[42]

---

[42] Board in Control, Box 5, November 1922 (1)

Yost responded to this article in a private letter to the columnist after the 1922 MAC game.

> There is no denying the fact that many of the students, and, I regret, some of the alumni and townspeople, have frequently expressed the sentiment as given in the article…In fact, many have spoken to me and I was frequently asked, "Why do we play MAC when all they do is injure our players?"
>
> The feeling has really been intense along this line on campus here…I gave a talk to the team and the coaches regarding this situation and asked the coaches to see those in charge of the MAC team and talk the situation over with them. I felt that if there was any act on the field that had the appearance of unnecessary roughness that our future relations with MAC would be at the breaking point so far as student opinion was concerned. Very fortunately the game produced no injuries…
>
> Personally, I have not found any evidence that justifies this extreme feeling. In my opinion the sentiment has been developed from the fact that numerous injuries have occurred to Michigan players in MAC games and this was especially so in the 1921 game when some five or six men were injured which kept them out of the Ohio State game the following Saturday and some of them practically for the entire remainder of the season…I am deeply concerned about the elimination of this condition and in the establishment of very pleasant relations between the students and the alumni bodies of these two institutions.[43]

Yost reminded angry Wolverines that, if one looked at all sports played, there was no school with which Michigan had more extensive intercollegiate relationships. Nonetheless, Yost did act to

---

[43] Board in Control, Box 5, November 1922 (1)

try to prevent a repeat of the previous experiences with MAC. He placed the Aggies later on the Michigan schedule in 1922, after the Ohio State game, and also insured an open week after the game so Michigan had two weeks to prepare for Wisconsin. He must have had some continuing concerns.

The game itself didn't seem to worry him. Yost left town again, this time to scout the Minnesota-Wisconsin game that would feature Michigan's last two Big Ten opponents. He left behind assistant coaches George Little and Tad Wieman to handle the team in the MAC contest. 4500 Aggie supporters detrained in Ann Arbor for the game and the crowd included virtually every student at the East Lansing school. Ferry Field attendees approached 40,000, exceeding by 7000 any previous Michigan-MAC game.

Yost's confidence was appropriate, however, as Michigan easily defeated its sister school, 63-0, handing them their worst defeat since 1902. Michigan fans were especially encouraged by the passing game in which Michigan completed 14 of 31 attempts with five players passing from different positions. The Wolverines survived the game this time without injuries, which must have been a relief to Yost. Michigan now had two weeks to prepare for the showdown with the Badgers. Up in Minneapolis, Yost saw Wisconsin defeat Minnesota, 14-0, to remain undefeated as well.

## The Wisconsin Game

The success of the Michigan team in 1922 yielded greater demand for tickets than anyone could have imagined. A few days after the MAC game, the *Daily* reported on page one:

> Every available seat in Ferry field for the Michigan-Wisconsin football game to be held on Nov 18 has been sold…[It has been] estimated that if more tickets were available they could have been sold at the rate of 1500 a day…The sale of tickets this year has completely shattered all previous records for all games. The MAC game drew 7000 more than ever before, the Illinois game filled the

field to capacity, and the Wisconsin tickets have sold out 18 days before the game, with thousands being refused on account of space. More applications for tickets have been received from alumni for the Wisconsin game than for any previous contest in the history of the University…The Athletic office said, "We have been completely landslided with applications, the heaviest it has ever been in any year."[44]

An editorial in the *Daily* made the obvious implications.

An epidemic of what may well be termed "stadium fever" has taken possession of a number of the larger universities of the middle west. It is the desire of each university to own a stadium which not only has an enormous seating capacity but is a marvel in concrete, an imposing structure which will call forth gapes of admiration from everyone.

It causes no end of wonderment when one views a stadium such as the one at Columbus, that such a titanic structure should be built to be used just half a dozen times each year. Seldom indeed does an institution erect a building costing over a million dollars unless it is to be used almost constantly.

Yet it cannot be doubted that a stadium such as the one at Ohio is a source of pride to the student body of that University.[45]

Despite the fact that Ohio State had constructed a new stadium, Illinois was building one, and Minnesota and Chicago were talking about it, there was no serious discussion about a new stadium in Ann Arbor. Ferry Field was Michigan's home, and the seating capacity there had been increased by several thousand just the year before. "Stadium fever" had not yet arrived in Ann Arbor.

[44] *Michigan Daily*, 11/7/22, p 1
[45] *Michigan Daily*, 11/5/22, p 4

Since Michigan had the week off after the MAC game, Yost again hit the rails, this time with his assistant coaches and several of his players, traveling to Madison to see the Badgers take on Illinois. Wisconsin was undefeated and heavily favored, but Illinois managed a major upset, winning 3-0. Wisconsin had 14 first downs to Illinois' two, but the Illini intercepted Wisconsin six times. Yost noted that several of the intercepted passes were short screen passes that gave Illinois the ball virtually at the Wisconsin line of scrimmage. This reaffirmed Yost's belief that there was little reason for a screen pass. If the ball is to be thrown, he taught, it should be thrown way down field.

By this time in the fall, darkness descended early on Ferry Field. Yost Fieldhouse was not yet built; the only indoor facility on campus was the old Waterman Gymnasium, which was wholly inadequate for football practice. To partially solve the problem, Yost years before had introduced the "ghost ball," a football painted white that could be seen well by the players as darkness fell. Practice lasted until the "ghost ball" could no longer be seen, and then sometimes the players would adjourn to Waterman where they would have signal drills.

For the first time all year, President Burton addressed the Thursday pep rally at Hill Auditorium. He wowed the student body by taking off his suit jacket, ascending the podium, and making it clear to all in attendance that from the top down, Wolverines were behind Michigan's title run.

At the last minute, one minor controversy developed. Ferry Field was U-shaped, with the curve of the U on the west side of the stadium, opposite State Street. Michigan's famous block "M" occupied the curve of the U, with students donning yellow or blue colors to make the configuration. The week of the Wisconsin game, it was announced that no women would be allowed into the block "M" configuration. This crucial decision came about because it seemed that women's attire, especially their colorful hats, interfered with the perfection of the block.

Two days before the game, the *Daily* put it this way.

> In order to make the block "M" at next Saturday's game strictly maize and blue in color, it has been decreed that absolutely no women will be allowed to sit in that section reserved for it. In past years it has always been noticed that the various colors that the women wore in the "M" tended to detract from its effectiveness…The block "M" will be formed in the west stand. Tickets for seats in this section have been stamped on the back with a large "M" by the Athletic Association and mailed out to men students only…Members…who are supervising the formation of the "M" will be at the stand in Ferry Field to see that no women bearing "M" tickets are admitted. These tickets are supposed to be held by men only and any women who come with them will be turned away.[46]

This sorry state of affairs did not go unchallenged. One co-ed relayed her response.

> The alleged purpose of this rule is for the "effect" it will give. It is averred that the varied colors worn by women tend to detract from the effect of the "M" of the maize and blue. It is also said that the cheering is not so vociferous because women's voices are not as voluminous as those of the men…What is the effect of such a sentimental idea compared with the effect of a dissatisfied student body? Students are separated from their friends and even from other members of their families…Worst of all, no particular individual or group is willing to shoulder the responsibility of the "rule." When complaint is made to the Athletic association they pass the buck to the Student Council and when members of the council are questioned about it they disclaim any responsibility and shift it back on the Athletic association. Whoever is accountable for

---

[46] *Michigan Daily*, 11/16/22, p 1

it should know by this time that it is opposed to the will of the student body.[47]

Nonetheless, the decision remained unchanged.

Wolverine fortunes depended upon the strength of the line. Michigan had suffered several injuries up front, and R. L. White, the substitute hero of the Ohio State game, was sick and couldn't play. Wisconsin was expected to use a powerful running game, but Michigan's offensive game plan was to focus on the forward pass. If the day were to be saved, the strength and ability of Michigan's reserves would be the key.

The Badgers left Madison to the largest send-off the town had ever seen. The team stayed in Jackson, Michigan, Friday night and arrived in Ann Arbor Saturday morning accompanied by 2500 fans and a 100-piece band. The whole outfit marched straight down State Street from the depot to Ferry Field.

The game was billed as a great defensive struggle. No team had scored on Michigan yet this season, while Wisconsin had allowed only one touchdown in two years. Adding to each team's offensive woes was the weather. Rain started Friday and kept up in spurts all night, letting up just before game time. Ferry Field, the same field upon which all the football practices were held, was a mud hole. With the defenses dominating on a wet field, it is not surprising that the two teams slipped and slid to a 0-0 halftime score.

However, in the third quarter, two consecutive pass plays covering 47 yards put Michigan in scoring position, and it was soon 7-0. Shortly thereafter, Michigan completed a 45-yard scoring pass to Kipke, the extra point was missed, and it was 13-0. Wisconsin, fighting to the end, scored in the last three minutes of the game, but the final was 13-6.

This game was a great victory, and the hometown crowd loved it. The Wolverines were only the second team to cross Wisconsin's goal line in two years, and they did it twice. Kipke's talents were lauded by all: his touchdown, his defensive play, and 12 punts for

[47] *Michigan Daily*, 11/18/22, p 4

an average of 44 yards. Old alums said that this Yost team reminded them of the great Michigan teams from the turn of the century.

Among the celebratory columns, the *Daily* found room on page one to say this about the block "M":

> Formation of the block "M" in the west stand was completed with every flag in place, making a perfect huge yellow "M" in a field of blue. 2500 freshmen and first year men made up the "M." The huge letter was the most effective and impressive "M" yet seen on Ferry field since its origin at the Pennsylvania game in 1907. With the absence of all distracting colors usually caused by different colored dress in the "M" the letter of maize stood out in its dark background a symbol of Michigan spirit and fair play.[48]

Henry Ford, the auto magnate, witnessed this match between Michigan and Wisconsin and afterwards was moved to write,

> It was a splendid victory for Michigan…The gathering Saturday was an impressive spectacle, indeed, and it occurred to me then that such a huge throng had not come together merely to witness a game—instead, that it had come in tribute to the man who had given so unflinchingly all through the years to maintain football on a plane of clean, American sportsmanship, unsullied by the professionalism that has degraded so much of our athletics.

> Mr. Yost well deserves the splendid machine he has created in the Michigan team and I know all in the University must feel as I do. And the University itself surely reflects the wholesome virility of our great Middle West. The young men and young women who are undergraduates of Michigan are fortunate indeed in having chosen an institution so expressive of the real America.[49]

[48] *Michigan Daily*, 11/18/22, p 1
[49] Board in Control, Box 5, November 1922 (1)

Mr. Ford, it turns out, did not have tickets for the game, but at his personal request he was placed in prime seats at the last minute. It was decided not to publicize this event for fear that those who could not get tickets would be "rather sore."[50] Again, notice was being taken of the limited seating capacity at Ferry Field in the face of exploding demand.

## The Minnesota Game

Three teams in the Big Ten were undefeated at this point: Michigan, Iowa and Chicago, but with the league limiting the season to a seven-game schedule, there were often shared titles. Michigan had only one game left, this one in Minneapolis. Since re-joining the Big Ten in 1918, Michigan had finished every football season against the Gophers. This was a traditional rivalry that dated back to 1892 and had led to the first great trophy to be contested between two college teams: the Little Brown Jug.

When Michigan journeyed to Minneapolis in 1903, Yost was in his third year at the Wolverine helm, and he had yet to lose a game. His early point-a-minute Michigan squads didn't just defeat other teams, but destroyed them, often winning by very lopsided scores. During this season, the Wolverine players made much of their giant water jug. "It went everywhere with them and the per-spiring warriors drank from its heavy mouth during every contest on the schedule. After each game, the score was emblazoned on the side of the jug."[51]

In 1903, the awaiting Gophers were very determined and a classic contest ensued. Michigan scored early in the game to take a 6-0 lead (touchdowns in those days were only worth five points, which makes the scores Michigan amassed even more astounding). Minnesota, however, fought every minute of this great game, and late in the fourth quarter, launched a tremendous drive that crossed the Wolverine goal with just a couple of minutes left. The point after was good, making the score 6-6. The field was immediately

---

[50] Board in Control, Box 5, November 1922 (1)
[51] *Michigan Daily*, 12/12/26, p 10

stormed by the thousands of excited Gopher fans. It was impossible to restore order and the game was called because of darkness, but in the chaotic gloom of that historic finish, Michigan's much valued water jug disappeared.

In 1922, the *Daily* told the story this way.

> In 1903, after the game, it was noticed that the Wolverine water jug had disappeared. The invaders hunted high and low all over Minneapolis for their container, but nowhere could it be found. As soon as they left for Ann Arbor, [a Minnesotan] bore it out from the armory basement as a trophy of battle. The student body and the athletic association took the suggestion and draped it with Minnesota colors, placing it in their trophy case as a challenge to all future Michigan elevens.
>
> Slightly wrought up over the happening, Michigan was led to see the joke, but insisted that the jug should be returned with due glory the next time they defeated the Gophers. And since then the tradition has grown up that the jug should be present at every Minnesota-Michigan football game, to be borne home by the victors.[52]

The students in Ann Arbor scheduled an emergency pep meeting to raise funds to send the band to Minneapolis, but this time the effort faltered. Minneapolis, no doubt, was just too far in those days, even though a Big Ten title was on the line. Special trains that had been scheduled were cancelled for lack of fans. The focus in Ann Arbor quickly became the Michigan Central railroad station, from which the 29 members of the travel squad would depart on Thursday afternoon. The *Daily* exhorted all Wolverine faithful.

> The student body has as serious a function to perform in this encounter as the team, for a victory without the moral support of those who benefit by it is only half a triumph. To fulfill this duty, every undergraduate should

---

[52] *Michigan Daily*, 11/24/22, p 1

be present at the Michigan Central station this afternoon to speed the team on its journey, and with cheers and song convey to the men who go to defend the honor of Michigan his confidence and trust in them…The team will give its all Saturday—the student body must do its share today.[53]

Today one must cross the widened area of Depot Street, turn and face the Gandy Dancer restaurant, to conjure up this scene. Thousands of delirious Wolverines are packed into the square. The team and the band are on the train platform, feeding the crowd spirit. Tad Wieman, an assistant coach, hauls out the Little Brown Jug, places it on his shoulders, and makes his way through the huge throng as they cheer, "Bring Back the Jug! Fight, team, fight!" Michigan's cheerleaders are on top of the boxcars, jumping and yelling and leading the crowd in "The Victors" time and time again. The roaring doesn't stop until the train finally pulls from the station and this great anticipating crowd makes its way back up State Street to campus.

The news from Minneapolis was not good. It had been raining all week for this late November contest and the Gopher field was six inches of thick black mud. There was not a blade of grass to be seen. Thursday afternoon the Minnesota athletic department had it covered with six inches of straw, hoping to somehow improve the conditions by game time. Fortunately, temperatures dropped into the low 20s Thursday night and the field froze solid. The Michigan team practiced Friday afternoon, taking the field in "Eskimo coats"[54] and kicking their way through the straw.

Back in Ann Arbor, the electronic grid-graph was again set up in Hill Auditorium so the home town crowd could watch the game in lights. Once more a telegraph line was in place, direct from Minneapolis to Hill for the play-by-play. The place was packed long before kick-off.

---

[53] *Michigan Daily*, 11/23/22, p 1
[54] *Michigan Daily*, 11/25/22, p 1

Minnesota's rock-hard home field was jammed with the largest crowd ever to witness a college football game in Minneapolis at that time. The first quarter belonged to the fired-up Gophers. Minnesota picked up a Michigan fumble, returned the ball to the Wolverine 8-yard line and shortly thereafter scored to make it 7-0. In the second quarter, Michigan seized the momentum and kept the Gophers in their own territory. Kipke finally scored on a short run to make it 7-6, but the point after was missed. Just before the half, Michigan's running game came alive, with the fullback breaking through the middle of the line for a 30-yard gain to the Minnesota four. Two plays later, Michigan scored to make it 13-7 at the half.

The second half was a legendary Kipke defensive performance. Minnesota threatened early in the third quarter, but Kipke intercepted a pass at the Wolverine 10-yard line. In the fourth quarter, Kipke again thwarted a Minnesota drive with another interception at the Michigan 30-yard line. Late in the game, Michigan launched a nice drive from their own 45-yard line to the Gopher 10, where they kicked a field goal. The score was 16-7 and it was over. The Wolverines had officially captured their first Big Ten title since 1904. On the same day, Illinois tied Chicago, so the title was shared only with Iowa.

The *Daily* could not be contained.

> Tonight all Michigan will turn out to greet those men who with a brand of football unsurpassed in gridiron history have brought back to their Alma Mater the championship of the West. Tonight, thousands of Michigan men, their faces glowing in the flare of torches and fireworks, will make "Victors" ring true as the triumphant Michigan locomotive rolls gloriously into the station.
>
> With a record that outshines that of any other important university football squad in the country, Michigan has opposed four of the most formidable elevens in the

Conference and emerged a decisive victor in each contest. Her goal line has been crossed but twice, while she has amassed high scores against every opponent…

And tonight, as 'Hurry-up' Yost steps off the train with the Minnesota jug under one arm and the winner's football under the other, eight thousand followers of the Varsity will take off their hats and cheer the man who not only developed an offensive machine of irresistible power, but who took raw material and whipped it into a line which added the finishing touch to a perfectly organized and unbeatable unit.

Tonight the Champions of the West come home and Michigan has just cause for rejoicing.[55]

Sunday afternoon, the freshman class threw together a huge pile of firewood at the foot of State Street, overlooking the train station where the Wolverine gridiron heroes would arrive at 7:00 P.M. The bonfire was lit at 6:00 P.M. and at 6:30 P.M. the band, playing "The Victors," stepped out from in front of Hill Auditorium, leading virtually the whole student body in a march down State Street to the depot. Placards proclaiming "The Champions of the West" were hung everywhere.

With the band playing and the crowd roaring, Michigan's heroes disembarked from the train at the station. The throng went into a frenzy over the reappearance of the Little Brown Jug, held high by the players and coaches. Slowly, in the glow of the bonfire, the mass of jubilant Wolverines made their way up the hill from the station and returned to central campus. On the Diag, in front of the library, there were short speeches by the coaches and players, songs and cheers, and a fireworks display. The Big Ten title was finally back in Ann Arbor and the victors were hailed as never before.

Two days later, Harry Kipke was elected captain of the squad for 1923. Three days after that, the annual football banquet was held at the Michigan Union. "Few persons realize," President Burton told the squad, "what a unifying force such a team is as Michigan has produced this year. It is the common ground where the interests of the people of the state, the town and the students is centered."[56] Coach Yost stated that at the outset of the season he thought the running game was most important, but he changed his ideas as the season progressed and began to emphasize passing more.

> As for the coaches, I am ready to back the statement that they have put in five hours of coaching to every hour put in by the coaching staffs of the average American university. They have worked practically 15 hours a day throughout the entire season…It was worth all my work if I could have lived only one hour after the Ohio State game to enjoy thinking about it!
>
> As for Harry Kipke, I never saw a player that gave more in every play than he did throughout the season. In the case of the team, if I were to take each of you individually and try to see the great team that has turned out, I could not do it. It is because you worked as a unit that you have done what you have.[57]

Kipke would receive another great honor. Several All-American teams were appointed in those days, but the greatest was the one compiled by Walter Camp. Even then, Camp, the former Yale coach, was recognized as the father of American football. He originated the All-American team in 1889, in which membership was considered the greatest athletic achievement for a player. Midwesterners grudgingly felt that Camp favored eastern players, but in 1922 Kipke, as a junior, was named to the first team.

University of Michigan President M.L. Burton was clearly an admirer of Yost. Even with this great championship season completed, speculation continued about whether Yost would or should continue as head coach. Burton privately wrote him:

---

[56] *Michigan Daily*, 11/28/22, p 1
[57] *Michigan Daily*, 11/28/22, p 1

I cannot let this football season close without expressing to you on behalf of the University our heartiest congratulations upon the success of the season. I think you know that I appreciate what you are doing here and how fully I am in sympathy with your general plans and standards…I want also to say that I for one have no sympathy with this constant discussion about whether you are to continue your services at the University. That question is not under discussion. You are the Director of Intercollegiate Athletics here; you are a man we want in every respect and I wish that the newspapers and everyone else could forget it and understand that you are a regular permanent part of the organization of the University of Michigan.[58]

Perhaps the significance of this team and this season has been lost to Michigan fans over the years. The great championship of 1922 gathers dust on placards and championship lists, but it should be remembered every time one walks up the ramps of Michigan Stadium. This was, in fact, the season that laid the cornerstone for the great stadium Michigan fans enjoy today. This sterling team filled Ferry Field with happy Wolverines, Wolverines who were excited when the game started and elated when the game ended. These Michigan fans wanted more, and when the season of 1923 rolled around, the demand for tickets remained impossible to satisfy. Looking around Ferry Field, Michigan alums began to wonder if a new stadium would not be needed in Ann Arbor. It wasn't a foregone conclusion and there would be plenty of obstacles, but the idea had emerged.

Fielding Yost, on the other hand, was not focused on a new football stadium in 1922. Rather, he was building the nation's very first field house.

---

[58] Board in Control, Box 5, November 1922 (2)

# Chapter 3

# The Building and Naming of Yost Field House

When Fielding H. Yost was appointed Director of Intercollegiate Athletics at Michigan in July 1921, the athletic facilities were wholly inadequate. Michigan's Ferry Field Stadium occupied the site extending southwest from Hoover and State Streets. A cinder track circled the football field in the same place as today's modern track. Except for a modest baseball facility and a few tennis courts south of the football stadium, the Ferry Field complex was undeveloped.

The only indoor sports facility for men was Waterman Gymnasium, which stood on the main campus where the new chemistry building is today. For the five winter months of the year, the only indoor space available for the intramural and intercollegiate programs was Waterman. If the weather was poor, the football team would sometimes retreat to Waterman for signal drills and light workouts indoors.

Michigan was the last school in the Western Conference to initiate basketball. Basketball became a conference sport in 1906 while the Wolverines were out of the league. Michigan's first team was fielded in 1909; in that season, one game was won and four were lost. After that, no scores were even recorded for the team until the season of 1917, when Michigan re-joined the Conference. The school's team was welcomed back, but ended league play in last place. There was no place to play the game except on the very short court in Waterman Gym, and there was virtually no room for spectators. It was widely recognized as the poorest basketball facility in the conference.

Needless to say, when the intercollegiate programs required use of the space at Waterman, the intramural program had no place at all. Even though Michigan, in 1913, had been the first university in America to implement an organized intramural athletic program, the entire situation by 1921 had become very unsatisfactory for the over 10,000 students enrolled at that time.

Many years later, Yost wrote,

> In 1921, I became thoroughly convinced that the University was not assuming its full responsibility in its all-around physical welfare program for every boy and girl at the University. There had been much talk of "athletics for all," but little had been done to provide the physical plant, the program, and the supervision necessary to make this a reality. But after I had talked with members of the Board of Regents of the University, I accepted an appointment to come here for the full year. My motto has been, since 1921, making athletics for all a reality instead of just a subject of conversation.[59]

Yost's commitment to the concept of "athletics for all" defined many of his initiatives when he was not coaching the football team. The idea provided the framework for most of his lasting accomplishments at Michigan. Yost felt strongly that education included more than mental exercises, that physical fitness was an essential factor in the development of a well-rounded individual. He never wavered from this commitment to intramural sports. Gradually, he made this belief much more than "just a subject of conversation" and the great physical plant that Michigan students enjoy today is a reality because of the foundation Yost put in place.

Eighteen months after becoming Michigan's Director of Intercollegiate Athletics, Yost knew the challenge he faced, what he

---

[59] Yost papers, Box 7, speeches (6)

wanted to accomplish, and the possible solution. The money that had begun to accumulate in the athletic department coffers would be used to foster better and more extensive intercollegiate athletics, to be sure, but it would also contribute to the funds to build the greatest university-owned intramural plant in the United States. This legacy would add to the one Yost bequeathed Michigan on the football field.

Following the Big Ten football championship of 1922, Yost was asked to address the meeting of the National Collegiate Athletic Association in New York City in December. In his wide ranging speech that defended the role of football on campus and also described the stressful life of a coach, Yost included these remarks:

> Our boys in too many homes live a life of luxury and ease and spend too much of their time on the soft easy cushions of automobiles. What they need and must have to fit them as men, real men, are the very things which are taught and developed on the football field, a strong alert body, a keen, quick thinking mind and that unconquerable fighting spirit which overcomes all obstacles in the end...
>
> The problem facing the colleges and universities is how best to put on a broad program of games, plays and physical education in the institutions throughout the country. Grounds, plays, equipment, instruction and supervision must be provided and a program adopted to encourage all students to participate. If a large part of the present student bodies take part in the plays and games it requires much space and a large expense. How is this money to be obtained except through the receipts from intercollegiate games? Football, so far as I know, is the only game from which profit for the maintenance of a broad program of athletics for all can be obtained.[60]

---

[60] Board in Control, Box 41, Articles by Yost, Book 2

At the time Yost became athletic director, Michigan supported six varsity sports: football, baseball, basketball, track, cross country and tennis. Yost was interested in adding others, including wrestling, swimming, golf and hockey, but, of course, any expansion of the Michigan intercollegiate program depended upon football income and appropriate facilities. In fact, the wrestling program was suspended in January 1923 for lack of funds and a place for meets. Yost's very first commitment at Michigan was to the building of the field house.

He wasted no time in realizing his vision. Clearly, a new indoor facility was needed on campus, but Yost wanted to be certain that it could accommodate both the football team and the baseball team in inclement weather. He originated the idea of a "Field House" and coined the name. It would be an enclosed facility that would encompass a field, a place large enough not only for football practice that could include punting (so crucial to his style of play), but also for the baseball team to practice hitting. Since his original concept was to make it as much like an open field as possible, he proposed huge windows to ring the facility so the field would be flooded with daylight. The structure would be the obvious facility for intercollegiate basketball and would include room for thousands of spectators. The field house would also allow for expanding the number of indoor intramural games. In addition, Waterman Gym would no longer have to be used by the intercollegiate teams, so it could be used exclusively by the intramural program.

Yost proposed this bold project as the winning football program began to fill the athletic coffers. He was, however, an astute businessman, who was well aware of the athletic department's financial history. As recently as 1919, the department had run a deficit. The concrete stands built on the south side of Ferry Field in 1914 took many more years to pay off than had been originally expected. Astute financial planning for a field house would be critical. The projected costs for the building were $235,000 (the equivalent of $2,642,350 today), an amount Yost and the Board in Control of Athletics felt to be quite manageable with athletic department income. Significantly, no tax money was to be used or solicited, a commitment Yost would make again and again as he expanded Michigan's athletic facilities. The financing and construction of the field house would give Yost critical experience that would be essential when it came time to initiate the football stadium project.

While the athletic department had an initial estimated cost of $235,000 for the project, there were, of course, cost overruns. By July 1922, even before the groundbreaking, the expected price had risen to $371,000. Yost was forced to write a long letter to the members of the Board in Control of Athletics explaining the problems.

> Naturally one would ask why this difference between the estimated cost of $235,000 and the actual bids of $371,000. In the first place, much was added to the original plans on the architect's own initiative. Under the original estimate it was figured that 600 tons of steel and 900,000 bricks would be necessary, but it turned out that 985 tons of steel and 1,400,000 bricks would be required. This difference takes care of about $50,000 of the cost of the building…
>
> The bids received for the steel per ton, the roofing, and the heating, lighting and plumbing were approximately as low as estimated. A very important factor in the high cost is due to the fact that there are no brick masons in Ann Arbor and few to be had anywhere at present. Brick masons are receiving $1.35 per hour and six months ago they were receiving $1.00 per hour. I am informed that these masons are doing from 25% to 50% less work per hour and that the contractors figured that they would have to pay about $1.50 an hour to get masons to come to Ann Arbor.[61]

---

[61] Board in Control, Box 5, July 1922

The chairman of the Board, law professor Ralph Aigler, expressed his dismay.

> I was astonished beyond expression at the news about the Field House. It is easy to see how the estimates should fail to meet the bids in view of the changes in structure and business and labor conditions, but how they should have *guessed* only about *half* the cost passes my understanding...I had supposed engineers and architects could figure those things almost exactly.[62]

Another member of the Board wrote,

> I am surprised to hear that the estimates have gone up. I would regret any changes in the building which would bring criticism on the Board...While I would regret delay in the construction of the building, I would rather wait a year or two than to erect something that would be a target for the critical. This building is likely to be on Ferry Field for some time after you and I have retired from active service.[63]

It was decided to proceed with the steel framework and hope that by the time the brick had to be laid, the bricklayers would be available and more affordable. A quick appraisal today of Yost Field House makes very clear the work the bricklayers had to do.

Delays continued. The steelwork was to be started on August 5, 1922, then the date was moved to August 20, but it wasn't until late September that the work actually began. Problems multiplied. There was a railroad strike, then a coal shortage. The necessary steel arrived in bits and pieces. The proposed opening date was pushed back to late 1923.

The *Michigan Daily* was, nonetheless, very pleased with the project. After noting that it would even be possible to hold football practice at night and in inclement weather, the editors stated:

[62] Board in Control, Box 5, July 1922
[63] Board in Control, Box 5, July 1922

The new field house will provide ample room for all conference sports including football and baseball; 340 by 160 feet rising clear of obstruction to 63 feet. The size of the room corresponds exactly with the dimensions of the standard football field (300 by 160).[64]

In the middle of all the building troubles, Yost received another warm letter from university President Burton.

I certainly do want to thank you for your letter of January 1 enclosing the clipping from the New York Mail, every word of which I have read with keenest interest…I do not need to tell you how happy I am over what you are doing here. I was down yesterday to look at the steel skeleton of the new field house. It is beginning to make a real impression. I think you know too how much I appreciate the standards for which you are champion and how much we appreciate the high honor you have brought to the University through her intercollegiate athletics this year.[65]

With the steel skeleton expected to be in place by the spring of 1923, Yost's focus turned to the bricks. Early in January, Yost placed a final order for the exterior brick, 325,000 in all, of which 20,000 were to be of a special type. He concluded his letter accompanying the order with:

This brick has been selected largely on my recommendation and I am more than anxious that this order be well taken care of and that the right colors in the right proportion be used.[66]

Despite his careful planning, the construction would not be so easy. In April, Yost wrote a sharper letter to the company.

---

[64] *Michigan Daily*, 11/2/22, p 1
[65] Board in Control, Box 5, January 1923 (2)
[66] Board in Control, Box 5, January 1923 (1)

I placed an order with you for some 300,000 bricks for our new Field House here on Ferry Field. It was definitely understood as regards the percentage of colors of these bricks. The bricks shipped here have had very few if any of the dark reds of which there were to be 30%...You know I was very interested in having you get the order as the bricks in my home in Nashville come from your plant. I wish you would wire me on receipt of this how your reds are running in comparison with the last car shipped. We are ready to start the brick work.[67]

The company responded with an encouraging note that the proper proportion of good red bricks were on the way, yet they never materialized. Yost wrote a letter in July clearly showing his exasperation.

It seems impossible to keep the outside face brick coming thru with enough reds to be in accordance with the original agreement. I do not believe that a car has ever come on the job that had the correct percentage of the right kind of bricks. The last car or two that came thru had almost as many browns and "sick" reds as the first car or two which were rejected. I have urged the architects to reject any more cars like these. Remember, we want a red building, not a brown one.[68]

At about this time, Yost wrote his wife that he felt he was under mental strain like he experienced during the football season and was suffering from "nervous indigestion."[69] Clearly, Yost's intimate involvement in every step in the construction of the field house was taking its toll on him.

In another letter, Yost indicated his preference for the interior brick to be buff in color. He ordered 260,000 of these bricks in February 1923, and even sent his own personal representative to

---

[67] Board in Control, Box 5, April 1923 (1)
[68] Board in Control, Box 5, April 1923 (1)
[69] Yost Papers, Box 2, April 1923

the plant where they were to be made. He wanted the manufacturers to know that thousands of people would be seeing the interior of the field house so the manufacturers should have every reason to supply him with premium bricks. This message got through and those special buff bricks remain visible throughout Yost Field House today.

However, obtaining the right bricks was not the only challenge. Brick masons remained in short supply, and for this reason the work progressed slowly. In mid-June 1923, Yost wrote that he only had 13 brick masons when he needed 50. By September, however, he could send a more positive note to the Board.

> Since the 18th of July all the necessary brick masons have been available and the work has been coming along fine. The brick work will be completed within the next two weeks. All the roof should be on in four weeks and all interior work should be completed by about the first of November…The outlook is that we will have the building ready for use before cold weather.[70]

September also brought other good news. It looked like four Michigan home football games would be sold out.

## The Naming of the Field House

As the steel skeleton began to rise over the field adjacent to the football stadium, the students began a movement to properly name the place. The *Michigan Daily* started the ball rolling with an editorial on November 22, 1922.

> At the present time the Athletic association is in the midst of an enterprise which is to result in a new athletic building for Michigan, known as the field house. This structure, well on the road to completion now, will be ready for use some time before the end of this school year.

---

[70] Board in Control, Box 5, September 1923

The field house is to be a center of athletic activities. It will shelter all indoor intercollegiate events. Vast audiences will proceed there often during each passing year to witness basketball games, track meets, and other athletic competitions.

In view of this fact, it seems only fitting and appropriate that a building of such importance in athletic activities, should be named after and dedicated to the man who during a quarter of a century of service has done more for Michigan athletics than any other could have hoped to do. Fielding H. Yost, for-ever-since-we-can-remember coach to Michigan's Varsity and now director of athletics in addition, merits the naming of the new field house in his honor.

When in the near future the Board in Control of Athletics meets, this matter should be given weighty consideration.[71]

Not only did the *Daily* initiate the idea, the paper was relentless in bringing it to fruition. Another editorial in January 1923, stated,

On November 22, 1922, the *Daily* suggested editorially that the new field house now being erected upon Ferry field should be named in honor of Coach Fielding H. Yost. Since that time many enthusiastic supporters have been won to the idea....Detroit papers have taken up the cry and alumni throughout the country have expressed their opinion that the naming of the new athletic structure in his honor would be a fitting acknowledgement of the services which Coach Yost has rendered the University.

Some objections have arisen to the proposition on the grounds that Michigan will have a stadium at some time in the future and this would provide a grander and more

---

[71] *Michigan Daily*, 11/22/22, p 4

fitting structure to bear his name. But Michigan cannot hope to have a new stadium for decades to come. Her stands now accommodate more than 40,000 spectators, and those in authority have serious doubts as to whether any larger stadium will be worth while financially.

The field house, on the other hand, has been described as "the greatest single athletic building in the country and the best and most complete all around college athletic plant in America." Ever since Coach Yost took his office as Director of Athletics his aims have been to obtain a building in which to house all indoor sports and it is largely through his influence that the present enterprise was undertaken.[72]

Michigan would soon have a new stadium, of course, but no one thought so in 1923. The editors refused to wait "decades" to name a facility after Yost. They wanted to honor him now. A few days later, the editors of the *Daily* announced a petition drive on campus to support the naming of the field house after Yost.

It is fitting that this building be dedicated to the man who has devoted a quarter of a century of service towards the placing of Michigan's athletes in the high place they now hold and whose value to the University is still undiminished. To those who believe that there should rather someday be a "Yost Stadium," let it be reiterated that such a structure cannot be hoped for inside of one or two decades.[73]

On January 21, 1923, the *Daily* announced that petitions had been distributed to all the fraternity houses, local restaurants, and the Union. The article emphatically stated that "neither the signatures of the faculty nor of the women are being solicited."[74] This was a man's show. Three days later, the *Daily* trumpeted that over

[72] *Michigan Daily*, 1/13/23, p 4
[73] *Michigan Daily*, 1/20/23, p 4
[74] *Michigan Daily*, 1/21/23, p 1

3000 signatures had already been gathered and soon 4000 would be topped. President Burton didn't hesitate to weigh in. "I think it would be very appropriate to attach the name of our Director of Intercollegiate Athletics to the new field house."[75]

The movement, however, didn't stop with a male student petition drive. Letters were sent to alumni clubs all across the country. The response was overwhelming. Within days, letters of support poured in. The University of Michigan Alumni Club of Detroit passed the first of many resolutions that would be presented.

> Whereas, Fielding H. Yost is the most prominent figure connected with collegiate athletics in the United States and has been of inestimable benefit and service to the University of Michigan for the past twenty-three years, and has won the respect, affection, and admiration of Michigan men and women everywhere; and
>
> Whereas, his followers have long sought some means of showing their appreciation of his varied services, not only in promoting the athletic prestige of Michigan, but in the far more important work of raising the standards of organized society by preaching year in and year out to tens of thousands the value of clean living, nobility of service and sacrifice and unselfish giving, fair play, generosity and magnanimity; and
>
> Whereas Detroit alumni were the first to urge that the proposed field house be named after Mr. Yost, and the occasion of its dedication be made a gathering of Michigan men and women from far and near to do honor to Mr. Yost and Michigan in the greatest celebration ever held in Ann Arbor; and
>
> Whereas, the naming of buildings and fields after college benefactors is fully justified by precedent; and
>
> Whereas, the new field house was conceived by Mr.

[75] *Michigan Daily*, 1/21/23, p 1

Yost, and made possible by his financing and executive ability, and the drawing power of his teams and his own personality; therefore

Be It Resolved, That the University of Michigan Club of Detroit urge and recommend to the Board in Control of Athletics at the University of Michigan that the new Field House be named after Fielding H. Yost.[76]

This type of resolution, in one form or another, was forwarded from alumni clubs all around the country.

Yost was very flattered by the idea. In a letter to a friend dated March 6, 1923, Yost wrote:

Sometime after the first of February the Student Council appointed a committee and passed resolutions in favor of naming the Field House and appointed a committee of three for the purpose of securing alumni and student sentiment. This committee wrote some prominent alumni, the secretaries of the alumni associations and placed some petitions about Ann Arbor where students might voluntarily sign them. More students volunteered their signatures than have ever been present at any regular election on the campus and girls were not permitted to sign the petition…Some thirty alumni associations have passed resolutions favoring this move, among them New York, Detroit, Chicago, and St. Louis.[77]

One person opposed to the idea was Chairman of the Board in Control of Athletics, law professor Ralph Aigler. When the time came, he would vote against naming the field house after Yost, but the enormous display of support impressed him. To a friend, Aigler indicated his ambivalence.

I have come to the conclusion that I am, perhaps, over sensitive in regard to the naming of the Field House, and

---

[76] Board in Control, Box 5, January 1923 (1)
[77] Board in Control, Box 5, March 1923 (1)

that my previous position, even if justified by my feeling that the university rather than any individual should be stressed, must be modified in view of the expressed wishes of so many, who are as well-qualified as I to determine what is proper and fitting.

I do this with less compunction because Mr. Yost represents a high type of integrity and loyalty. His services to and his love for Michigan justifies us in going much beyond ordinary recognition of such service. His long years of service—probably never to be duplicated —another factor, and for myself, a real affection. All these things are influencing me when I say that I am in favor of naming the new building, "Yost Field House."

I have just returned from a luncheon…at which the Coach spoke to some 100 Michigan men and perhaps twice as many more from other Colleges…The Coach was at his best, in fact I have never heard him speak so well—he has improved wonderfully during the last year or so—and his talk was dignified, forceful and inspiring. He has also his own inimitable way of putting things and his own peculiar humor, all of which kept his audience at attention the whole distance. I heard several, from other Universities I think, who had evidently never heard him before, comment on his sincerity, his directness and his conviction in what he was saying. He certainly did the Athletic Department of the University of Michigan no harm today.[78]

Another Board member, John Hibbard, changed his mind.

Perhaps with a supersensitive desire to bring "Michigan" to the fore where ever possible, my first impression was that the new Field House should bear the name of the University; like the "Yale Bowl" and the "Harvard

---

[78] Board in Control, Box 5, March 1923 (1)

Stadium," but soon realizing that it was the evident wish of many of the Regents; of the Faculty and of a large majority of the Alumni and Students, and with the greatest personal pleasure, I wrote…that I was unqualifiedly in favor of naming the new building "Yost Field House."[79]

Congressman Robert Clancey, a University of Michigan alumnus and friend of Yost, responded to Hibbard's declaration.

I am certainly overjoyed at your coming into the Yost camp. There is really not a good argument against our proposition. The fact that his opponents proposed finally to "dedicate" the building to him but not name it after him shows they are splitting hairs. We should try to honor him while he is alive and the main thing in my mind is to get out his admirers to warm the cockles of his heart at the demonstration…when the building is dedicated. He has taken a lot of grief for Michigan.[80]

All that was required now was the official vote by the Board in Control of Athletics. The Student Council presented 3500 signatures at the Board's meeting on March 11, 1923, but the Board deferred discussion of the issue. The editors at the *Daily* were not pleased.

This is not the first time that the matter has been tabled…From now until the April meeting members of the Board will have considerable time in which to deliberate the request. They have the facts in hand. They must realize the weight of alumni and student opinion; almost a quarter of a century of exceptional service on the part of Coach Yost is worthy of recognition; the greatest athletic structure in any university of the country today provides an appropriate tribute.[81]

---

[79] Board in Control, Box 5, March 1923 (1)
[80] Board in Control, Box 5, April 1923 (1)
[81] *Michigan Daily*, 3/13/23, p 4

Finally, on May 5, 1923, the Board in Control of Athletics voted to officially name "the greatest athletic structure in any university of the country today," Yost Field House. The vote was not unanimous. At this time, the Board in Control consisted of 11 members: Yost, three alumni representatives, three student representatives and four from the faculty. Professor Aigler of the law school was the chairman and had been for years, but Yost almost always controlled the student and alumni votes so his wishes tended to dominate the Board. This makeup of the Board irritated the faculty and would lead to some of the opposition Yost would face when he would eventually propose building a new stadium. Clearly, Yost was very influential on campus and, no doubt, some faculty members resented that fact. In any case, on this day, all four faculty members, including Aigler, voted no, while the students and alumni voted yes.

Nonetheless, the final vote was in and the *Daily* celebrated.

> To perpetuate the name of one who has contributed so greatly to the prominence which the University of Michigan has attained, the new Field House is to be named after the grand old man of football, Fielding H. Yost. In bestowing this name upon Michigan's greatest achievement in athletic structures, the Board in Control of Athletics voices for the entire body of both alumni and undergraduates, the sentiment which they have so ardently express through petitions and innumerable letters.

> Under the able guidance of "Hurry Up" Yost, Michigan has attained prominence in both competitive and instructional athletics, so that today to be a member of Yost's team means more than merely being a football player. No tribute can be too great as recognition of the service this able leader has rendered to Michigan.[82]

---

[82] *Michigan Daily*, 5/6/23, p 4

This affectionate tribute to Yost as "The Grand Old Man" was widespread in the Michigan community at this time. In 1923, though, Yost was only 52 years old. There is nothing to suggest he objected to this nomenclature. Yost was born in 1871 when life expectancy was probably about 45 years. A male who reached 20 years of age in 1891 would have been expected to live about another 40 years, to age 60. In this context, Yost as "The Grand Old Man" was no doubt quite fitting. He would live, though, to the very respectable age of 75.

So it would be Yost Field House. The only remaining issue was to determine when the dedication would occur. Many alumni wanted it to be at a home football game, with the Ohio State encounter being a clear preference. However, Michigan was playing Ohio State in October, and Yost, ever cautious, did not want the dedication to suffer the embarrassment of occurring before construction was complete. Michigan had scheduled a home game with the Quantico Marines for November 10, 1923, and Yost chose that date for the dedication ceremony that would precede the game.

# Chapter 4

# 1923: The Season That Built the Foundation

Until 1922, the Big Ten faculty representatives had insisted on a seven-game football schedule as the maximum commitment possible for student athletes. However, at the end of that season, an eight-game schedule was approved for the future.

The Big Ten athletic directors met at the end of each football season to set the schedule for the next year. Since Iowa and Michigan had tied for the Big Ten title in 1922, it was agreed to arrange a game between the two teams in Iowa City the following year. Other Big Ten teams that Michigan would play in 1923 included Ohio State, Wisconsin, and Minnesota. However, because of scheduling difficulties, Illinois would not be an opponent. Non-conference competition would be provided by Case, Vanderbilt, the Michigan Agricultural College, and the Quantico Marines.

Yost was met by one of the largest turnouts ever for spring practice. Eighty-five men initially showed up, and the squad quickly increased to one hundred. Letters of invitation to likely candidates had been sent out, but the coaching staff made it clear they were desirous of recruiting every man on campus "who can play, thinks he can, or would like to learn."[83]

Michigan's chances for 1923 looked promising. The starting quarterback, Irwin Uteritz, was returning, as well as the All-American, Harry Kipke, and most of the line. The *Daily* set the tone.

[83] *Michigan Daily*, 4/3/23, p 6

Michigan has a difficult schedule to face next fall—one of the hardest that has been waiting for a Wolverine team in many a day, but those who will control the destinies of the 1923 team feel that Michigan will have an aggregation on the gridiron that will be more than fit to meet that schedule. We cannot afford to disappoint those who have arranged it, and, further, we cannot afford to disappoint ourselves, for Michigan knows where Michigan belongs—always leading.[84]

Unfortunately, all was not rosy. Yost learned over the summer that three promising players were lost due to academic ineligibility. Another player the coaches were very keen about was disqualified following an objection by Ohio State. The young man had apparently played summer baseball for money at one point and was, therefore, under Big Ten rules, ineligible for college competition.

In July, Yost sent the following missive to his players,

Michigan has an eight game schedule, the first one since 1905 and seven of those games will be hard ones. You should do everything possible to give yourself a 'fair chance' to be a real asset to the football team…How well you are prepared along these lines, I want to impress upon you, is a continuous day by day proposition…Again, let me say, DO NOT CHEAT YOURSELF, but GIVE YOURSELF A FAIR CHANCE…Practice, PRACTICE, PRACTICE.[85]

The football ticket situation in Ann Arbor in September 1923 was, simply put, unbelievable. The *Daily* provided this assessment,

Applications for 13,000 seats for the Ohio State game, the entire alumni allotment, had been received at the Athletic association office by September 13. Since that

[84] *Michigan Daily*, 4/6/23, p 6
[85] Board in Control, Box 5, July 1923 (2)

time 12,600 have been returned to applicants because of the ticket shortage…

Up to the present season, the largest pre-season sale of tickets for any one game was 4967 for the Illinois game last year. The total number of reservations made by September 20 in 1921 was 8460. A new record was established last year when 9722 tickets were sold by the same date, but already this season 32,934 reservations have been made, tripling the previous record.[86]

One can only imagine the receipts being counted by the athletic department. Of course, much money was returned, generating chagrin and anger from those who were denied seats. Yost, unable to comply with the multitude of requests, wrote to a friend that "the ticket problem is awful in regard to the Ohio State game."[87]

Nonetheless, he retained a cautious approach to the problem of more seating in Michigan's stadium. At the end of the 1922 season, Yost wrote the following in response to a complaint about the lack of decent seating:

The plan of distribution of tickets has received long and careful study by those experienced in this work. Every year the experience of the directors and those in charge of tickets at all the larger institutions meet and exchange ideas and submit to each other the plans used at the various universities. The demand and conditions are different at each university. At our university, the stands are divided as follows: beginning at the center of the field, the students receive one section and the alumni and general public another. These sections are alternated between alumni and students all the way around. The great difficulty, of course, of satisfying everyone is the fact that all applicants want tickets on the 50-yard line or very near it. All objections come to us from those who receive

[86] *Michigan Daily*, 9/24/23, p 1
[87] Yost papers, Box 2, 1923

their allotment, perhaps, beyond the 25-yard line. If the stands are to be filled, of course, some one must take the end seats. Except for four or five occasions, our problem has been one of intense publicity to sell out the stands.

*This year with a winning team we had no trouble of doing so, but only about five times in the history of our athletics has every seat been sold, which means only three times in the history of football previous to this year* [italics mine]…One must remember that one quarter of the good seats in the 'center' of the field are allotted to supporters of the visiting team. I still feel that our problem in the future will be to fill our stands unless we maintain a winning team when all the fair weather friends come out.[88]

Yost was cautious. He had lived through some very sparse football years, including one as recently as 1919. While 1922 had been a great and wonderful success, Yost knew it was his job to keep the seats filled. He was no doubt impressed by the amazing good fortune of the athletic department as football ticket requests piled up in September 1923, but he wasn't about to predict that such success could last indefinitely. Even so, it had to relieve some of his concern as the giant field house neared completion.

By the end of September, the ticket office could report truly astonishing news. Not only had the alumni allotment for the Ohio State game been sold out in its entirety, 13,000 seats, but $17,000 had already been returned to disappointed alumni for just that game. Just two years earlier, only 7000 seats for the Buckeye game had been sold by the end of September. In 1922, the two biggest home games, Illinois and Wisconsin, had sold just 13,600 tickets by the end of September, but one year later the two home games with Ohio State and Wisconsin had already sold 25,400 tickets. The four biggest home games had sold an incredible 35,600 tickets by September 30. Even students and faculty were joining the parade.

---

[88] Board in Control, Box 5, December 1922 (2)

By September 1922, those two groups had claimed only 4300 tickets. One year later, the number jumped to 15,700. Michigan football fans were showing up in unbelievable numbers. Such a demand, if it continued, could eventually provide the money for all kinds of projects.

Wolverine adherents had every reason to be very pleased with the achievements of Michigan's intercollegiate teams in the previous year. In September 1923, Yost issued this assessment and challenge to the returning student body.

> So far as I have been able to learn, Michigan's 1922-23 record in athletics has never been equaled. We won six Conference championships and one National Championship. We were not beaten in the Conference in football, cross country, indoor track, or baseball. The championship in outdoor track and in tennis singles also came to Michigan as did the National Championship in outdoor track.
>
> No Michigan man or woman can help but be proud of such a record. It will go down in history as an achievement without parallel.
>
> But what of today? Our life is now—not yesterday.
>
> Real winners differ from ordinary performers in their reaction to victory. The real champion enjoys the thrill of WINNING. The ordinary man enjoys the thrill of HAVING WON. In other words, during the very minutes that the average fellow is sitting back and enjoying past victories, the true champion is out achieving more.
>
> This year will be perhaps as difficult a testing time as Michigan has ever experienced. Because of our record all eyes will be directed our way and the country will watch more keenly than ever our progress.
>
> Are we going to be content to spread our wings and soar

on reputation or are we going to put the past behind us and tackle the job ahead? The former is the course of least resistance—but of sure defeat. The latter is the course of possible victory.

Turning to our most immediate problem, the 1923 football team, we find a very mistaken idea permeating the campus. Instead of having a full team of veterans as most followers seem to think, we are really beginning the season with only 5 men who started the Ohio State game last year. These are Captain Kipke, Blott, Muirhead, Vandervoort, and Uteritz. These men constitute a good nucleus but represent less than half a team.

The coaches and candidates realize the situation and are doing everything possible to build up another strong team. But this isn't enough. There must be the right background of student attitude. The campus must appreciate the problems at hand and must assist in their solution. First of all, the vacant places on the team must be filled. This means work. There must be work of reserves, work of freshmen, work of everyone. Enthusiasm is fine but *work wins*. There must be full quotas of good men for freshmen and reserve teams. There must be the active cooperation of the entire student body…

No victories can be won nor any physical growth or development attained by recourse to soft cushions, low lights, and pink teas. Every Michigan student must put his shoulder to the wheel and push. Remember, we can't win today on what we did yesterday.[89]

Team workouts began September 15. The initial scrimmage of the year on Ferry Field was lackluster, with poor line play of real concern to the coaches. New ends and a fullback were needed, as none had returned from the previous year's team. The coaching staff

---

[89] *Michigan Daily*, 9/24/23, p 6

had been very pleased with Michigan's strong aerial attack of 1922, and much practice time was devoted to improving and refining it. Unfortunately, several promising players from the previous year's freshman squad did not return to school.

Captain Kipke, quarterback Uteritz, and the returning center, Jack Blott, were kept out of practices to act as officials and to avoid any unnecessary injuries. On September 25, the varsity squad was cut from 50 to 35. Before practices were closed to the public, a full scrimmage was finally played out on September 27. One enthused student wrote,

> Our esteemed contemporary, Fielding H. Yost…is doing a great social service for the student body. This service, we need hardly say, is the daily scrimmage…This super spectacle is daily witnessed by thousands of interested spectators: some who come there to sit and think, some who bring rushees to give them a thrilling afternoon, and some who want to back the good ol' team. It's a fine thing for the boys to have this innocent place to pass their time; without it they might be forced to go to the movies or even, possibly, to study. Thank God for Mr. Yost.[90]

With the onset of October, the football squad practiced behind closed gates. On October 4, the varsity defeated the reserves, 22-7, in a spirited game that drew many spectators. The next day, the varsity blasted the freshman team, 26-0, but note was made of the play of a promising halfback for the freshman team, Benny Friedman, an Ohio lad from Cleveland.

Michigan's first game of the season was again with the Case Scientific School of Cleveland. Once again, Yost did not stay in Ann Arbor to coach the game. He took the train to Columbus to scout the Buckeyes in their opener against Ohio Wesleyan, but the team he left behind performed admirably. Michigan handily defeated Case, 36-0, but there was concern by those who watched the game

---

[90] *Michigan Daily*, 9/28/23, p 4

that the offensive line was not opening holes. Much of Michigan's scoring came through the air and on end runs. The amazing Kipke, however, wowed the crowd with a beautiful 38-yard drop-kick field goal and an average of 45 yards on punts.

## The Vanderbilt Game

The next game was a return engagement with Vanderbilt in Ann Arbor. This would be a true grudge match. Vanderbilt had been undefeated in 1922 with its only blemish the tie with Michigan. In fact, the Commodores had not lost a game in two years, and several returning lettermen insured a powerful squad. More than one special train had already been arranged from Nashville, and a large portion of the student body was expected to follow their team. "Beat Michigan" was the byword on the Nashville campus.

Vanderbilt had opened its season with a 27-0 victory over Howard College of Birmingham. Michigan and Vanderbilt both followed their opening victories by holding secret practices for the week of preparation before the contest. The Ferry Field stands were cleared of spectators as Michigan worked on new signals and drills.

The *Daily* ran a request on page one.

> Cars are wanted by the athletic reception committee to meet the Vanderbilt team when it arrives in Ann Arbor Friday afternoon. This sort of welcome has never been carried out for a visiting team, but the committee wishes to try it this year. All men who have cars available are urged to turn them over for this purpose…The Vanderbilt team will have its headquarters at the Union during the stay here and will both eat and sleep there.[91]

Vanderbilt's football squad was accompanied by 35 band members and 800 fans. The school's total enrollment at the time was about 1000 students, so this was a considerable entourage for them. The *Daily* was ready for the challenge.

---

[91] *Michigan Daily*, 10/9/23, p 1

The Maize and Blue squad will not be outdone…The work of the Varsity on Ferry Field during the past week has been evidence of that fact. Every man who showed a flaw in last Saturday's game…has been driven hard in order to overcome his imperfections and all of them have taken their work-outs in a spirit which hails back to the time when Coach Yost drilled his point-a-minute eleven in 1903. Not a man on the squad has shown any signs of laziness and if work counts for anything, Vanderbilt will face a real football team tomorrow.[92]

The appearance of the Commodore band, however, led to some soul-searching. The Michigan band remained underfunded and was often unable to make trips to away games. The *Daily* lamented,

Today we have with us a team which has traveled more than 500 miles to meet Michigan on the gridiron and it brought its band along. Last year we played this same team on its own field, but the Varsity band stayed in Ann Arbor. It stayed here because its finances would not permit a journey to the Southland…Today the Board in Control will consider the student council petition regarding financial support of the band that it may accompany the team to the Iowa and Wisconsin battlefields…It merely asks the Board to temporarily rescind its ruling which prohibits bucket collections in the Ferry Field stadium. It asks to take up a collection at the Ohio State game…If the Board will suspend its ruling for one day the student body will do the work. Otherwise we must remain in the class with the small college which either does not have a band or cannot afford to send it with its team.[93]

The Michigan Band traditionally paid its way to games on foreign fields by holding "tag day" sales on campus. Band mem-

---

[92] *Michigan Daily*, 10/12/23, p 6
[93] *Michigan Daily*, 10/13/23, p 4

bers used to beg for contributions from the student body, but this effort was hopelessly inadequate. A trip away from Ann Arbor for the band often cost in excess of $3000 and campus fundraising simply couldn't raise this revenue. The student council proposed fundraising among the crowds at the stadium, but the athletic department was initially quite opposed to the idea of student hawkers approaching alumni. Nonetheless, the athletic department finally relented and agreed to allow a collection at one home game, the Ohio State encounter, which would follow the Vanderbilt game. Although students were restricted to collecting funds only at the gates to the field, the band hoped it had solved its problem.

The contest against Vanderbilt was a fiercely fought football game. In the first quarter, Michigan drove to the Vanderbilt 10-yard line, but with fourth down and one yard to go, they were stopped. Michigan scored the only points in the game in the second period when the center, Jack Blott, kicked a 10-yard field goal, making it 3-0.

The game was a punting duel since Vanderbilt's Coach McGugin was, of course, Yost's most astute student. Both teams made strategic decisions to punt often on third and sometimes even on second down.

Kipke did not have a great day. In the first period, he missed a 40-yard field goal, and in the third period he had one blocked. Surprisingly, Kipke was outpunted, averaging 40 yards per kick to Vanderbilt's 42. Yost knew the quality of the Vanderbilt team, however, and he was very pleased with the 3-0 victory.

## The Ohio State Game

Knowing that Michigan next faced Ohio State, McGugin, the Michigan graduate and letterman, wrote a quick note to Yost after the game explaining that Commodore players had told him that Michigan's fullback wore a certain facial expression that gave away when he would be carrying the ball. Yost was happy for the tip and corrected the problem.

The Michigan ticket office estimated demand for the Ohio State game to be twice the 37,000-seat capacity of Ferry Field. OSU had been granted 9000 tickets, 7500 in the stands and 1500 in standing room only at the east end of the field. Michigan's ticket manager stated the obvious, "The Michigan-Ohio State game is fast becoming one of the football contest classics of the country and the demand for accommodations is increasing yearly in proportion to this fact."[94]

While Michigan's passing game thus far had not been as effective as the previous year, Wolverines were most upset about Kipke being outplayed in the punting category. It was noted that Vanderbilt players put great pressure on him, forcing him to hurry several kicks, and it was assumed the Buckeyes would attempt to do the same.

In both Columbus and Ann Arbor, the teams prepared for the game with secret practices. Yost took the whole team off Ferry Field to the inside of the unfinished field house where there could be no prying eyes. He finally had a perfect place for secret practices.

Ohio State seemed to have a better passing game than the previous year, but their defense looked suspect. The Buckeyes had beaten Ohio Wesleyan, 34-7, in the game scouted by Yost, and subsequently tied Colgate, 23-23.

The day before the game, the little community of Ann Arbor was packed. The *Daily* exclaimed,

> All vacant rooms, not to mention hotels and dormitories, are filled to capacity with double-deck beds and temporary cots much in evidence...Special trains will arrive in the city tomorrow at the rate of nearly one an hour...from Chicago, Columbus, Detroit, Kalamazoo, and Grand Rapids.[95]

The editors noted the significance of the first pep rally of the year,

---

[94] *Michigan Daily*, 10/16/23, p 1
[95] *Michigan Daily*, 10/20/23, p 1

The pep meeting is more than a mere blowing off of steam or foolish display of pomp and ceremony. It is a period of time set aside…in which the football team has a few minutes to understand and estimate the support of the student body. Such meetings are necessary to produce winning teams. Players are given added stimulus. They are made to understand that their efforts are appreciated; more than that, they see that while they are fighting and suffering, the student body is also ready and anxious to do everything possible to support the team.[96]

President Burton was a true friend of the athletic program at Michigan. He would never join the voices that called for the elimination of intercollegiate sports, and he was comfortable with the role athletics played on campus. He issued the following game day statement:

The University of Michigan welcomes with joyous enthusiasm all of its guests today. In particular, we greet warmly the friends and allies of Ohio State University. We believe, with you, in the spirit of play, in wholesome recreation, and in true sportsmanship…It would be very easy to misinterpret this spectacle today. Some critics will say, "So this is higher education!" Such a person forgets that this is not all that a university does.…Only on one or two afternoons in the year do we see such a stimulating sight as this. It is a powerful agent in unifying large and growing institutions. It gathers up and weaves together into one strong bond the loyalties and enthusiasms of thousands of virile, throbbing youths. Such results are highly to be desired.[97]

The game itself was no contest as Michigan dominated every aspect and won, 23-0. For the second straight year, the Buckeyes

[96] *Michigan Daily*, 10/17/23, p 4
[97] *Michigan Daily*, 10/20/23, p 1

had failed to score on Michigan. Kipke revived, scoring a touchdown in the third quarter and averaging 50 yards a punt. In fact, he nailed two punts for more than 60 yards. The modern reader, reviewing the play-by-play, would likely be amazed by the number of times the two teams punted on first, second, and third downs.

The *Detroit News* hailed Michigan's senior quarterback, Irwin Uteritz,

> Having had two years' experience, Uteritz was qualified to reach his best form this season and Uteritz delivered against Ohio State on Ferry Field last Saturday. In our opinion that was the best job of quarterbacking that has been seen in Ann Arbor since the open game was introduced…There had been a great deal of talk about the Michigan forward passing attack and Ohio State came prepared to halt the overhead game. However, Uteritz did not launch into a passing game but opened with a running attack. Then, when he had the Ohio secondary defense pulled in to support the first line and stop the Michigan plunges, he began forward passing.[98]

A fervent alumnus and friend of Yost wrote to him,

> The victory over…Ohio was as gratifying to me as I believe it could possibly be to you. In view of all the circumstances of the past few years it proved conclusively that victory is sweet indeed. No team ever played a more intelligent game than Michigan did on that day. They seemed to take advantage of every opening and won so decisively as time went on that I think there will be no question in the minds of even the Columbus newspaper reporters about the knowledge that Michigan and Yost have about all phases of football, including the so-called modern forward passing game.[99]

[98] *Michigan Daily*, 10/23/23, p 1
[99] Yost papers, Box 2, 1923 (2)

Yost was, no doubt, feeling quite vindicated. He had suffered much criticism a few years earlier for allegedly not understanding the "open" passing game of football. Now he seemed to be its master. Michigan's winning streak now went all the way back to the Ohio State game of 1921.

A few days after the game, one enterprising Michigan student wrote this prophetic letter to the *Daily*.

> Ohio State rather than Minnesota has come to be our great rival. What does an old brown jug matter? Its story is that of other days and of a stale rivalry. Ohio State should be given the last date on our schedule.[100]

Should this young man have an honored place at the Michigan table? All prophecies take some time for fulfillment, and it would be many years still, 1935 in fact, before Ohio State would assume its rightful place at the end of Michigan's schedule.

After this great game, the only frowns in Ann Arbor were those of the band members. The much heralded collection for the band at the game netted only $800, not nearly enough to send the band to even one away encounter. The editors at the *Daily* remained in the band's corner.

> The band is one of the proudest boasts of Michigan. It renders invaluable service to the University and particularly to the athletic interests of the University… For the support of the band the Athletic association contributes each year the sum of $700 which goes toward the buying of equipment and supplies…otherwise, the band exists on the money it can raise itself…

> It's very distinctly the duty of either the Athletic association or the University to take over the support of the band.[101]

---

[100] *Michigan Daily*, 10/25/23, p 4
[101] *Michigan Daily*, 10/23/23, p 4

## The Michigan Agricultural College Game

The next contest on the schedule was the annual tussle with the Aggies from East Lansing. The game was made more interesting for the fans because "Stub" Kipke, Harry Kipke's younger brother, played at end for the Michigan Agricultural College. However, the Aggie team was not taken seriously in Ann Arbor as shown by this *Daily* comment.

> It is expected that Saturday's game will not warrant starting the first Varsity team and in view of the fact that the Iowa game which follows will without a doubt be a terrific struggle the coaches are allowing the men to take it easy this week.[102]

In fact, the word from East Lansing was not threatening. The Aggies lost their star starting tackle to diphtheria, and there was concern the rest of the squad had been exposed. As a result, the whole team was inoculated, and players had arms so sore that contact practice had to be deferred. Yost just paid no attention to this game. He left town as he had the previous year, this time to scout the Iowa game with the Buckeyes in Columbus.

As the game approached, the *Daily* was merciless, and trumpeted its confidence in a front-page article.

> It is expected the Wolverines will have little difficulty in trouncing the Farmers today as in previous years…While the game has no bearing on the Conference standing of the Wolverines, the members of the squad are anxious to defeat the East Lansing aggregation by a large score. The Aggies have already stacked up against Chicago and Wisconsin and the Varsity is anxious to roll up a larger score than either of those two Big Ten teams could against the Farmers.

> If the eleven men who start the game today show as high

---

[102] *Michigan Daily*, 10/25/23, p 6

a quality of form as they did in the Ohio State game last week there is no question but that the issue will not be long in doubt.[103]

The Aggies arrived with enthusiasm and a 60-piece band, but they weren't enough to ensure victory. Michigan overwhelmed MAC, 37-0. Kipke scored two touchdowns in a brief appearance. The *Daily* summed it up: "Overwhelmed by the same attack which downed the Buckeyes a week ago, the Green and White of MAC bowed to Michigan by the score of 37 to 0 in a fracas that had all the aspects of a slaughter."[104]

## The Iowa Game

Michigan emerged from the game with no injuries and most of the starters well rested, important factors for the showdown with Iowa. This game took on added significance because Michigan and Iowa had tied for the Big Ten title in 1922, but did not play each other that year. However, at the end of that season, the two schools decided to schedule a game in Iowa City for 1923 with a return game in Ann Arbor in 1924.

This would be Michigan's first game against Iowa since rejoining the Big Ten. The two teams had only met three times previously. In 1900, the year before Yost arrived in Ann Arbor, Michigan lost 28-5. In 1901, Yost's inaugural year, the two teams played in Chicago on Thanksgiving Day. Michigan won 50-0, and the following year Michigan plastered the Hawkeyes 107-0, racking up the largest margin ever achieved against a conference team. By 1923, however, the long absence of competition had no doubt dulled the Hawkeye memory of this humiliating defeat.

There was no enthusiasm in Ann Arbor for making the trip to Iowa City. A special train was arranged, but for it to be economical, 200 students were needed to pay the round-trip cost of $34. The *Daily* complained,

[103] *Michigan Daily*, 10/27/23, p 1
[104] *Michigan Daily*, 10/28/23, p 1

Iowa's gridiron warriors will be backed by cheering thousands of…supporters. Thus far Michigan backs its team with a grand total of 18 students…At least 102 students must give tangible evidence that they are backing the team by signing up by tonight for the special train to Iowa or the train will not run.[105]

The train did not run. The *Daily* quickly promoted the traditional send-off at the station, but later reports stated that only 1000 students followed the band down State Street to the station. For whatever reason, Michigan's run for the title did not seem to be generating the same enthusiasm as the year before. Perhaps students were already complacent. Michigan was on top of the Big Ten, and the world was as it should be.

The Iowa football team would be a challenge. The Hawkeyes had a heavy line averaging 210 pounds and an awesome ground game that was pivotal in their 20-0 defeat of Ohio State. Sportswriters claimed the 1923 Iowa attack, while not credited with much of a passing game, nonetheless moved like a steamroller on the ground. The Hawkeye defense against the pass was sterling, having intercepted Ohio State eight times.

Once again, both teams instituted secret practices. Michigan fans were unhappy to learn that three inches of snow had fallen in Iowa City two days before the game. Adding to the concern, Michigan's travel plans were complicated. The team left Ann Arbor at 3:50 P.M. Thursday afternoon. In Chicago, they took buses to another station where sleeping cars were waiting for them. The team was to arrive in Cedar Rapids, Iowa, Friday morning at 6:15 A.M. where they would have a light workout and stay overnight before moving on to Iowa City Saturday morning. Meanwhile, even though the proposed train with fans from Ann Arbor wouldn't run, special trains with Michigan alumni would leave from Chicago, Minneapolis, Omaha, Kansas City, and St. Louis.

---

While snow had fallen on Iowa City two days before the game, by game day, November 3, 1923, the weather had cleared. Michigan scored first, but missed the extra point, and it was 6-0. Later in the first quarter, Kipke dropped a beautiful punt out of bounds at the Iowa 3-yard line. On first down, Iowa punted to their own 39-yard line. On the very next play, first down for Michigan, Kipke drop-kicked a perfect field goal to make the score 9-0.

In the second quarter, Iowa drove to the Michigan 12-yard line and drop-kicked a field goal, making it 9-3. These were the first points scored against Michigan in 1923, but there was no more scoring by either team, and Michigan escaped with a hard fought victory.

Back in Ann Arbor, the electronic grid-graph that had been so popular the year before was re-erected in Hill Auditorium to show the progress of the game. However, it didn't work so well this time. Somehow the line to Iowa City kept getting disconnected, so game reports were running as much as an hour late. Anxious fans were not happy with the technology, but the game's end result was satisfactory compensation.

The grid-graph was sponsored by the alumni association, and a nominal fee was charged for entrance to the event. The alumni had agreed to give a portion of the profits to support the band. Everything would be tried to finance the band.

Michigan didn't emerge unscathed from this game. In what would be the first of a series of catastrophic injuries for this team, two starters went straight to the hospital upon arrival in Ann Arbor. Several others were banged up enough that they avoided contact drills for a few days.

## The Quantico Marine Game

Fortunately, the next game was the non-conference encounter with the Quantico Marines. The Leathernecks, however, were a predictably tough bunch. They had won their games the previous year against other service teams and were anxious to test themselves against the Wolverines. Any member of the Marine Corps was eligible for the team, even if he had already used up his college eligibility prior to joining the Corps. It was, therefore, a group of veterans who knew how to play the game. Some of these Marines flew to the game by airplane, the first time in Michigan intercollegiate history that members of a visiting team traveled that way.

The peculiar timing of the Marines on the Michigan schedule was due to the vote by the Big Ten representatives to expand the season to eight games. The United States Secretary of the Navy at the time was Edwin Denby, who had played at center on the Michigan football team of 1896. He eagerly jumped at the chance to go west to play the Wolverines. He was determined not only to bring his team, but the renowned Marine Band and 1500 cadets as well. Notables planning to show up for this event included the Governor of Michigan and, once more, Henry Ford.

Yost had selected this game months earlier for the dedication of the field house. The *Daily* initiated the celebration by proclaiming on page one, "With a record of championships greater than any other team in the west and 11 All-America players since 1902, Michigan's Grand Old Man stands today as probably the greatest football authority in the country."[106]

The University of Michigan alumni in Detroit planned "the biggest day Detroit has ever seen."[107] Trains arrived in the city early Saturday morning carrying the Marine contingent. The cadets and their band marched through the streets of Detroit to Grand Circus Park before huge and enthusiastic crowds. Later, they re-boarded the trains for the short trip to Ann Arbor.

This would be the first time the University officially dedicated an athletic facility, and it would be done in grand style. The Marines were met at the station by the University of Michigan Band. Before thousands of onlookers and football fans, the Michigan Band led the Marines down Main Street to Liberty, up Liberty to State Street and down State Street to the stadium and the beautiful new Yost Field House. Ann Arbor had never witnessed such a gathering.

---

[106] *Michigan Daily*, 11/10/23, p 1
[107] *Michigan Daily*, 10/28/23, p 1

Eventually, the Michigan Band led the contingent into the field house. The parade marched down the center aisle of the great new building, and the Marine cadets assumed their place in front of the speaker's stand. The Michigan band and invited guests sat in the east stands while the Marines and other government officials were in the west stands. There was not an empty seat. The ceremony opened with "The Victors" and closed with "The Yellow and Blue." The *Daily* described the scene,

> Thousands jammed their way into the new Yost Field House today to see the dedication of Michigan's new athletic plant. The great building was literally a sea of color and faces. Flags of the allied countries, of the Marine Corps, the national colors and above all the Yellow and Blue were blended together in one great symbol of glory and achievement becoming the opening of such a great monument to athletics and physical manhood.

*The dedication of Yost Field House—November 10, 1923*

"The Marines, 1500 strong, together with their famous band, made an inspiring sight as they entered the field house. They marched in a column of squads the full length of the

*Photo courtesy of Bentley Historical Library*

*The dedication of Yost Field House*

building in an aisle between the thousands of spectators seated in the stands and standing on either side."[108]

When the crowd was finally in place and the music had died down, James Murfin, chairman of the Board of Regents, spoke on behalf of the Board:

> This splendid building is unique. It is a realization of a dream many have had. Its accomplishment at this time is due in no small measure to the long head and stout heart of a Michigan institution sometimes called "Hurry Up."
>
> A future period will more accurately gauge the value of his services and the influence of his character upon the men and women of Michigan. Nor is this the time perhaps to do more than remark in passing they have been magnificent and are being appreciated more and more every day by those who observe and know this splendid man—Fielding H. Yost.
>
> May I express the hope that this wonderful building, this splendid addition to our athletic plant may be dedicated

---

[108] *Michigan Daily,* 11/10/23, p 1

to a continuation of clean, college sport—sport for the love of the game, sport for the enthusiasm of the college men and women, sport of the clean and wholesome type of which, for so many years Michigan has been so justly proud.[109]

President Burton then took the podium,

The University of Michigan today takes genuine and justifiable pride in the dedication of the Yost Field House. The modern university has come to see that the physical welfare of its students lies at the basis of its educational effectiveness. Moreover, the spirit of true and manly sportsmanship has a place in actual life which none will deny.

We take particular pride in this occasion because this building represents not only sound principles, but because it stands as a fitting recognition of the life work of a man whose nationally recognized skill as a football coach, with all its dazzling success, has not been able to blind our eyes to the merit of the man whose character and ideals have been such a powerful influence in developing staunch men. Yost, the man, is the heart of this occasion today. May this building, bearing his name, stand through the years as a silent but compelling witness to the worth of loyalty, integrity, and manhood.[110]

Finally, Fielding Yost himself stood before the cheering crowd.

Secretary Denby, President Burton, Friends and Visitors: Deep appreciation and a very real sense of humility are uppermost in my emotions. The great name of Michigan fills my heart with pride, and with gratitude for all she has done for me.

[109] Board in Control, Box 5, November 1923
[110] Board in Control, Box 5, November 1923

This inspiring occasion instills within me a renewed purpose. I shall go forth determined to be of better service to Michigan. I shall live in the hope of repaying in some small measure this high honor.

Service has many compensations. My intimate relationship for twenty-three years with the flower of young manhood and with older Michigan men, and the friendships resulting therefrom are among my most cherished possessions. It is an inspiration to be a part of such a wonderful University and to have the confidence and cooperation of Michigan's great leader, President Burton.

My long association with our University and the responsibility I feel cause me to subscribe most earnestly to the Michigan creed. With all my heart,

> I believe in the University of Michigan,
> The maker of men,
> And in Michigan Spirit
> Conceived in loyalty and democracy,
> And in her traditions
> Cherished by all her sons.
> I believe in the spirit of service
> To the University and all her activities.
> All these I promise to uphold
> To the best of my ability,
> For the greatest of all universities, Michigan.
> My heart is so full I cannot say more.[111]

And so the Michigan community honored and celebrated this revered man in his own time.

But there was still an important football game to be played following the dedication ceremonies. The crowd was the biggest of the year, eclipsing even the packed house that showed up for the Ohio State game. Nonetheless, some perceived a tangible lack of

---

[111] Yost papers, Box 2, 1923 (2)

football enthusiasm in Ann Arbor in the fall of 1923. The *Daily* was compelled to editorialize on the day of the Quantico game,

> Sing the Victors! It is customary for the band to play this piece as it parades across the field just previous to the appearance of the team. In fact this is an old tradition, the genesis of it being that 'The Victors' is Michigan's fighting song, the song in which Michigan men shout out their defiance to the invader and their loyalty to the team that is about to defend their colors.
>
> At the previous games when the band played 'The Victors' there has been no response…Can it be that Michigan men no longer care for their school songs? In 'The Victors' Michigan has a fighting song that cannot be equaled. If everyone joined in to sing it when the band triumphantly parades the length of the field to its strains, it would be a big influence in giving the team the feeling of confidence and support which is so necessary for a victory.[112]

The game began badly for Michigan, as a blocked kick led to a Marine touchdown and a 6-0 lead. It was the first time the Wolverines had been behind the whole season. However, Michigan scored in the second period to make it 7-6 at halftime, and totally dominated the second half to capture the victory, 26-6.

This game, however, was not without controversy. In those days, there was no clock for the fans to follow, just a stopwatch run by a timekeeper on the sidelines. The first period was 23 minutes long instead of the usual 15 because the timekeeper somehow lost track of the minutes. Although the other periods were kept at 15 minutes, Michigan scored two touchdowns in the fourth quarter, and the Marines claimed that if the game had been the usual regulation time, the latter two touchdowns wouldn't have occurred. Even so, Michigan had the lead, 14-6, at the end of the third period.

---

[112] *Michigan Daily*, 11/10/23, p 4

After the game, a fan wrote to Yost, criticizing the timekeeper and suggesting that a game clock be placed at the end of the field, large enough for all the players and even the fans to follow. Yost wrote back that he was not impressed with this novel idea.

> The timer of the game was a fellow…recommended by the Marines. The trouble with him, no doubt, was that he never before kept time and if so he stopped his watch and forgot to start it. The first period, with a high wind, was 23 minutes long, yet his watch showed but nine minutes. When I first talked with him he said his watch stopped. "Of course," I said, "it is stopped. It is a stop watch. The trouble with you is that you did not start it again." I do not see where an electric clock or any other device would be more valuable than a stop watch as you would have to stop and start these the same as a watch.[113]

Unfortunately, the Wolverines suffered a serious loss in this game. Their senior quarterback, Irwin Uteritz, who had performed so well for the Wolverines for three years, was carried off the field in the fourth quarter with a broken ankle and was lost for the season. Perhaps this injury would have been prevented if the game had been the appropriate length. Knowing that the season was over for his veteran quarterback, Yost issued this statement,

> Irwin Uteritz was one of the very few great quarterbacks I have seen. He was the most sure and certain tackler on defense that I ever saw play the backfield position…He was the most accurate and efficient passer who ever played on a Michigan team. Since Uteritz became a quarterback three years ago, Michigan has lost but one game and that was his first one.[114]

Clearly, the loss of Uteritz was a severe blow to Michigan's title hopes. The coaching staff worked feverishly to try to find a replace-

---

[113] Board in Control, Box 5, November 1923
[114] *Michigan Daily*, 11/13/23, p 6

ment. Substitutes off the bench and the other running backs were given a try. For a time, even Kipke ran the team from the quarterback position. Finally, the coaches settled on a sophomore back-up, Tod Rockwell. However, he wouldn't be expected to throw. The passing chores would fall to the two halfbacks, Kipke and Steger. Obviously, the Michigan offensive attack would require major adjustments. To make matters worse, the Wolverines had also lost their starting right guard and tackle, so untried substitutes were manning the line for a backup quarterback.

## The Wisconsin Game

Michigan was undefeated in the Big Ten at this point, along with Illinois and Minnesota. The Wolverines next played at Wisconsin before ending the season in Ann Arbor against their traditional final opponent, the Golden Gophers.

A special train to Madison had been filled with rooters as well as the Michigan Band, which had finally cobbled together enough money to make the trip. Eighty-five women were included in the travel party, each paying a special chaperone fee of 75 cents. Furthermore, permission for any woman to stay overnight either in Madison or Chicago had to be obtained from the Dean of Women by presenting a written invitation from an appropriate female hostess. The ladies, so the administration was assured, would be closely watched.

The *Daily* tried to get the students fired up,

> A crippled football team representing the University of Michigan will leave Ann Arbor at 11:27 P.M. to engage in one of the most crucial gridiron battles in the history of Wolverine football. If their student body, thousands strong, cheers them off at the station, the memory of those thousands at home tomorrow afternoon anxiously watching the report of the game will remain vividly in their minds as they face the Badgers.[115]

---

[115] *Michigan Daily*, 11/15/23, p 1

Despite these efforts, this would not be one of the great memorable railroad send-offs. As noted in the editorial, the team's train left at 11:27 P.M. Their sleeping cars were on a siding in the Ann Arbor station, and the players boarded at about 9:00 P.M. and went to bed. Around 11:00 P.M., about 500 students tramped down to the station and started singing "The Victors." Suddenly, one of the football trainers came running out of the train and told them to quiet down. The team was already asleep, he said, and they didn't need any cheering tonight. Astonished and disappointed, the scolded fans made their way back to central campus.

The grid-graph would again be available for homebound fans in Hill Auditorium. This time, though, organizers had made arrangements to have an open phone line to Camp Randall so they wouldn't have to depend solely upon the telegraph.

Yost spent two full hours with his new quarterback on the train to Madison. The sophomore would need to be sharp. The Badgers had tied Minnesota earlier in the season and had lost a tough game to Illinois, but they were a solid 11, especially on defense. While a great game was expected, few could anticipate the controversy that would result from this contest in Madison.

Wisconsin started it off with a beautiful drive in the opening period to the Michigan 5-yard line, where they were forced to settle for a field goal and a 3-0 lead. Then disaster struck the Wolverines. Michigan's veteran center, Jack Blott, broke his leg in two places in the first period and was out for the season. Now Yost had to put in an untried center in addition to his right guard, tackle, and quarterback.

The great controversy occurred in the second quarter. Wisconsin punted to Michigan's substitute quarterback, Tod Rockwell, who took the ball and scooted 60 yards for a touchdown. Or so it was ruled. What seemed to happen was that Rockwell caught the ball, ran toward the sidelines, was hit by one Wisconsin defender, escaped, but was then hit and knocked down by a second defender. In 1923, the rule for whether or not a player was down was like the one the professional football leagues use today. A player had to be knocked down by another player; in fact, he had to be in the grasp of the defender. Simply falling down was not downing the ball, and a player could get up and run. According to Yost and Rockwell, Rockwell was not hit by the second defender. Seeing him coming, Rockwell threw himself out of the way and was missed by the player, but in so jumping to miss him, Rockwell fell down. Not considering himself downed by a Badger, Rockwell jumped up and ran in for the eternal touchdown. Fortunately for Michigan, the referee saw it as Rockwell saw it and called it a touchdown, making the score 6-3, Michigan. There was much more football played, but no more scoring. The game ended this way, and Michigan kept its undefeated season intact.

The *Daily* described the postgame melee,

> Badgers thought the runner had been grounded at the 40 yard line, but the referee said no. The rooters continued the argument with the referee during the remainder of the game...Shouting "robber," "thief," and repeatedly accusing him of "throwing the game to Michigan," the rooters worked themselves into such a frenzy at the end of the game that they rushed onto the field intent on mobbing the referee. With cries of "get the robber" several hundred pushed their way past a squad of remonstrating policemen and were only checked when the Wisconsin coaching staff, realizing the danger to the referee, called upon the Badger team, weary from the bitterly fought game, to escort the referee from the field.
>
> The players formed a cordon about the referee and with the aid of the police hurried him safely to the field house with the hooting crowd following.[116]

The referee was not the only one targeted. A rabid Badger fan reportedly confronted Yost as the coach walked off the field and was getting ready to pop the Grand Old Man a good one when

---

[116] *Michigan Daily*, 11/18/23, p 1

a Michigan student stepped up and took the blow instead. The commotion didn't end there; even the bands got caught up in the ill feelings. To the great consternation of the Michigan contingent, at halftime the Wisconsin band started playing "On Wisconsin" while the Michigan band was still playing "The Yellow and Blue." The Wisconsin band director later said that an elaborate program had been worked out for the halftime entertainment, but the Michigan band refused to cooperate. According to the Michigan band, the Wisconsin plans left no room for the formation of the block "M" and the Michigan rooters present wanted the block "M." Unable to come to agreement, the bands performed their own shows simultaneously. The Wisconsin director subsequently apologized for the breech in protocol, saying he was "driven to it by the clamor from the stands."[117]

After the game, the referee issued a statement that no doubt added to the confusion.

> The play in question came after Rockwell, the Wolverine quarterback, juggled one of Taft's punts. The Michigan player finally obtained possession of the ball and started to run. He was hit by a Wisconsin player and spun partially around. He was struck by a second Badger player…who was on top of the play and knocked to the ground, but the field judge stated emphatically he was not in the grasp of an opponent at the time he struck the ground.
>
> After the second Wisconsin player struck Rockwell, the latter was rolling on the ground as I came up to cover the kick. At that time Rockwell was not in the grasp of an opponent. He regained his feet and ran for the touchdown. I asked the field judge if Rockwell had been held on the ground in the grasp of an opponent. He answered by saying that at no time was Rockwell legally tackled.[118]

[117] *Michigan Daily*, 11/20/23, p 2
[118] *Michigan Daily*, 11/20/23, p 1

The *Daily Cardinal*, the Wisconsin paper, issued a bitter editorial the next day stating, essentially, that their team had been robbed and they didn't want to ever see that referee set foot in Madison again. In the *Michigan Daily*, Yost said the referee made the right call and pointed out that these were all experienced referees, one with 25 years on the field, two with 15 years, and one with 10 years. The *Michigan Daily* editors had their own axe to grind,

> The tumultuous disturbance at Randall field Saturday and subsequent incidents in Madison, Saturday night, when visiting rooters were subjected to indignities at the hands of people representing the city of Madison and the University of Wisconsin are without parallel in the history of Conference athletics. Wisconsin is doubly unfortunate in losing the game and in being a poor loser.

> There are certain standards which have until Saturday been considered sacred to major college football. Two of these unwritten but loudly propounded ideals are "competition" and "sportsmanship"…

> The misfortune to Wisconsin is the misfortune of the Conference. The poor spirit displayed was a shock which startled every Westerner…The affair passed the last possibility of recall when the student newspaper, carried away by the same madness of a bitter defeat, launched a grossly unreasonable attack upon the referee, the innocent target of more abuse than has ever before been heaped upon an official in an intercollegiate event. The editorial published in the newspaper was an adolescent attempt to criticize and offer an alibi…

> Wisconsin owes an apology to organized football and to the referee.[119]

This game was remarkable for another reason. A few years later, an enterprising sports reporter asked Yost what was the greatest play

---

[119] *Michigan Daily*, 11/20/23, p 4

he had seen in all his years of football. Yost's memories returned to this contest in Madison for the answer, but not to Rockwell's controversial run. With 16 seconds left in this game, Wisconsin stood on their own 35-yard line. The Badgers needed a touchdown to win, so Michigan expected a pass, and Yost had his defenders playing deep. Wisconsin, however, used an unexpected formation and surprised the Wolverines by putting three receivers on one side of the line. With the snap, the receivers sprinted for the goal. The Wisconsin quarterback launched a perfect strike, 50 yards in the air. Michigan defenders and the Wisconsin receivers went up for the ball, but somehow it bounced away into the arms of a Badger who then sprinted for the goal a few yards away. Staving off a last second disaster, a Michigan player came from nowhere and tackled the Badger receiver short of paydirt just as the final whistle blew.

The Michigan player who had saved the game was the All-American left guard, Edliff "Butch" Slaughter. When, after the game, Yost asked Slaughter what he, a guard, was doing way back there, Slaughter replied that he knew it would be a pass play so he saw no reason to stay on the line. When the ball was hiked, he started running down the field to be in place in case a Wisconsin receiver eluded the Michigan backs. That is, of course, exactly what happened, and Michigan's left guard was there to save the day. Said Yost, "For a guard to leave his position as Slaughter did and go down the field was an unheard of thing and so unexpected I could hardly believe my eyes when I saw that it was he who made the tackle."[120]

To Slaughter, a linesman, Yost awarded the greatest play he had ever seen.

## The Minnesota Game

What is a football season without a little controversy? Michigan had emerged victorious in Madison, and the Wolverines now faced a final showdown in Ann Arbor against the Golden Gophers. Min-

[120] Board in Control, Box 8, July 1926 (2)

***The University of Michigan Football Team of 1923***
***This team won a second consecutive Big Ten title***

*Row 4: Hoyt (trainer), Kunow, Hawkins, White, Neisch, McCabe (student manager)*

*Row 3: Steele, Slaughter, Vandervoort, Lot, Muirhead, Babcock, Brown*

*Row 2: Coach Little, Curran, Steger, Uteritz, Coach Yost, Captain Kipke, Miller, Coach Wieman*

*Row 1: Marion, Rockwell, Vick, Grube, Herrnstein*

nesota was still undefeated, having impressively beaten Iowa while the Wolverines were in Madison.

The eyes of the football world now focused squarely on Ann Arbor and Michigan's badly battered team. The right side of the line, the center, and the senior quarterback were gone. Only five starters were left from the team that had taken the field in October against Ohio State. Yost still had his starting left tackle, left guard, right end and two halfbacks, but all the other players were substitutes off the bench. Under total secrecy on Ferry Field, the Wolverines were put through light practices to prevent any more injuries. Yost tried new players at center and up and down the line. Rockwell had performed well at Madison and would stay at quarterback. With Uteritz gone, Yost decided to insert Dutch Vick at fullback because he was a reliable passer. Late in the week, the team retreated to the confines of Yost Field House because of inclement weather.

The usual pep rally was held at Hill Auditorium. Yost dramatically appeared on stage with the Little Brown Jug in his arms and,

> This was the signal for a veritable stampede from the assembled students who gave volley after volley of cheers, as Coach Yost placed the prized trophy upon a stand in the middle of the stage.

> Harry Kipke said, "The fellows are not discouraged. They are in there to win. Tomorrow you will see the hardest hitting and hardest fighting team that Michigan has put on the field this year."[121]

Yost concluded the rally with an eye on the fracas in Madison. He stressed Michigan's reputation of fair play and the students' responsibility to the team. He appealed to the fans to support and to respect the referee's decision in all cases. "If we lose," said the coach, "we will take our beating like men."[122]

The *Daily* worried, "Can a team composed of five regular members and six men who have been substitutes for most of the season successfully keep clean its record of straight victories against an opponent which is in the pink of condition and without a defeat chalked up against it?"[123]

That Saturday, Ferry Field was packed with an estimated crowd of 45,000, and the fans were treated to a classic coaching job by Yost. This victory is perhaps most impressive when one considers that all these substitutes were playing on both offense and defense. Yost's patched-up Michigan line dominated the undefeated Gophers for most of the game. Most surprisingly, the responsibility of passing was turned over to Michigan's fullback, Dutch Vick. In the second quarter, Vick hit Kipke for a nice gain and then threw a perfect touchdown scoring pass to Rockwell, the quarterback. Michigan

---

[121] *Michigan Daily*, 11/24/23, p 1
[122] *Michigan Daily*, 11/24/23, p 1
[123] *Michigan Daily*, 11/24/23, p 1

led 7-0 at the half. In the third quarter, Kipke hit a beautiful 35-yard drop-kick field goal and the game was 10-0. Two Minnesota drives in the fourth quarter were squelched by Kipke interceptions. For the second consecutive year, Michigan was the undefeated Big Ten champion.

The *Daily* exulted,

> Once more Coach Fielding H. Yost, Michigan's Grand Old Man, gained the honor of having produced an undefeated team. For the Wolverines, playing in the hardest game of the season, defeated Minnesota's hitherto unbeaten football team yesterday afternoon on Ferry Field by a score of 10-0, thereby winning the Big Ten title.
>
> The Yostmen played as they had never played before. Forced to start the game with only five men who had been regulars at the beginning of the season, the Varsity went into the battle and fought against great odds as only Michigan teams can fight. Playing against a line which was much heavier and, to a large extent, more experienced, the Maize and Blue warriors brought all their power into play and stopped the offense of the Gophers.[124]

On the same day, Illinois defeated Ohio State 9-0 and as a result shared the title with Michigan. Somewhat ominously, the talk in Champaign-Urbana all season had been about their sensational sophomore halfback. The youngster had not only scored three touchdowns and gained 202 yards against Nebraska in his very first game, but he was, by far, the leading scorer of touchdowns in the Big Ten. His name was Harold "Red" Grange. Ironically, Michigan had dropped Illinois from its schedule the year before in order to play the 1922 co-champion Hawkeyes. Now fans at both Illinois and Michigan wanted the rivalry resumed. Illinois' student paper, the *Daily Illini*, graciously laid down the challenge:

---

[124] *Michigan Daily*, 11/25/23, p 1

We would like to see a championship game with Michigan of course. We would like to have the football supremacy of the Western Conference settled once and for all by such a game. Yet we realize that a post season game is impossible…to Coach Yost and Michigan our heartiest congratulations. May the teams meet next year.[125]

The *Michigan Daily* replied, "The Big Ten season ended in a tie which only the most rabid of partisans would venture to break by calling either a better team. But we look forward to the battle next year. Congratulations, Illinois."[126]

The great Kipke, who would one day be Michigan's head football coach, finished his college career without ever playing in a Michigan defeat. Since he was named a member of Camp's 1922 All-American team, he was a marked man in every game he played in 1923. Still, he excelled on both sides of the ball. A Detroit sportswriter exclaimed,

> Kipke's greatest claim to fame probably is his ability to place punts where the opponents are unable to return them. He was called upon to do the kicking in the last two games of the 1921 season and did all the kicking in the games played in 1922 and 1923.
>
> In all of these games he never had a punt blocked and only had one punt returned for more than five yards. He placed practically 75% of his punts out of bounds and had a grand average of better than 45 yards from the line of scrimmage to where the ball hit the ground on all the punts he made in his three years.[127]

Following the 1923 season, Michigan placed another player on Camp's All-American team. While Kipke didn't make the first team, Jack Blott, the Wolverine center, did. This was a surprising development because Blott had gone down with a broken leg in

[125] *Michigan Daily*, 12/1/23, p 1
[126] *Michigan Daily*, 12/1/23, p 1
[127] Yost papers, Box 2, 1923 (2)

the Wisconsin game, and it was very unusual for a player to make Camp's list without completing the whole season. Blott was from a small town in Ohio where he had played fullback in some games in high school, but he hadn't planned to play football at Michigan. Yost grabbed him off the baseball team in his sophomore year and had him in pads and at the center of the line when autumn came.

Yost always developed great centers. He was fond of saying, "The center position is the most important on the team. If I could have but one exceptionally good player on my eleven, I would select a center. The quarterback is important…but a quarterback without a good center would be at a big disadvantage."[128]

There was much complaining in Columbus when Blott's great achievement was announced. The question tormenting the Buckeyes was perennial: why was this Ohio boy playing for Michigan?

Upon learning of Blott's award, Yost said,

> Blott had everything a football player needs. He was intelligent, fast, and powerful. His coordination was perfect and his muscular reaction instantaneous. He had the faculty of coming through in an emergency and was best under fire. He had plenty of reserve power, never quit, and was always in the right place. His ability to diagnose plays made him invaluable on defense and his uncanny accuracy in passing and powerful drive made him an ideal offensive lineman…
>
> I never once heard him lose his temper or commit an unsportsmanlike act…
>
> Coaching would be a snap if all players responded as readily to the coach's efforts as did Blott…He took coaching the best of any man I ever had.[129]

At the end of this championship season, Yost received another letter from President Burton with the salutation, "My Dear Mr. Yost":

---

[128] *Ann Arbor News*, 11/15/23 p12
[129] Board in Control, Box 41, Articles by Yost, Book 1

> I cannot let these days go by without expressing to you my unqualified satisfaction over the football season. As I have so frequently said to you we do not want to place an undue emphasis upon the necessity of winning every game, but when it has been done it is perfectly natural for one to express his unbounded enthusiasm for the result. I do not know when I have seen a game which was so satisfying to me as the one last Saturday. It is a remarkable tribute to the team, to the coaches, and to Michigan morale and I for one want to extend to you my heartiest congratulations.[130]

A few days after the Minnesota game, the team met and elected Herb Steger, the halfback who played opposite Kipke, captain for 1924. The usual football banquet was held at the Michigan Union, but otherwise the *Daily* recorded no on-campus event to celebrate this second Big Ten title in as many years.

Nonetheless, this remarkable football achievement contributed dramatically to the exponential growth in demand for football tickets in Ann Arbor. By once again bringing the title home, this Michigan squad laid the foundation for the great stadium Wolverines know today. The demand for football tickets in 1924 would inundate the Michigan athletic department and make the inadequate seating capacity of Ferry Field obvious to everyone.

Rumors swirled about for a time that Yost might give up coaching. Speaking to the University Press Club in mid-November, Yost intimated that 1923 could be his last year on the bench. He cited the ever-increasing duties as Athletic Director and the unending stress associated with being head coach.

> There is more uncertainty in the coaching game than in any other I know. You've got to win, win, win, when only one team out of the 10 in the conference can win. Nine teams have to lose.

---

[130] Board in Control, Box 5, November 1923

How many coaches are there who have been in the game for 10 years? Count them. Most any coach I know would trade his salary and position for that of a professor, with his certainty of position.[131]

Yost went on to say that, although he had received offers from other institutions with salaries two and one-half times as much as what he had received in Ann Arbor, he could not leave. "My heart is with Michigan. Football is my recreation. For three years I have not received any salary from the university as football coach. My contract with the university expired three years ago."[132] However, no final decision was announced by Yost. Similar rumors had developed after the 1922 season, too, but had come to naught. A sportswriter recorded,

Michigan's eminent football instructor is trying to make up his mind to retire from active leadership and concentrate upon general athletic development. But even after two unbeaten seasons and twenty-seven years of coaching he finds the decision hard to make. No man ever loved a profession as Yost loves coaching. "I have wanted to quit before," he once told the writer, "but I couldn't. It meant too much, and if early fall ever comes on when I am not out working with a football team it will be the longest three months I ever knew."[133]

Around the Midwest, stadiums continued to be built or planned. The Ohio State stadium story has been told. Illinois would open a great new arena in 1924 and so would Minnesota. Indiana had announced major new expansion plans.

Even the Michigan Agricultural College was getting "stadium fever." Facilities in East Lansing were so dilapidated that MAC couldn't get quality football teams to play there. Michigan had provided MAC with home and away games years earlier, but in the

[131] *Ann Arbor News*, 11/19/23, p 8
[132] *Ann Arbor News*, 11/19/23, p 8
[133] Yost papers, Box 2, late 1923 (newspaper article)

last few years Yost refused to go there. MAC was having trouble getting other Big Ten teams as well. Finally, a scheme was hatched whereby the state of Michigan would loan the school some money to build an acceptable facility and then MAC could repay it over time.

In Ann Arbor, however, there seemed to be little official enthusiasm for a new stadium. Michigan's Board of Regents met in October 1923, and, perhaps in one of its least prescient meetings ever, registered its opposition to a new stadium. On a motion by the Chairman of the Board, the Regents passed a resolution against the idea. The minutes from their meeting detail the reasoning.

> We should seriously regret any policy that would strengthen the tendency to transform the amateur collegiate contest into a public spectacle with some of the evils which seem inevitably to accompany some events in the world of sportsmanship.
>
> Intercollegiate athletics should be conducted primarily for the students and alumni of the competing institutions, for their friends and families, and for the immediate constituencies of the participating schools.
>
> Consideration must be given to certain very practical aspects of the problem arising out of the limitations of a small city such as Ann Arbor. Spectators must be provided with meals and housing facilities. Special trains require railroad yards which do not exist and could only be provided with great difficulty. The parking of automobiles is already a perplexing problem.
>
> The solicitation of a fund amounting to one and a half million dollars would not at this time meet with our approval in view of other very proper demands that have been and may be made upon our graduates and the constituency of the University.

In view of the foregoing observations and with the thought of avoiding an undue emphasis upon intercollegiate competition and one which in our judgment is frequently misinterpreted, we venture to suggest that those primarily in charge of the matter may find the most satisfactory solution of the problem by proceeding to the completion of the concrete stadium heretofore planned, the south unit of which has rendered and is now rendering such satisfactory service. By this method we understand about thirteen thousand seats would be added making it possible to accommodate approximately fifty thousand spectators.[134]

So the Regents, the University's board of governors, were not about to join the stadium stampede. The most critical point they introduced was that raising $1.5 million from alumni and university friends for a stadium would detract from other crucial projects on campus. Ohio State, Illinois and Minnesota built their stadiums with solicitations from students and alumni.

Michigan already had a long tradition of giving on campus. Michigan's alumni association was formed in 1860, making it the oldest association for any state university. In 1923, Michigan graduates had given more to the university than had alumni of any other state university in the country. The Union, Alumni Hall, Hill Auditorium, Betsy Barbour and Martha Cook dormitories, Clements Library and the Law Club were alumni gifts, comprising over one-third of the buildings on campus at that time. The Regents believed these buildings were appropriate needs for a great university, but not a new football stadium.

Ironically, the University of Illinois cited the record of Michigan alumni contributions when it initiated its stadium drive. Said the president of the University of Illinois alumni association at the stadium groundbreaking, "The memorial stadium is the first great act of generosity on the part of the students and alumni of

---

[134] Proceedings of the Board of Regents, September 1923 to June 1926, pp 115-116

the University of Illinois."[135] He went on to express his hope that it would be just the beginning of similar gifts to the university. Michigan alumni and friends, he said, have given one-third of the buildings on campus to that institution, and he declared that such an achievement should be a goal for Illinois alumni. So while Illinois was building a classic stadium with student and alumni contributions, Michigan's Regents saw no place for such an effort for a building that would only be used six times a year.

The football program at Michigan wielded no more ardent support than that shown by the *Michigan Daily* editorial staff. Somewhat surprisingly, then, the editorial staff sided with the Regents on this issue. After complaining that the school had no swimming pool and no golf course for students, and that such facilities should take precedence over a larger stadium, the editors wrote,

> The Board of Regents is to be congratulated upon the good sense and acumen which it manifested at its recent meeting…In forthright terms which must have delighted everyone intelligently interested in the University's welfare, the Regents denounced the fatuous proposal recently advanced that $1,500,000 be solicited from alumni with the intention of making Michigan "the sport center of the Middle West" by enormous expansion of the football stadium at Ferry field…

> It is no secret that in recent years the University has drifted far afield from the legitimate activities of an "institution of higher learning." In common with most American universities, it has become so enslaved by the mania for athleticism and "campus activities" that the only really important activity, namely intellectual improvement, has practically ceased to exist…President Burton's dictum that "education still has something to do with the mind" has fallen upon deaf ears in a student body whose fetish

---

[135] Board in Control, Box 5, July 1922, Memorial Stadium Notes

is "popularity" and whose conception of a "100 percent Michigan man" is realized by…getting off dull jokes about prohibition and roaring for the team…

The leading universities of the country are feeling this trend back to an education which stresses the primacy of the mind. At the University of Chicago, at Dartmouth, at Yale and at Columbia we have seen recent manifestations of the change. Entrance requirements have been raised and sterile athleticism discouraged.

In the light of these facts, we cannot but applaud the Regents' action.[136]

Law Professor Aigler, Chairman of the Board in Control of Athletics, gave a more practical reason for forgetting about a new stadium: there was simply no money.

Unless somebody will provide the financial means, there is no use of the University of Michigan talking of building a new stadium or even of completing the present one in the immediate future. Nevertheless, with the increased demand for tickets the past few years and the huge demand this year, the problem of just what to do about the stadium situation is naturally in the mind of every Michigan man…At the present time, the U-shaped stadium on Ferry Field composed of the cement south stand and the north and west wooden stands has a seating capacity of 37,000 people. The small wooden standing room platform at the east end of the field will accommodate 4000, bringing the total number that can be handled in the present stadium up to 41,000.

Finishing the stadium which was started with the building of the cement south stand by erecting cement stands on the north and west sides would increase the seating

---

[136] *Michigan Daily*, 12/4/23, p 4

capacity about 6000 or 7000. In addition to this, by making some arrangement for the east end, the total number could be brought up to 50,000…The athletic association will be in debt nearly a quarter of a million dollars at the end of this year, after funds are used for the construction for the field house…It is for this reason that it is impossible for a new stadium to be built in the near future or even to complete the present one. With such a large indebtedness as there will be after this year, it couldn't be expected that we would be able to borrow enough money to attempt to solve the stadium problem.[137]

What Professor Aigler didn't appreciate was the incredible amount of money that would soon flow into the Michigan athletic coffers from sold out football stadiums, home and away. In the fall of 1923, though, the idea of a new stadium in Ann Arbor seemed most implausible.

Of course, many Michigan alumni refused to accept this conclusion. Some alumni were angry over the lack of tickets; others, seeing huge stadiums rise on comparable campuses, couldn't countenance the idea that Michigan would retain the present facility. The Michigan athletic files from the fall of 1923 are filled with complaints from unhappy alumni and proposals for a new stadium. The Detroit alumni club seemed to take the lead on this issue. In a letter dated October 3, 1923, the President wrote,

We in Detroit are hearing bad things from businessmen and alumni because they have not been able to secure seats to the Ohio State game. A majority of our most enthusiastic backers are not Michigan men and we must tear to pieces the argument…that football should be played before alumni and students only.[138]

Yost was very sensitive to this argument. The University of Michigan was a tax-supported public institution, after all, and

---

[137] *Michigan Daily*, 10/20/23, p 1

Yost would never endorse the idea that taxpaying citizens should not have access to the games. Yost always insisted that taxpayers of the state be given the same preference for game tickets as alumni.

A letter from Irvin Huston, dated October 5, 1923, states that the writer is considering accepting an appointment as Chairman of the Stadium Committee for the Detroit alumni club. Huston writes, in what is the earliest available document to make such a proposal,

> Personally, I would be very much pleased to see a stadium at Ann Arbor that would seat 100,000 people and to have the finest one in the country if possible.[139]

But Huston wanted Yost's thoughts. Before accepting the Chairmanship of the Stadium Committee, Huston wrote Yost,

> Will you kindly advise the writer what your present plans are relative to a stadium at Ann Arbor and whether or not you think that I could be of any assistance to you by taking the chairmanship?[140]

Yost responded to Huston a few days later, but he was obviously not yet convinced about the proposals for a new stadium and wasn't ready to take a position. "I have not yet had time to go over this matter with any members of the Board." He agreed that the need for more seating at the games was a "pressing problem." He concluded by thanking Michigan alumni for their "great interest in reference to a new stand or increased seating capacity of the present one."[141]

A handwritten letter, undated, but in the athletic department's file for October 1923, is from C.E. Wise at the General Motors Building to Coach Yost. Wise unequivocally wanted a stadium:

> I am still strongly of the opinion Michigan cannot take a back seat on the stadium question. Why let other

---

[138] Board in Control, Box 5, October 1923
[139] Board in Control, Box 5, October 1923
[140] Board in Control, Box 5, October 1923
[141] Board in Control, Box 5, October 1923

universities lead in this matter? Michigan does not have to follow. Let's make our stadium with a capacity for 125,000. It will pay…Big.[142]

In a letter dated 9/21/23, Yost writes Wise, "I note what you say in regard to additional seating capacity or a new bowl. This is quite a problem we are facing. It would take about a million and a half dollars to build a new stadium to take care of the crowd."[143] Wise was not to be dissuaded, and he wrote another letter to Yost in mid-October, in which he says,

> Since receiving your letter, advising that it might not be quite feasible to build a new stadium, I have been doing quite a little thinking about the cost of the new stadium and I cannot see but it would be a success…A new stadium should be built that would accommodate at least 100,000, in other words, you should build for the future…With the tremendous demand there is for seats, I cannot see any reason for anything but success in building a new stadium.[144]

While Yost was not yet ready to jump on this bandwagon, he was clearly mulling over the idea. Obviously, the Regents would not allow a solicitation campaign like other universities had used. In addition, Yost knew that filling a new stadium would require winning teams, and he knew whose responsibility that would be. Nonetheless, he did present the issue to the Board in Control of Intercollegiate Athletics as recorded in the minutes for October 13, 1923:

> Coach Yost read a communication from Detroit Alumni in reference to a new stadium or increased seating capacity of the present one. Moved by Professor Johnston and seconded by Mr. DuCharme, that a committee of three

---

[142] Board in Control, Box 5, October 1923
[143] Board in Control, Box 5, September 1923
[144] Board in Control, Box 5, October 1923

be appointed by the Chairman to study the problem of increased seating capacity or a new stadium, this committee to work with the Detroit Alumni Committee and report back to the Board.[145]

This 1923 Michigan Big Ten championship team again brought unprecedented numbers of spectators to Ferry Field. The home games against Ohio State, the Michigan Agricultural College, the Marines, and Minnesota were virtually sold out. Many loyal fans were unable to obtain tickets, and Ferry Field appeared to some to be an inadequate facility. Such an incredible demand for seating could not be ignored, and now some alumni, especially, were actively promoting the idea of a new stadium in Ann Arbor.

Fans were mobbing other stadiums in the Midwest as well. An article in the *Daily* after the close of the football season trumpeted the totals. Big Ten football games drew an unbelievable 1,000,000 spectators and yielded gate receipts of $2,000,000.

> It was the greatest football year in the Western Conference with stadiums crowded while thousands clamored for seats to several of the feature games without avail.
>
> Michigan and Chicago, each with six home games, stood out as the principle drawing cards. Michigan's estimated attendance was set at 183,000 while Chicago attracted 163,000...
>
> At Ohio State, five home games drew 148,000...In five home games, two of which were played in her new stadium, Illinois had crowds totaling 117,000... Wisconsin...estimated that 66,000 saw its home games, while Purdue and Indiana claim 14,000 and 20,000 respectively. Minnesota, Iowa and Northwestern, each with five home games, would have added approximately 100,000 each to the total.[146]

---

[145] Board in Control, Box 48, Minutes 1910-1927, p 195

With his second consecutive Big Ten football title under his belt, Yost left Ann Arbor for the annual meeting of the Big Ten directors in Chicago. It was at these meetings that the schedules for the following year were developed. The *Daily* reflected the interests of Michigan and Illinois fans.

> The meeting of the directors and gathering of the football coaches buzzed with excitement today over the prospects of arrangements of intersectional games for next season…The prospects for a 1924 battle between Illinois and Michigan which divided honors this season appeared bright. Coach Yost of the Wolverines said he would be glad to arrange a game provided a satisfactory date could be agreed upon. Yost said Minnesota, Ohio State, Iowa and Wisconsin would be played in 1924, and, if dates could be arranged to accommodate Illinois, he would be pleased to do so.[147]

Illinois officials indicated that not only would they like to have Michigan on their schedule for the following year, but they would be honored to host Michigan for their stadium dedication game. Illinois had played two games in their new Memorial Stadium at the end of 1923, but the facility was then only partially finished. An official dedication game was to be held in 1924. Yost was particularly flattered to schedule that game, as Michigan had already agreed to provide the competition for Minnesota's stadium dedication game to be held November 1, 1924. So the two schools agreed on an Illinois Memorial Stadium dedication game to be played October 18, 1924. Thus, the stage was set for what would likely be the most storied game in American college football history.

At the same meeting, the Big Ten faculty representatives, as a direct result of the November melee in Madison, passed a resolution "that decisions of officials be accepted without bitterness and

---

[146] *Michigan Daily*, 11/29/23, p 8
[147] *Michigan Daily*, 12/1/23, p 1

urged sportsmanlike conduct upon the spectators."[148] Who could vote against such a hopeful premise? In addition, it was decided to have a Big Ten committee appointed to select the referees for each game. Prior to this decision, the coaches selected the referees before each game, jettisoning some they didn't like and picking out those they thought more favorable. Such a system no doubt led to abuse and the Big Ten chose to have a new committee constituted that would select the referees for each game before the season started. The coaches would no longer be involved. This proposal may have been developed as a result of the controversy in Madison as well.

Back in Ann Arbor, Yost Field House was an instant success. Overnight, Michigan went from having the poorest basketball facility in the Big Ten to having the best. The first intercollegiate contest in the facility was played against the Michigan Agricultural College on January 11, 1924. Michigan won the game, 23-19, and athletic officials were pleased to see all 8,000 seats taken. Plans were quickly made to expand the capacity to 12,000. Perhaps this relatively new intercollegiate sport could eventually generate some athletic department income, too.

There were, however, some kinks to be worked out. The Michigan Band refused to show up in February for a game against Indiana because of a dispute with the athletic department. The band felt the acoustics were best at either end of the court, but the athletic association put them up in a balcony where some of the members couldn't even see the game. After a bit of a standoff, and following a game without the band playing "The Victors," the musicians ended up courtside.

Another remarkable event occurred in the new field house. A group of enterprising students in the engineering school set up a radio station and broadcast the first play-by-play of a Michigan basketball contest on February 16, 1924. Michigan's team defeated Purdue, 34-20. Phone calls from across the nation flooded the athletic department the next day, confirming the effectiveness

---

[148] *Michigan Daily*, 12/2/23, p 1

of this initial effort. The University of Wisconsin had pioneered radio in the Big Ten and Illinois, Ohio State, and Purdue all had radio stations by the time Michigan first hit the airwaves. Students clamored for funding for an official university station, but the Regents, clearly not a very imaginative bunch, couldn't envision the utility of radio. Funding was refused, and the effort patched together in the engineering school soon closed down for lack of financial support.

All of Michigan's athletic trophies were retrieved from storage around campus and displayed in the 23 beautiful new trophy cases in the field house. Michigan had won or tied seven of the 11 Western Conference Football Championships in which the school had participated, and the souvenirs of victory were now displayed. Many people thought the most interesting exhibit was the one displaying the 12 game balls, including the one from the Rose Bowl, representing the 550 to 0 score achieved by the 1901 team.

The *Michigan Daily* continued to complain that much more needed to be done to optimize the intramural sports program, but they were pleased with the progress.

> Intramural athletics have given rise to many minor sports which have attracted undergraduates…With so many games to choose from, for example, boxing, speedball, hockey, golf, and wrestling, in addition to the major sports of baseball, basketball, track, and others that are now offered a student can not fail to find at least one form of athletics that will interest him…The largest field house in America for athletic purposes has been constructed, more minor sports have been recognized in the past year than ever before, the coaching staff has been increased in size and Weinberg's Coliseum has been leased for student skating this winter.[149]

But the editors went on to caution that "it must be remembered

---

[149] *Michigan Daily*, 1/6/24 p 4

by the student body that greater buildings and enlarged coaching staffs obtained for their benefit do not make them stronger in body, and consequently in mind, unless they utilize them."

The athletic department eventually put the final cost of Yost Field House at $475,000 (the equivalent of $5,247,250 today), nearly double the initial estimates. Fortunately, the overruns did not create a crisis in the athletic budget because football revenue filled the athletic department treasury. The whole cost of the project was paid off in three years.

Yost's concept of a field house was a huge success. In 1926, the coach wrote,

> There is no question of the great value of such buildings. They are being built all over the country now. A realization of the necessity for more "space" for boys to use indoor during the time they can not exercise outdoor requires buildings of this character for its solution. Generally speaking, the building, its arrangement and everything, have been very satisfactory.[150]

What would Yost say of this monument today? Now home to the Michigan hockey team, the name has been changed to Yost Ice Arena, but "Yost Field House" is eternally etched above the north entrances. Yost would no doubt be very proud and very pleased to know that the most raucous and spirited Michigan crowd to collect anywhere fills the place to the rafters in support of the Wolverine hockey team. In 2003, one of Michigan's hockey players said, "Yost is known nationwide as the toughest place to play. We can ride the crowd's emotion—it's tough to get down when you have the crowd behind you like that."[151] Yost Ice Arena has become famous in American college hockey circles. The building erupts in an exuberant living tribute to Yost every time the Michigan team takes the ice.

---

[150] Board in Control, Box 8, June 1926 (1)
[151] *The Wolverine*, April 14, 2003, p 20

# Chapter 5

# The Founding of the Big Ten Commissioner

The Western Conference, the forerunner of the Big Ten, can trace its roots to 1895 when university presidents from Michigan, Northwestern, Minnesota, Illinois, Wisconsin, Chicago, and Purdue met in Chicago to try to create rules to govern the increasingly popular game of football. In 1899, Indiana and Iowa joined the conference, and some sportswriters referred to it as the Big Nine. Then Michigan left in 1907, but in 1912 Ohio State joined. When Michigan once again became a member in 1918, the conference finally achieved the Big Ten moniker.

The conference members served as a model for the nation by agreeing to police their athletic programs according to specific regulations. In 1895, the Western Conference presidents were the first to require that each school create a committee on college athletics that would be responsible for enforcing conference rules. The schools agreed that a player had to be a student in the school for which he played, he could not be paid for playing, coaches couldn't play, players couldn't take the field under an assumed name, and "no student shall be permitted to participate in any intercollegiate contest who is found by the faculty to be delinquent in his studies."[152]

For college football at the time, these rules were revolutionary. Later, the Western Conference was the first to institute "the fresh-

---

[152] **Big Ten Football**, McCallum, J., 1976, p 7

man rule," which stated first year students could not play and that each player had a three-year playing limit. Students who played at another school and then transferred to a Western Conference school had to count the years played at another school against the three-year eligibility limit. The Conference strongly encouraged the schools to hire full-time coaches who would be on campus all year. Finally, the "amateur rule" was to be strictly enforced. Any student who played for money at any time, anywhere, was automatically disqualified from further Western Conference competition.

However, making rules and enforcing rules were (and are) two very different projects. What if, for instance, members of the Michigan athletic department thought that Wisconsin had an ineligible player? What if Wisconsin disagreed? What if a coach for Iowa saw a Purdue first baseman playing summer baseball for money under an assumed name? What if Purdue denied the accusation? Enforcement of the rules was left to each athletic department, and, of course, interpretation could vary. So could the degree to which an athletic department pursued enforcement.

Sometimes the violations were obvious and glaring. The National Collegiate Athletic Association reported in January 1922:

> Nine University of Illinois and eight Notre Dame football players have recently been declared ineligible to compete as amateurs in intercollegiate athletics because, without authority, they participated in a football game at Taylorville, Illinois, November 27, 1921, between teams representing that town and Carlinville. A great deal of money was wagered on the contest and it is a glaring instance of the inroads professional football is making on college players. It is stated in the public press that many other noted college football players during the past season played professional football, especially in Sunday games. Evidently concerted action is necessary and such is being initiated by the local leagues made up of our members.

All the members of the NCAA must recognize that intercollegiate athletics are in a very serious condition. It is doubtful whether or not the crisis that caused the formation of this body in 1905 was any more threatening than the present one. Those who believe in using athletics as a means of education and an agent for character building should join in an organized, efficient effort to correct the existing abuses. If the colleges themselves do not take the necessary steps, the situation may get entirely out of hand and result eventually in the suspension, more or less permanent, of intercollegiate athletics.[153]

As a response to these problems, Michigan's Fielding Yost strongly promoted the idea of a Conference Commissioner, an officer who would preside over the league and enforce conference rules. The Big Ten was the first conference in the nation to hire such a person. John L. Griffith left the Department of Physical Education at the University of Illinois to take the job in July 1922. In a statement for the press, the Big Ten Athletic Directors stated,

In defining the duties of the newly created office, the Directors have stressed the educational side of the problem and the officer elected will devote the greater part of his time to an educational campaign for amateur athletics…by public speeches to alumni and students. This Commissioner will also assist the Directors in the enforcement of the eligibility rules.[154]

Some sportswriters reported that the state of amateur athletics must be especially corrupt in the Midwest for the schools to find it necessary to hire such a commissioner. This charge particularly irritated Yost, and he responded,

The Western Conference has always taken the lead for better intercollegiate athletics…The fact that the Western

---

[153] Board in Control, Box 5, December 1922 (2)
[154] Board in Control, Box 5, July 1922

Conference Directors have appointed a Commissioner does not mean that conditions are bad in the Conference, but rather that the Directors are all practical athletic men and are not afraid to adopt progressive measures…in order to bring collegiate athletics to a higher plane.[155]

Commissioner Griffith hit the ground running. In an August 1922 letter to Yost, he indicated that he had already secured "definite information"[156] on six conference baseball players who were earning money over the summer by playing in city leagues. Some were playing under assumed names, but Griffith had found them out. In fact, Griffith wanted to hire some assistants to help with further investigation. He wanted to show that the rules "can be enforced and if a few boys are disqualified the rest will take the rule seriously."[157]

Now that Big Ten athletic directors had someone to whom they could complain, Griffith was kept busy. But he didn't only hear from athletic directors. Griffith recorded an incident that occurred before the fabled Ohio State stadium dedication game with Michigan. Just three months into his new job, he "received an unsigned card with a Detroit post mark which charged"[158] that Michigan's starting fullback, Douglas Roby, had used up his three years of eligibility and shouldn't be allowed to play. A quick investigation on his part, however, indicated that Roby had played one year for a preparatory school, and such play did not count toward college eligibility. Thus, Roby was allowed to take the field, but there was some smoldering resentment in Ann Arbor over this episode, and accusations persisted that it originated in Columbus.

The following year, Yost became very angry over a complaint from Ohio State that a Michigan athlete was ineligible because he had played in some games for pay as a high school student. No one had suggested in the past that the amateur clause should extend to

---

[155] Board in Control, Box 5, January 1923 (2)
[156] Board in Control, Box 5, August 1922
[157] Board in Control, Box 5, August 1922
[158] Board in Control, Box 5, October 1922

what a student did before enrolling in the university, but, in this case, Big Ten Directors upheld Ohio State's complaint. Yost was not happy.

> During the past year Michigan had five men barred for professionalism and about thirty were barred in the conference. So far as I know, Ohio State did not have any declared ineligible…[the student barred for high school activities at the behest of OSU] beyond any question was one of the best athletes entered at Michigan and would have won nine letters in the three major sports, football, baseball and basketball.[159]

Of course, these complaints cut both ways. A few years later Griffith wrote to Yost,

> Some time ago you called my attention to the fact that some Michigan alumnus thought that some Ohio athletic club had a pot of $35,000 which it was using as a means of getting athletes. I took this matter up with Mr. St. John [Ohio State's athletic director] without mentioning any details and he writes me that if such a fund exists he does not know about it and would like to find out whether or not it is true. Of course, I can well understand that a group of alumni might start something of this sort and the athletic director might be kept in the dark.[160]

In the summer of 1923, Griffith surveyed the schools in the Big Ten to see which had the most out-of-state athletes on their teams. Michigan had the highest number at 42 percent, and there was insinuation that such a number was an indication of illegal recruiting. Yost was quick to respond to this allegation, however, by pointing out that 45 percent of all of Michigan's undergraduates were from out-of-state.

---

[159] Board in Control, Box 5, June 1923
[160] Board in Control, Box 9, March 1927 (2)

I understand the object of your report on the percentage of athletes coming from out of the state...Michigan is, perhaps, one of the most cosmopolitan universities in America having students from nearly every state in the Union and from some forty different countries and having over 50,000 alumni scattered all over the world. These alumni have sons and daughters, nephews and other relatives who come to Michigan...

There were 900 students in attendance here from the state of Ohio last year, nearly 10 per cent of the student body. I would appreciate it if you would forward such information as you deem best to the other directors so that there cannot be any improper reaction on the minds of anyone...[161]

Griffith embraced his new appointment. For the most part, his job was one of detective and investigator. Griffith believed that protecting the amateur athlete was his most important responsibility, and he proceeded vigorously. If Big Ten players were paid money over the summer in city baseball leagues, then clearly they violated the amateur rule. Right from the start, Griffith used his job to identify and exclude athletes who were cheating by being paid for play.

On the other hand, in some circumstances Griffith had trouble knowing what to do. In 1922, a few months after Griffith took his new job, Michigan made its great run for the Big Ten football title. In the middle of all the excitement in Ann Arbor, a group of Lansing businessmen proposed giving Harry Kipke a new Oldsmobile during the halftime of the Michigan-Wisconsin game. Kipke, after all, was a Lansing boy and the businessmen wanted to recognize his achievements on the gridiron.

Griffith wrote to Yost,

I was just called up by someone from Lansing, Michigan.

---

[161] Board in Control, Box 5, August 1923

He stated that the businessmen of Lansing wanted to present Kipke with an automobile at the time of the Wisconsin game and asked if there would be any objection. I told him that in my judgment such a thing was perfectly all right…[162]

Griffith, who had been disqualifying baseball players for receiving a few dollars for a game, somehow felt that receiving an automobile in front of 45,000 fans would be all right. The situation resulted in a most agonizing letter sent to the Oldsmobile representative over Yost's signature, written by one of Yost's assistant coaches:

It is only with the greatest hesitation that I write this letter—as it is, because I dislike very much to take a position that might in the remotest degree stand between Harry and an automobile. I have grown to like the young man very much, indeed, and on purely personal grounds I would be delighted to see him get an automobile… However, there are some aspects of the situation that I think deserve the most careful thought before you go through with your proposed plan.

We must start, of course, with the realization that Harry Kipke has been a very much talked of young man both in respect of his accomplishments while here and in his coming to college in the first place. We must realize further that the publicity attendant upon his coming led an unfortunately large number of people to think that in some way he had been improperly persuaded to come to Ann Arbor. Let me hasten to say that I entertain no such thoughts myself, but at the same time we must recognize that there are a great many people who do have such notions. If an automobile were now presented to him, however, while you and I and the few of us who

---

[162] Board in Control, Box 5, November 1922

would know the actual inside of the story realized that there is nothing in the least out of the way in making the present, there would be a vast amount of publicity and thousands of people (I hesitate to guess how many) would at once conclude that this automobile had something to do with his coming to Michigan…Now is it quite fair to put the University, and the boy particularly, into that unfortunate position? If you people wanted to make this present to Harry, say the latter part of next year, when he is nearly through his college course I am sure there could not possibly be any criticism…

We realize perfectly well that it is not within our province to say that any group of people that may be so disposed cannot make a gift of an automobile to a boy who happens to be an athlete…I think it is equally clear that the acceptance of such an automobile would not prejudice the boy's eligibility. After all, it is not a question of rules and regulations, but a question of propriety and good taste…

We feel very clearly that it would be out of place to have any sort of presentation in connection with the game at Ferry Field. This, too, is merely a matter of propriety—it would smack too much of the presentations made to professional baseball players in connection with baseball games.[163]

The question of what exactly constituted a violation of the "amateur rule" confounded the Big Ten commissioner right from the start. Following the 1924 season, when "Red" Grange of Illinois was named to Camps' All-America team for the second year in a row, a movie producer wanted the player to star in a film. It was to be made over the summer between Grange's junior and senior years. Of course, he would portray a football player, and he would

---

[163] Board in Control, Box 5, November 1922

be paid $2000 a week for four weeks, an astronomical sum for the time (the equivalent of $22,100/week today). Again, there was much agonizing over this unexpected proposal, but the athletic directors, in consultation with Griffith, finally decided that accepting the role would jeopardize Grange's amateur status.

If the Commissioner was confused at times, then the Big Ten alumni were in a complete quandary. What, exactly, could an alumnus do to encourage an athlete to attend his beloved alma mater? In response, the Big Ten athletic directors met in Ann Arbor in the summer of 1923 and published a statement directed to all alumni groups:

> 1. Is it proper for alumni associations or groups to collect a fund from which loans may be made to needy athletes? NO
>
> 2. Is it proper to give financial aid without any obligation on the part of the athlete? NO
>
> 3. Is it proper to furnish scholarships to athletes? NO
>
> 4. Is it proper to give banquets to high school athletes for the purpose of inducing them to enter their respective colleges? YES
>
> 5. Is it proper for an alumnus to pay the expenses of an athlete whom he knows and in whom he has a personal interest? NO
>
> 6. Is it proper for an alumnus to pay the expenses of an athlete in whom he has no interest except that the latter is an athlete? NO
>
> 7. Is it proper for an alumnus to join with one or more others in furnishing financial aid to athletes? NO[164]

In the spring of 1924, the Directors took another step and voted unanimously that it was inadvisable for alumni to pay the

---

[164] Board in Control, Box 5, November 1923

expenses of groups of high school and preparatory athletes to visit their respective universities. Furthermore, Commissioner Griffith contacted all the state high school associations in the Big Ten area and asked them to directly notify him if they perceived a violation of the rules.

Under Yost's leadership, the Big Ten led the nation in the vital effort to preserve the ideal of the "amateur athlete," but from the beginning the struggle was difficult. For every rule made, violations were inevitable and enforcement was problematic. Nothing about this effort has become easier with the passage of time, but Yost could be quite eloquent and also very prophetic, in defending what he felt was a most important ideal:

> Once given official sanction, professionalism would spread to all branches of sport in all seasons…The problem is not merely a question of whether or not college athletes are to be permitted to play baseball for money during the summer. Much more is at stake. Followed to the logical conclusion the answer to this question will determine the whole nature of collegiate athletics in the future. Answer it one way and it is only a matter of time before our college teams would be composed of more or less an isolated group of professional athletes. Answer the question in the other way and we will continue to have high-class amateur athletics which will be an important part of every student's life and an activity in which every student will have an equal opportunity with each other student of taking part. The question is, "Which of these two situations do we want?"

> What would be the results if the question were answered in favor of permitting college athletes to sell their skill?

> In the first place the college teams would be composed almost entirely of professionals. The ordinary student could not hope to compete against the professional with

his great advantage in practice and training. All incentive to the mass of students to try for the team would be lost. A comparatively few would be set aside by themselves as "the athletes." They would be trained and developed at the expense of the University under coaches paid by the University, to be turned over at the close of their college career to the managers of the professional teams. Athletic contests would become mere spectacles...

College athletic associations would become "feeders" for the regular professional organizations...It is easily possible that under this system there might be a more perfect technical exhibition, but after all, is it the end of athletics to afford only a technically perfect exhibition? In reality athletics have a much more important function to perform in our colleges.

Fundamentally, the underlying aims of college athletics are these three: to develop and maintain the physical health of all the students; to promote recreation through self-expression, and a wholesome spirit of competition and rivalry; to form habits and inculcate ideals of right living.

To attain these ends the program of athletics in our colleges should be to make participation as nearly universal as possible. "Athletics for all" should be the aim. Each student should have an equal right and opportunity with every other student to participate...

To be sure, only a comparatively small number actually participate in intercollegiate athletics...However, the possibility is always open to any one to try for the team and the probability of his making it is sufficiently great to make the effort worthwhile.

Furthermore, the influence of athletic professionalism

is, in itself, detrimental to a college man. It tends to make him dissatisfied to play the game for its own sake and makes his athletic powers a marketable commodity, rather than a means of recreation and self-expression. The game is robbed of the exhilarating inspiration of achievement merely for achievement's sake, and many of the very important character building qualities which form a part of collegiate athletics are lost the moment the incentive of personal gain is introduced. The ideas of generous service, loyalty, sacrifice, and whole-hearted devotion to a cause are all taken away.

And is it not a very questionable benefit to a young college man to make it possible for him to receive large fees and salaries for short terms and comparatively easy work? Does not this tend to minimize some of the more desirable qualities of industry, hard work, and continued application to a difficult task? The athlete would become unwilling to put in the hard, tedious work at a small compensation that is usually a necessary part of one's preparation for the greater successes of life. The comparative ease with which an athlete could get money would foster habits of idleness and the desire to "get something for nothing" which would make it difficult for him to undergo the discipline and hard work of ordinary business when he had finished his athletic career...

The sacrifice of self to a group or institution for the attainment of a common goal is the first lesson taught by athletics. This means cooperation, team play, loyalty and service. The qualities of determination, will power, persistence and courage, both physical and moral, can no where be better learned than on the athletic field. Self-confidence, self-control, alertness, aggressiveness, obedience, reliability, friendliness, leadership, mental and moral poise, resourcefulness, decision-making—these qualities and many more are brought out in marked degree by athletics…

It is readily granted that some very worthy and needy men may be compelled by these rules to give up their eligibility and take money instead of college glory. This is regrettable but unavoidable. The rules must be made for the many and not for the few. It must be remembered that participation on college teams is a privilege rather than a right. Excellent facilities, high-class coaching and all the atmosphere of the big University games are provided for the college athlete freely and gladly by the school. The student must choose between these advantages and the financial gain of playing outside. It is merely a question of which the student most desires—those things which go with college and amateur athletics, or those things which go with outside and professional athletics. He may choose either, but NOT both. They do not mix.[165]

In another speech, Yost asserted the importance of amateur athletics at an even higher level, placing it at the very core of American culture.

Since the people of America have shown such increasing fondness for sports, we believe that through intercollegiate contests we can stress the moral qualities which are the embodiment of good citizenship and that these lessons are being taught not only to those who play the games, but also to the thousands who witness them.

In support of this contention we cite the testimony of history which tells us that from Greece down to Great Britain and America, the countries that have been most successful in democratic self-government have invariably been the countries that have placed the greatest emphasis on competitive games and athletics.

---

[165] Yost papers, Box 7, Yost speeches, folder (1)

All who have enjoyed them will agree that athletic games inculcate qualities much to be desired in citizens of a democracy. They teach, indeed, self-control in the individual which is the first essential of self-government in the nation. They develop the habit of cooperating with fellow players. And they give, as perhaps nothing else can, the ability to respect opponents. Democracy is based upon respect for the opposition.[166]

Who could not fight to protect the amateur athlete who was placed on such a pedestal? The new Big Ten Commissioner had a heroic job to perform.

---

[166] Board in Control, Box 6, April 1924 (1)

# Chapter 6

# 1924: The Decisive Year
# "The Dedication Season"

Would Fielding H. Yost coach the 1924 team? Rumors had swirled about for some time that Yost might relinquish his coaching duties. It is obvious that, as athletic director, Yost had much on his mind besides coaching a football team. While building the field house had been a very stressful experience for him, the athletic department now proposed to field a hockey team, a swim team and other varsity sports. Accommodations and arrangements had to be made for all of them The university would need to hire coaches, arrange schedules, and properly monitor the programs. Selling football tickets had by itself become a full time job.

To some of his dear friends, Yost intimated that the strain of being athletic director and football coach was becoming excessive. In August 1924, before the season started, Yost had a physical exam and weighed in at 211 pounds. The subsequent admonition from his doctors would find many sympathizers today.

> Your general physical condition has not changed materially since your examination some years ago with the exception of the blood pressure which is now slightly elevated. This emphasizes the need of reducing your weight for overweight means extra work for the circulatory system…we do not know whether you have restricted your diet according to our instructions…We

hope that you will give our advice more consideration than you have in the past…The benefits which will come to you as a result of this examination depend upon your cooperation in carrying out our recommendations.[167]

In 1922, Yost had hired George Little, the head coach at Miami of Ohio, to be his primary assistant. Little had previously played guard for three years at Ohio Wesleyan and was an assistant coach for two years each at Ohio State and Cincinnati. He had compiled a 46-3-3 record over six years as head coach at Miami of Ohio. His hiring was warmly greeted by Michigan fans, many of whom saw him as Yost's eventual successor.

While Yost had said that he was slowly turning over coaching responsibilities to his assistants, there was no official declaration made that he wasn't in charge of the 1924 team. The idea that Yost might give up his coaching duties worried some alumni groups. The Chicago Alumni Club passed a resolution urging him to remain at the helm of the football program. "We hereby request Coach Yost not to retire from his well earned position, but to continue in his present capacity, in which capacity the entire athletic world has learned to love and respect him."[168]

While Michigan's official record books list George Little as the head coach in 1924, there was no such confirmation at the beginning of the season. The *Ann Arbor News* put it succinctly, "Within the last year or so, Yost has turned over much of the details to George Little, his assistant, but the 'Hurry Up' one's word is still final."[169] There was no official announcement at the beginning of the 1924 season in either the *Michigan Daily* or the *Ann Arbor News* that Yost had given up his coaching duties. In fact, both newspapers referred frequently to the team as the "Yostmen."

But some changes seem to have been in the works. In the spring of 1923, Yost extended Tad Wieman's contract as an assistant coach. Wieman wrote,

[167] Board in Control, Box 6, August 1924 (1)
[168] *Michigan Daily*, 12/14/23, p 5
[169] *Ann Arbor News*, 9/23/24, p 12

When we talked about terms you had not yet mentioned the fact, of which you later spoke—namely, that you did not expect to take an active part in the coaching next season but, rather, would create a committee in which would be vested entire authority and responsibility for the season's work. As a member of such a committee I would be inclined to rate my services at a figure somewhat higher than the one I named which was to cover services in the capacity of your assistant only.[170]

Yost replied,

When I was with you I spoke about having in mind a program covering the coaching of the team by a committee. I have not yet definitely decided on that and above all would not want this known until the beginning of the football season so I have not discussed this proposition with any one except Mr. Little, and for that reason did not take up the matter of additional compensation in case this program was adopted.[171]

The key phrase here seems to be: "I have not yet definitely decided." There is little to suggest that Yost ever did make that decision. Clearly, he retained primary control over the team when the 1924 season began.

Two major college football rules were implemented in 1924. First, kicking tees were made illegal. Artificial tees had never been allowed, but players were permitted to mound the dirt on the field and place the ball on top for kick-offs. Soon some enterprising players were mounding mud on the sidelines, molding a tee, and then bringing it on the field for kick-offs. This approach was banned in 1924, but since the ball was to be kicked right off the ground, the kick-off was moved up from the 40-yard line to the 50. Secondly, the attempt for the point after was moved from the

[170] Board in Control, Box 5, April 1923 (1)
[171] Board in Control, Box 5, May 1923 (1)

5-yard line to the three. Very few teams would attempt a running play from the five, so by moving the ball to the 3-yard line, it was hoped that more teams might try to run rather than kick. Even so, only one point could be scored with either approach.

Michigan's schedule for 1924 originally listed home games with Miami of Ohio, the Michigan Agricultural College, Wisconsin, Northwestern, and Iowa. However, Yost agreed to move the game with MAC to East Lansing. Michigan hadn't played there since 1914, but MAC had received funds from the state to build a new 20,000 seat stadium, and Michigan was invited to be the guest team for the dedication game. Yost issued a statement,

> I will be very glad to take the team to East Lansing next fall to dedicate the new stadium that the Michigan Agricultural College is erecting. They have come to Ann Arbor for the annual game every year since 1914 and it is only right that we should return the courtesy on such an occasion as this.[172]

Thus, the 1924 season quickly became known as the "Dedication Season" in Ann Arbor since Michigan would provide the competition in the stadium dedications at MAC, Illinois and Minnesota. No school had ever been so honored in a single season.

However, without question, the pre-season focus of the Michigan camp was the game to be played at Illinois. Illinois and Michigan had tied for the conference championship the year before, and this game represented the major clash in the Big Ten. Red Grange, Illinois' legendary halfback, had been named to Walter Camp's All-American squad after the 1923 season, his sophomore year. Michigan fans knew it would be a tough game.

George Little had laid down the challenge to the Michigan team in a letter to the players during spring training, 1924:

> Our team faces the greatest test in Michigan football history when we meet Illinois at Urbana Oct 18, in the

---

official dedication game of their new $2,000,000 stadium. Our efforts must be concentrated on this game because of its great importance to students, alumni and citizens of Michigan…We must start now to prepare. There will be 80,000 spectators watching the outcome of the contest and many hundreds of thousands of interested alumni and friends listening for reports throughout the country. It means too much for you and Michigan to neglect any opportunity to make of yourself a more valuable factor in this great game.[173]

Yost, vacationing in Tennessee in August 1924, received a note from an assistant coach hoping "that your vacation may be thoroughly enjoyable and that you will be able to forget the 18th of October for at least a part of the time."[174] In another letter, the same assistant wrote,

We'll be able to get down to some concentrated work in preparation for the 18th. Believe me, there is one team that is going to be ready for the battle on that day or I don't know three fellows that have their headquarters around the Yost Field House. Every player I see is rearin' to go and every one else I see says he is going to be in Urbana on October 18th. I'll bet it will be just about the greatest game of football ever played. I get all excited thinking about it now.[175]

In mid-September, Yost wrote a former assistant coach,

A few days ago there came to my desk a copy of "Football Technique and Tactics" by Robert Zuppke [the Illinois coach] with notes by you. This was a very thoughtful idea on your part. This is going to aid me very materially for the Illinois-Michigan dedication game at Champaign. I

[173] *Michigan Daily*, 4/22/24, p 6
[174] Board in Control, Box 6, August 1924 (1)
[175] Board in Control, Box 6, August 1924 (2)

am counting on going to the Illinois-Nebraska game at Lincoln October 4th. I will take this book along and will study it very carefully with your notations.

This, as you will imagine, is a very busy place just now. Every effort possible is being made to prepare for the Illinois game. In a way, if possible, more effort is being made than for the Ohio State game two years ago. I believe there has been more work done to date to have this team ready than there was for the Ohio game. This is a high spot and we are determined if possible to go over the top at Champaign. We realize we have a difficult game and that our team must be largely rebuilt.[176]

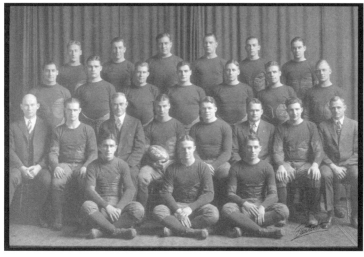

Photo courtesy of Bentley Historical Library

**The University of Michigan Football Team of 1924**
*This team did not win the Big Ten title, but played before more spectators than any team in college football history*

*Row 4: Parker, Babcock, Kunow, Dewey, Domhoff, Gregory*
*Row 3: Flora, Hawkins, Steele, Slaughter, Edwards, Grube, Stamman*
*Row 2: Coach Wieman, Marion, Coach Yost, Captain Steger, Brown, Coach Little, Miller, Hoyt (trainer)*
*Row 1: Friedman, Rockwell, Herrnstein*

[176] Board in Control, Box 6, September 1924 (1)

Major work would be required to get the 1924 team ready for its remarkable schedule. The great Kipke had graduated, Uteritz, the quarterback, was gone and so was the All-American center, Jack Blott. The *Daily* noted that 60 participants showed up for drills on the first day of practice and worked "under the guiding eyes of Coach Yost and Coach Little."[177] The first scrimmage was held four days later, but the varsity had problems defeating the reserves, 14-0. Tod Rockwell was looking good at quarterback, but an undiscovered talent, Benny Friedman, was lost amongst the reserves. In another scrimmage, the reserves tied the varsity, 7-7, in a spirited game. Finally, on September 28, the varsity proved its good form, defeating the reserves, 24-0. By October 2, the backfield was set. Rockwell would be at quarter, captain Herb Steger and Fred Parkman would play at half, and Red Miller would be the fullback.

Ignoring any supposed transfer of head coaching duties to Little, the *Daily* proclaimed, "Coach Fielding Yost, Michigan's grizzled head coach, will direct his players in the first game of the 1924 season."[178] In fact, the *Daily* went on to say that Michigan and Miami of Ohio had never played each other before, but "they have a bond of relationship in George Little, *assistant coach* [my italics] of Michigan football teams."[179]

However, Yost didn't stay in Ann Arbor for this game. He traveled all the way to Lincoln, Nebraska, to scout the Illinois-Nebraska game and to get a good personal look at the Illinois phenomenon, Red Grange. Illinois won the game, 9-6, and Grange had an impressive day, running for 116 yards and passing for another 127.

Little stayed behind and guided the Michigan squad to a 55-0 whipping of Miami. Michigan substitutions were numerous, and the press corps found it impossible to identify the players because the team took the field in old jerseys that didn't have numbers. While Michigan had new jerseys with numbers from 23 to 82, they were being saved for the game at East Lansing the next week.

[177] *Michigan Daily*, 9/20/24, p 6
[178] *Michigan Daily*, 10/3/24, p 6
[179] *Michigan Daily*, 10/4/24, p 4

Despite the one-sided victory, the *Daily* noted some worries:

> Nine days hence Michigan's Varsity will trot out onto
> the field to meet the Illini in what promises to be one
> of the most important football games in the history of
> Michigan. If Michigan is to come through in that game
> the days between now and then must see a marked
> improvement in the performance of the Wolverines.[180]

To make matters more serious, the varsity was almost held to
a tie by the reserves in Wednesday's scrimmage.

## The MAC Game

A capacity crowd of nearly 20,000 spectators turned out for
the new stadium dedication at the Michigan Agricultural College.
The Governor of Michigan and both university presidents were in
attendance. The *Ann Arbor News* described the scene:

> Michigan's proudest educational institutions clasped
> hands across a new monument to athletes and spat rivalry
> at each other across the gridiron here today.

> From early morning thousands of alumni and students of
> the University of Michigan poured into this little college
> town to help the graduates and undergraduates of the
> Michigan Agricultural College dedicate a new stadium.
> The heads of the university pledged enduring friendship
> and warm regard for the East Lansing college while the
> students pledged their equally enduring rivalry on the
> football field.[181]

The teammates for MAC played their hearts out before a packed
stadium, the largest crowd to ever watch a game in East Lansing.
The *Daily* related that, "Eleven Aggies, urged on by thousands of
rooters and the thought that they had a chance to take the haughty

---

[180] *Michigan Daily*, 10/9/24, p 6
[181] *Ann Arbor News*, 10/11/24, p 12

Wolverines in their new stadium, fought as an Aggie team has not fought for a decade."[182]

While most of the second half was played in Michigan territory, the Wolverines finally struck paydirt in the last four minutes of the game. Halfback Fred Parker completed a 47-yard touchdown strike to the other halfback, Herb Steger. As the final minutes ticked away on a 7-0 Michigan victory, Wolverine cheerleaders led the relieved Michigan crowd in a mocking repetition: "Dedication, Dedication."

Michigan's offense was less than impressive. The Wolverines made only two first downs in the game and tried only 12 passes. Seven fell incomplete and three were intercepted. The team was lucky to stagger out of town with this dedication day victory.

Yost missed this game as well. He traveled to Champaign to watch the match-up between Illinois and Butler. Illinois easily won this game, 40 to 10. Grange showed his brilliance by gaining 104 yards on the ground and scoring two touchdowns in 16 minutes of play.

Poor George Little would retrospectively carry the blame for coaching the coming disaster at Illinois, but Yost scouted the Illini twice and surely directed the game plan for Champaign.

## The Illinois Game

The Memorial Stadium at Illinois would be the second great Big Ten stadium built during the 1920s. In 1921, Illinois' home field had a capacity of 17,000. The place was packed that year for the game against Ohio State, and Illinois officials estimated they had turned down 30,000 ticket requests.

Even before that season, however, a drive was initiated to build a great new memorial stadium, "the greatest college stadium."[183] University students initiated the effort with a huge rally on campus that raised $700,000 from student pledges alone. Alumni and friends of the University contributed the remainder for a total of

---

[182] *Michigan Daily*, 10/14/24, p 6
[183] Board in Control, Box 5, July 1922, Memorial Stadium Notes, September 1922, p 4

$1.7 million. To stimulate subscriptions, the athletic department announced that,

> With each $100 pledge you will receive an option on one good seat in the Stadium for 10 years, or on 2 good seats for 5 years. As your subscription increases, the number of seat options increases in the same ratio. A $200 subscription entitles you to two seats for 10 years or 4 seats for 5 years…$1000…entitles you to an option for 10 years on 20 seats or for five years on 40 seats.[184]

Ground was broken in September 1922, but this stadium would be a place for more than football. It would be a great memorial to those Illini who had died in World War I. An Illinois alumni publication asked, "Why a stadium as a memorial?"

> First, nothing could be more beautiful in an imposing, monumental way than a Stadium. Think of the Coliseum, the Circus Maximus, the Stadia of Greece…Picture the massive, graceful structure, gleaming in the Illinois sun.

> Second, nothing could better commemorate the men and women who represented Illinois in the Great War than an athletic Stadium. Three things characterized the American soldier in the war: resourcefulness, physical training and morale. All of these were in large measure the product of the athletic contests of American youth. All are best typified in a great Stadium where stamina and physical prowess reach their highest expression. For our soldiers and sailors, the Stadium is the one most fit monument.[185]

The edifice would be a great horseshoe with two levels of parallel stands so that more than 70% of the fans would sit between the goal lines. Designed by the same architect who created Soldier Field in Chicago, the structure was graced with 200 columns. One

---

[184] University of Illinois Archives, Box 1, Stadium Drive Publications, Stadium Promotion Book
[185] University of Illinois Archives, Box 1, Stadium Drive Publications, Stadium Captain's Book

column would be dedicated to each of the 184 Illini, 183 men and one woman, who gave their lives in the Great War.

The *Daily Illini* of October 18, 1924, relates that arrangements had been made to dedicate nine of the columns in the Stadium to honor the war dead from each of the other Big Ten universities. This gracious plan was never completed, but a Michigan column was dedicated to "Col. Curtis G. Redden, an '03 graduate of Michigan who was a colonel in the 149th field artillery. He died shortly after the Armistice."[186]

Buried in the July 1922 folder of the University of Michigan athletic department records is an Illinois Loyalty Pledge Card in the name of Fielding H. Yost, marked "paid in full, $500." Why would Fielding Yost contribute $500 to the Illinois stadium project? In the same year, Yost was contacted by the principal at his old high school. They were planning to name the football field after Yost, and they wondered if he might provide them with a contribution for football equipment. Yost promptly sent $25, and the principal replied, "I am writing to thank you most earnestly and kindly for the honor that you have conferred upon us by your very liberal subscription to our equipment fund."[187] When his own alma mater, West Virginia University, announced a stadium drive in 1923, Yost sent $100.

There is every indication that Yost was generous with his personal funds. However, Yost's income statement for 1922 shows he received $8500 from the university, $2770 from stocks and bonds, and $1400 from rents for a total of $12,670. A $500 contribution, then, to the University of Illinois Memorial Stadium fund would have been no small amount for him.

So who was Curtis G. Redden? Curtis G. Redden was a 1903 graduate of Michigan, all right, but from the law school, not the undergraduate school. Redden, originally from the state of Illinois, had initially matriculated in 1900 and had played on the football team that year. When Yost arrived in 1901, Redden became a

---

[186] *Daily Illini*, 10/18/24, p 17
[187] Yost papers, Box 2, 1922 (4)

stalwart at left end, participating on the first great point-a-minute team that accumulated 550 points to the opponents' 0. Following the 1902 season, when Michigan again went undefeated, this time overwhelming their opponents with a combined score of 644 to 12, Redden was honored with a full page tribute in the *Michiganensian*, the university yearbook.

> Of all the players on this year's team there is no one whose work has been more satisfactory to the coaches and students than that of Redden…Throughout the whole season he has labored hard and earnestly to perfect his playing…He began the season by playing faultless games against Albion, Case and Indiana and by the time of the Wisconsin game he had fully developed his great faculty…Wherever the ball was there you found Redden.[188]

At the close of the 1902 season, Curtis G. Redden was elected captain of the team for 1903. Even though he graduated from the law school in June 1903, Redden still had a year of eligibility left, and he agreed to stay to captain the football team in the fall. In 1903, with captain Redden at the helm, Michigan rolled up 565 points to their opponents' 6, but the six points were big ones as the Wolverines were tied by Minnesota (this was the game that initiated the Little Brown Jug tradition). Incredibly, Redden had also been elected captain of the baseball team, and he remained in Ann Arbor to play his final games for Michigan in the spring of 1904.

Redden, who practiced law in Danville, Illinois, returned to Ann Arbor each autumn from 1909 to 1912 to serve as an assistant football coach for Yost. Following the outbreak of World War I, he voluntarily enlisted and eventually commanded an artillery regiment in the famed Rainbow Division. He participated in virtually every major engagement on the western front, but contracted pneumonia after the Armistice and died in a field hospital in France a short time before he was scheduled to return home.

---

[188] *Michiganensian*, 1903, p 139

photo courtesy of Diane Marlin

*Ilinois Memorial Stadium—West Stand*
*Redden column is farthest to the right*

The University of Illinois Alumni Association has confirmed that the $1000 pledge for a column to honor Michigan's war dead, inscribed with the name of Michigan's 1903 football captain, was paid for with a $500 contribution from the 149th field artillery unit along with $500 from Fielding H. Yost. So this great Memorial Stadium that meant so much to the University of Illinois community meant much more than just football to Yost, too. (If one is outside facing the west stand at Illinois stadium, the column farthest to the right is the one dedicated to Colonel Redden. An adjacent plaque confirms "F.H. Yost" as a primary donor)

When Yost paid his Memorial Stadium pledge, he contributed more than many an Illini. A December 1922 note from Illinois' athletic director, George Huff, to the stadium subscribers described the situation and again made the ever-present comparison to Michigan.

> The carelessness of those of you who are delinquent has been a great disappointment to me. But I still have an abiding faith that encourages me to believe you will hasten to make your pledges good.
>
> I appeal to you to pay up immediately the amount you are behind…Unless you who are behind in your payments

soon make good your delinquencies, instead of hurrying the Stadium to a greater degree of completion next fall, it is even possible that we will have to slow up the work to a considerable degree.

Michigan tells me that it collected 93 percent of the subscriptions to its great Union building. I hold that the pledged word of the sons and daughters of Illinois is at least as good as that of Michigan's.

What have you to say?[189]

Further on in the same newsletter, Huff was very blunt, "Do not ask for cancellation or reduction of your pledge. That such a request cannot be granted was decided by the Stadium executive committee one year ago. Death alone is accepted as a ground of cancellation."[190] The October 1923, stadium newsletter said, "The Stadium will soon be broke. Because delinquent subscribers owe upwards of $290,000…it will be necessary either to halt work or borrow money."[191]

In fact, work was slowed to some degree, which allowed for Michigan to play the dedication game. The original dedication was planned for November 1923 against Chicago, but the stadium was only partially finished, and thus the game was moved to 1924.

Of course, Yost was aware of this financial struggle at Illinois. The same problem had developed at other universities trying to build stadiums. It would influence him greatly when it came time to raise money for Michigan's effort.

Nonetheless, the Illinois community rose to the occasion and completed its hallowed Memorial Stadium in time for the 1924 season. This eternal inscription on the outside columned walls greets visitors:

[189] University of Illinois Archives, Box 1, Stadium Drive Publications, Memorial Stadium Notes, December 1922

[190] University of Illinois Archives, Box 1, Stadium Drive Publications, Memorial Stadium Notes, December 1922

[191] University of Illinois Archives, Box 1, Stadium Drive Publications, Memorial Stadium Notes, October 1923

"This stadium is erected in grateful memory of those sons of Illinois, who in the great war with brave hearts and eager feet went out in defense of an ideal. The memory of their courage, their willingness to suffer and to sacrifice and, if need be, to give their lives to the cause they served will be an inspiration to men long after these bricks shall have crumbled into dust."

photo courtesy of Diane Marlin

*Illinois Memorial Stadium*

In this great place, these two teams would meet for an official dedication game on October 18, 1924. "Beat Illinois" and "Stop Grange" were the words on everyone's lips in Ann Arbor. Practices for the week were closed, but the *Daily* chronicled the preparation.

> Michigan's determination to give Illinois everything she has this weekend was manifested by the appearance in uniform of Coach Fielding H. Yost Monday afternoon. "Hurry Up" showed that he is still the same old coach when he blocked, tackled, and gave demonstrations of plays in the same way which won for him his popular title years ago.[192]

Yost was back in uniform on Tuesday.

> It was "Hurry Up's" driving voice that kept the players on the run. Whenever an individual made a mistake,

no matter how trivial it was, he got "caught up" by the coaches…

Not a backfield man on the Illinois team failed to have his individual tricks considered and "Red" Grange was the subject of plenty of advice handed out to the regulars by Coaches Yost and Wieman who took in the Illinois-Butler contest at Urbana last weekend.

Grange, Grange, Grange…is the way in which Michigan's coaches have been talking to the Varsity during the past few days.[193]

The *Ann Arbor News* put it this way.

Frantically the Michigan coaches are preparing for the struggle. Coach Yost has been out in uniform every night this week working with a vigor which cannot help but instill pep into his men.

Those who have watched Coach Yost in action…realize that to the veteran coach the Illinois game looms up as one of the greatest events in his career. A defeat will add years to the man who has piloted Michigan teams through a quarter of a century. A victory will make him the happiest man in the world…

There is nothing being overlooked at Ferry Field these afternoons. There is no joking, there is no time wasted. From the minute a player reports for practice he is kept busy until darkness ends the workout.[194]

Needless to say, there was much ferment on the respective campuses. This game would also be homecoming at Illinois, the university that originated the event in 1910. However, the homecoming celebration had been discontinued at a few schools because some believed they had become little more than drunken orgies. Of

---

[193] *Michigan Daily*, 10/15/24, p 6
[194] *Ann Arbor News*, 10/15/24, p 12

course, 1924 fell in the midst of Prohibition, but this fact seemed to matter little. America was losing its first war on drugs. Alcohol was everywhere, often smuggled to campus by returning alumni.

The Interfraternity Council at Illinois conceded that a dry homecoming would be impossible and declared that it would never do to antagonize Michigan fraternities by asking them not to bring liquor. Nonetheless, the Council agreed to do "all in its power" to bring about a dry weekend and "to point out to the Michigan men that Illinois students are gentlemen and they would expect Michigan to live up to that standard."[195]

The *Michigan Daily* chimed in with an editorial that could be written every autumn.

> Coincident with the appeal of representative organizations at Michigan and Illinois for temperate conduct on the part of students at the dedication game Saturday, comes a feeling akin to shame that such action should be necessary. It remains to be seen what effect the movement for a "dry homecoming" will have, but even if it succeeds entirely, which is doubtful, the fact that it has proved necessary to urge supposedly intelligent students to remain sober while attending a football game is a reflection on American universities.
>
> It should be made clear at once that Michigan and Illinois are no worse than an hundred other institutions of the country when excessive drinking is concerned…The fact that a considerable minority of our compatriots in the field of learning feel it essential to their happiness to lose their mental balance entirely during football games is simply a condition which every honest American educator must recognize…
>
> Prohibition has assumed a definite place in our life and seems to have brought with it a feeling of bravado con-

---

[195] *Daily Illini*, 10/9/24, p 1

cerning the excessive indulgence in the forbidden beverages. The principal problem for us is found not in the fact that students drink, but that they get drunk in places where their conduct is both disgusting and slanderous…

The good name of the entire student body is affected. The public comes to believe that each and every student is as weak as the person reeling up the aisle of the stadium…

It is time that those who have principles in the matter take a stand and make it known, that the capacity for drunkenness become a matter of sorrow instead of humor, that the ability to imbibe to excess lower rather than raise social standing.[196]

The obligatory pep rally occurred Thursday night before the game. Fred Lawton, the composer of "Varsity," gave an inspiring address that was interrupted again and again by applause. The *Daily* recorded the event.

Last night 5000 Michigan men and women gathered in Hill auditorium and cheered themselves hoarse for a Michigan Day at Illinois Saturday. Everyone there pledged himself to stand with the Michigan team in victory and defeat. Today the hearts of 11,000 students are with the team as they start on their journey of conquest.

A greater force…which the team must feel is the spirit of comradeship in a mutual undertaking for the glory of Michigan—to fight for victory, but to conquer in victory or defeat.

The team, the student body, and the alumni, are one in their wish for victory. They commence their invasion of Illinois tomorrow. Upwards of 10,000 Michiganders will be on hand Saturday to cheer eleven men of Michigan worthy to represent that greatest of all universities.

---

[196] *Michigan Daily*, 10/16/24, p 4

Then—MICHIGAN WILL RULE THE WEST![197]

After the pep rally, student volunteers lined up in their cars to drive the football team to Milan, Michigan, from where they would take an overnight train to Champaign.

From this pep rally, however, there came some controversy. In a letter signed, "Amazon," a co-ed forcefully stated her case: the seating at the pep rally was segregated, with women getting the poorest seats. Even worse, the Michigan Union at that time was off-limits to females.

> Do the men on the Michigan campus lack the fundamentals of courtesy or is it true that Michigan women are intentionally being frozen out of Michigan athletics? If plans had been carried out by the [women] who gathered outside the library after the pep meeting last Wednesday evening there might have been a little discourtesy shown by Michigan women. Had not better judgment prevented them from tearing open the sacred portals of the Union, stacking the furniture, and breaking a few windows, Michigan men might have learned that Michigan women back the team as well as men; also that they have…"Hearts for Michigan" that can be roused.

> The first thing that greeted us upon arrival at Hill Auditorium Wednesday evening was a janitor's voice, "All women to the balcony," while the main floor remained empty. After delaying the pep meeting for some fifteen or twenty minutes for enough "men" to get there, the fun began: which fun consisted mostly of addressing Michigan "men."

> After the ceremony the audience was informed that there would be music and "eats in the tap room of the Union." The result was that the women should go promptly home, squelched and happy.

A placard advertising a cheering squad on the fifty yard line "for men only" was the first red flag of the season and the first pep meeting all too definitely bore the same stamp. University officials state that Michigan men and women are on an equal status. Is that mere words and may I ask again?

1. Do Michigan men lack the fundamentals of courtesy?

2. Do not Michigan women back the team or

3. Are we being intentionally frozen out?[198]

Despite the problems they faced at the pep rally, more than 100 women had signed up in the office of the Dean of Women to go to the game and a special train for them, along with chaperones, would depart Ann Arbor Friday at 10:00 P.M. Several other chartered trains would leave on non-stop runs to Champaign at half-hour intervals. After the game, railroad officials said the traffic represented the largest movement of railway cars in the history of Chicago. Twenty-one trains averaging 13 cars per train left Chicago for Champaign between Friday night and Saturday morning.

The Michigan Band was finally satisfied as Ann Arbor businessmen had agreed to raise money to send the 77 musicians to Champaign. Very quickly, the local Chamber of Commerce came up with $1400 to help defray the travel expenses.

Sometime during the week WGN, the major radio station in Chicago, notified the Michigan athletic department that they would broadcast the game. "The announcer would describe every play in the game as it occurs and his voice…would be put on the air to be heard by listeners for many hundreds of miles in all directions."[199] It would be the first live radio broadcast of a football game for both schools.

The little community of Champaign-Urbana witnessed the

[198] *Michigan Daily*, 10/18/24, p 4
[199] Board in Control, Box 6, September 1924 (1)

largest influx of visitors in its history. A little ditty had made the rounds all week,

> Don't send my boy to Harvard
> A dying mother said;
> Don't send my boy to Michigan
> I'd rather he were dead
> But send my boy to Illinois
> 'tis better than Cornell
> But rather than Chicago
> I'd see my boy in hell.[200]

A crowd of 20,000, including veterans and their families, attended a solemn dedication ceremony at the stadium on Friday afternoon. The *Daily Illini* wrote,

> Inspired by the memories of their immortal heroes, loyal Illini are making their first great gift to posterity.
>
> We stand ready today to answer the challenge flung to us from Flander's field. We have won the right to hold high the flaming torch as a symbol that Illini did not break faith with the dead. It is they who have incited us successfully to accomplish a noble work of which we are justly proud.[201]

Perhaps it was on this afternoon that Fielding Yost found the time to walk the solemn ramparts and first gaze upon the column dedicated to Michigan's war dead, inscribed with the name of a former Michigan football captain.

The stadium was finished, but the area around it was a sea of mud. Townspeople were urged to walk to the game and to leave their cars at home. Visitors were assured that teams of horses would be available if needed to extract vehicles from the mud.

Before a capacity crowd of 67,000, the curtain was about to rise on perhaps the most remarkable individual performance in

---

[200] University of Illinois Archives, Box 1, Stadium Drive Publications, Stadium Drive Record
[201] *Daily Illini*, 10/18/24, p 4

the history of American college football. Fielding Yost, the living legend, was about to witness the birth of another.

Illinois' great halfback, Red Grange, had made Camp's All-America team in 1923 as a sophomore. However, the *Michigan Daily* had posted their own such team, and they put Grange on the second team. The *Daily* complained "that all Grange can do is run."[202] This assertion was made to slight Grange's ability to pass and to play defense, but Grange says in his autobiography that this insult by the Michigan student paper inspired much of his preparation for this game.

Robert Zuppke, the great Illinois coach, always searched for any possible psychological edge. According to Grange, in this game it became the Illini socks. During the pregame warm-ups, Zuppke mentioned how hot it was, and in the locker room before the game, Zuppke suddenly ordered his players to shed their woolen socks. Grange said the whole team was surprised, but they nonetheless followed orders. So the Illini then took the field without socks.

Immediately, Yost and Little protested this event. The referees said that, to their knowledge, there was no rule that said a team must wear socks. The Michigan staff suspected the Illini had greased their legs, so Michigan's captain, Herb Steger, accompanied by a couple of the officials, actually felt the legs of some of the Illini players. He found nothing but hairy extremities, but Grange felt in retrospect that this episode was enough to alter Michigan's focus.

Every football fan knows what happened next. Grange achieved football immortality by scoring four touchdowns in the opening 12 minutes of the game against a Michigan team that had allowed only four touchdowns in the previous two years. How in the world did he do it?

Here's the play-by-play: Illinois won the toss and elected to receive. Michigan's captain, Herb Steger, lined a kick-off from the 50-yard line straight down the middle that Grange took in full stride at the five. He was beyond the Michigan defenders in

---

[202] **The Red Grange Story**, University of Illinois Press, 1993, p 51

a flash and went the length of the field. With the point after, it was 7-0. Michigan had the option to receive or kick-off again and they elected to kick once more. Grange took the kick-off, this time returning it to the 20-yard line, but Illinois was penalized half the distance to the goal for illegal use of hands. A run on first down gained two yards. On second down, Illinois punted to their own 35-yard line.

Michigan's Rockwell passed nine yards to the fullback. A run gained two yards and a first down at the Illinois 24. Steger gained one yard on a run to the left, but then lost a yard on a run to the right. Rockwell threw an incomplete pass. On fourth down, Rockwell fumbled, recovered, and was thrown for a 10-yard loss. It was Illinois' ball.

Illinois gained a yard over right guard, but on the next play Grange sprinted around left end, cut back toward the middle and raced 66 yards for the touchdown. The extra point was good, and the score was 14-0.

Michigan kicked off again, and Grange returned it to the 20. Michigan was offsides on the first play and the ball was moved to the 25. Illinois gained a yard off left tackle; then Grange got four yards on the other side. Illinois punted on third down, lofting one 60 yards to the Michigan 20. Steger gained two yards off left tackle, but Michigan punted on second down to the Illinois 43-yard line. Illinois' fullback hit the line for two yards and then Grange raced around right end, cut back to the middle, and scored his third touchdown. The extra point was missed and it was 20-0.

Once again, Michigan elected to kick off. Perhaps it was time for someone in the Michigan camp to suggest keeping the ball, but one can only imagine the pandemonium by this time on the Michigan sidelines. Anyway, it was tried and true Yost philosophy to use the kicking game to pin the opponents down in their own end of the field. This time Steger put the ball in the endzone, and it came out to the 20. Grange fumbled, but recovered for a five-yard loss. Illinois punted on the next play to the Michigan 45, but Michigan's Rockwell fumbled the ball and Illinois recovered. Illinois ran exactly the same play that had just worked so well: Grange scooted around the right end, cut back to the middle of the field and had clear sailing to the endzone. The point after was good, and the game was 27-0.

Michigan kicked off again, but with three minutes still left in the first quarter, Zuppke called time out and took Grange out of the game. The Illinois crowd gave him a great and stirring ovation. Grange remembered being completely exhausted.

In all, Grange had gained 303 yards in 12 minutes of play, handling the ball eight times and scoring four times. He said afterwards that in both the Nebraska and Butler games he had taken his runs around end to the sidelines, but against Michigan it was decided to cut back to the inside. As a result, the Michigan defenders were posted too far to the outside, and the Illinois blocking was perfect.

Grange didn't return until after the half, but upon his return he accounted for another 85 yards rushing, including a 12-yard touchdown run to make the score 33-7 at the end of the third quarter. It was then that the visiting Michigan crowd experienced a most awful event. Slowly a crescendo spread through the stadium. As the fourth quarter opened, 60,000 Illinois fans chanted, "Hurry up, Yost! Hurry up, Yost!" One chagrined Michigan fan who witnessed the episode said he would never forget it for as long as he lived.

Michigan would score again, but so would Illinois, this time on an 18-yard pass from Grange to make the final score, 39-14. Incredibly, this football game was the first one Michigan's senior captain, Herb Steger, had ever lost. He had never played in a losing game in high school, and he had never lost one before in a Michigan uniform.

Grange had amassed 402 yards on the ground, 78 yards passing, and five touchdowns in 41 minutes of playing time. This would represent the most yardage for Grange in any single game during his college career. Today, a permanent monument, "The Grange

Rock," stands at the north end of the field in Memorial Stadium, proclaiming Grange's great accomplishment in that October 18, 1924 game.

This game, and the remarkable exhibition Grange put on against Penn before the eastern press in 1925, were his two greatest outings and brought him enduring national fame. In 2000, several publications named Grange the greatest college football player of the century.

The contest also represented the most points scored against Michigan by a Big Ten team up until that time. Minnesota had scored 34 twice—in 1893 and 1919—and Wisconsin had done it once, also in 1893.

The day after the game, the jubilant *Daily Illini* proclaimed that the "Champions of the West" had seen their domain reduced to somewhere around Ypsilanti. After celebrating the great dedication game, the paper noted:

> Even if defeat seemed inevitable from the first minutes of play, the Wolverines fought untiringly to the end. Never did the invaders rely on dishonorable tactics, even in the face of defeat…Nor were the visiting fans unsportsmanlike.

> At the close when the Michigan band struck up the strains of 'The Yellow and Blue,' the Wolverine players stood by the band, while their followers sang their praise.[203]

The *Michigan Daily* had no banner headline this time. Way over on the right side of the front page in a single column was the bad news, "Illini Vanquish Wolverines."[204] The editors were philosophical.

> Michigan and Illinois have enjoyed a close rivalry…but all contests have been marked with the same spirit of good sportsmanship which characterized the game yesterday. It

---

[203] *Daily Illini*, 10/19/24, p 1
[204] *Michigan Daily*, 10/19/24, p 1

was thus particularly auspicious that Michigan should aid in the dedication of the new stadium—that monument to the men who gave their lives in the greatest of all battles. The future will see many games there between the two schools…It is to be hoped that all will be played in the same spirit…

To the team that was technically defeated yesterday go the hearts of their fellow students. They did not lose as men. They gave their best for victory. The season is hardly begun. Yesterday's experience will make possible future victories. Michigan is never beaten.[205]

At the bottom of the editorial page, by itself and with no other commentary was this: "Maybe, after all, Grange does eat raw meat."[206]

Two days later, the *Daily* editors were ready to take some people to task. After commending those Michigan supporters who stuck by their team, the editors wrote,

And then there are those who will say with the alumnus coming out of Memorial Stadium Saturday: "Well, I guess Yost has seen his day. He didn't have a thing this afternoon." Others among the knockers are spreading wholesale criticism of the team that fought Illinois off its feet in the last three quarters of the crucial contest…Only when the team is winning will they support Yost, Little and the team.[207]

The *Daily* was not pleased with the crowd support.

One of the biggest disappointments of the game was the fact that 10,000 or more Michigan supporters attending the game lost their heart with Grange's first run and their "support" amounted to practically nothing during

[205] *Michigan Daily*, 10/19/24, p 4
[206] *Michigan Daily*, 10/19/24, p 4
[207] *Michigan Daily*, 10/21/24, p 4

the entire game…Had the Michigan stands let loose a volume of sound after Grange's first touchdown instead of remaining silent as the dead, Grange might have been stopped.[208]

There was only one happy group to be found in all of Ann Arbor: the Michigan Band. Said the band manager, "Never was a band more royally treated than was the Michigan Band last Saturday night at Urbana. Every man is shouting the praise of the Ann Arbor Chamber of Commerce…the band was better cared for than if it had been under the management of the University."[209] Despite an attempt by the local police to prevent it, the Michigan Band paraded through the streets of Champaign before the game with about 2000 followers, tying up traffic in all directions. A great time was had by the musicians, despite Michigan's disappointing loss.

Charles Baird, Yost's dear friend from Kansas City, attended the game, but the two never found the time to get together. Baird wrote afterwards,

> As it is not my habit to indulge in post mortems, I will not attempt to comment on the game. You know better than I the causes of our defeat and I am sure you and your associates are doing all in your power to prepare the team for the strenuous contests ahead…I can well imagine under what a severe strain you are laboring, and I hope you will not let the situation worry you beyond reason. We cannot hope to have a successful team every year and with such a heavy schedule for this season, we must realize that the going will be hard.[210]

Yost replied, "I regret very much that I did not see you in Champaign. This game was like a nightmare. The boys simply blew up. I know of no better way to express it."[211]

---

[208] *Michigan Daily*, 10/21/24, p 6
[209] *Michigan Daily*, 10/21/24, p 1
[210] Board in Control, Box 6, October 1924 (2)
[211] Board in Control, Box 6, October 1924 (2)

A couple of months later, Yost wrote to a friend,

> Red Grange, in my opinion, is one of the most dangerous men that has ever played football insofar as carrying the ball itself is concerned. I do not think he is one of the greatest all-around players and I consider his blocking and tackling only average. No doubt he has been one of the most sensational players that ever flashed across the grid iron.
>
> The game in which he played against Michigan did more than all of his other work to give him this reputation. His ability and the weakness and demoralization of our defense all combined, made this possible. So much has been written and said about him…Far be it from me to want to take anything away from him. I saw him make four touchdowns in the Michigan game without a single Michigan man touching him so far as I could see. In fact, only two or three were close enough to dive for him. This does not seem possible, but, yet, it was true. Once he ran from the kick off and the other three times from the scrimmage, starting about seven yards back of the line running to the side lines each time and then reversing the field back to the center, describing the figure "S" in his runs to the goal line.[212]

## The Wisconsin Game

There would be, however, a silver lining in this most dark Michigan cloud. Upon returning to Ann Arbor, the chastened coaching staff started over from scratch. Every position was up for grabs, and the whole team was reevaluated. Everyone felt the ends had played badly on defense, and several players were given a chance at the position, but the final decision was to move the fullback, Jim Miller, to one end position and put the end, Dutch Marion,

---

[212] Board in Control, Box 7, December 1925 (1)

at fullback. Tod Rockwell, the quarterback, had played perhaps his poorest game at Illinois, and rumors swirled around the campus that he was quitting the team. It didn't happen, but Rockwell was switched to left half and Steger was placed at quarterback. The silver lining, though, would be the Jewish kid from Cleveland, Benny Friedman. The sophomore Friedman, Michigan's next great All-American, had been riding the bench up until now. After the Illinois game, Friedman started at the right halfback slot, and he would never sit for Michigan again.

Despite the crushing defeat on the football field, there was some unfinished business back in Ann Arbor. The *Daily* made sure to find a place to respond to the complaints registered by the letter writer, "Amazon,"

> Considerable antagonism between the sexes has been aroused in the past week by the ill-considered attempts of a Michigan woman…to awaken the dead controversy concerning the position of women at Michigan…The question has long ago been settled to the satisfaction of men and the majority of thinking women…Women are at Michigan to stay…"

> Being excluded from the Union hurt their feelings to think that the men were doing something in which they could not take part…

> And now Amazon confronts us with new trouble. She and several other upperclass women have received poor seats for the games. The blame is immediately shoved on the male cheering section which is to have its tryout Saturday. Do they for a moment suppose that there are not hundreds of men whose seats are poor? These same men do not blame it on the fact there are 2100 seats being reserved for a cheering section. They realize that this cheering section is something which has been needed for years, that it will promote good cheering,

singing and a spirit to an extent never before realized at
Ferry Field…

Amazon says the Michigan women demand an equal right
to participate in campus affairs. In what way are they
excluded now? Every activity except the Union has its
women workers…Michigan men have no feelings against
Michigan women but they insist that there are some activities which should be exclusively reserved for men…Do
Michigan women want to make themselves conspicuous by
loud conduct in connection with a man's sport? The *Daily*
believes worthwhile women have no such desire. It is only
women like Amazon…who give the world its conception
of the unpopular "coeds" at Michigan.[213]

"Amazon" must have been invited to reply, for her response
was on the same page and she wasn't yielding ground.

The point is—a pep meeting is a University function held
for the purpose of arousing all there is of Michigan spirit
and backing the team. Women back the team heartily
and have Michigan spirit…This year upperclass women
have been deprived of good seats at the games because
of the cheering squad…and certainly no invitation has
been extended for their support of the team when this
movement is furthered by the courtesy of balcony seats
[at the pep rally] and free entertainment for only the men
half of the campus population.

Women are at Michigan. Furthermore, it is understood
that they are here to stay and so long as this is true they
want, and will demand, an equal right to participate in
Campus affairs. This is true especially when it comes to
a thing of such vital interest to them as the success of
Michigan's teams.[214]

---

[213] *Michigan Daily*, 10/24/24, p 4
[214] *Michigan Daily*, 10/24/24, p 4

The contest against Wisconsin was in Ann Arbor. A "Back to Victory" pep rally was held Thursday night. Michigan students packed Hill Auditorium in support of their team. Following the rally, the band led a snake dance to the Union where the male students were invited to further entertainment.

Yost spoke to the Michigan cheerleaders, no doubt with the previous year's contest in mind.

> Sportsmanship is the quality of honor that desires always to be courteous, fair and respectful…When two universities meet each other in an athletic contest, they agree to two tests, one to determine which has the stronger team, and the other to determine which has instilled into its team and students the better quality of sportsmanship. It goes without saying that supremacy in the latter is of much greater permanent value than victory in the contest itself…

> Sportsmanship…also means courtesy and respect for opponents, officials, and the game by both players and spectators.[215]

A capacity crowd of at least 45,000 witnessed this game on Ferry Field. Both WWJ of Detroit and WGN of Chicago announced they were broadcasting the game.

However, it was a somber and unfocused Wisconsin contingent that arrived. Tragically, their starting fullback had been accidentally electrocuted and killed in the engineering laboratory Thursday afternoon, shortly before the team was to leave for Ann Arbor.

The game provided the background for Michigan's Benny Friedman to emerge as a future star. In the second quarter, Friedman completed a 35-yard touchdown pass to Steger, the quarterback, for the first Michigan touchdown. In the third quarter, Friedman scored on a brilliant 26-yard run. Late in the fourth quarter, Dutch Marion, the end moved to fullback, scored on a 5-yard run, and the

---

[215] *Michigan Daily*, 10/25/24, p 1

final score was 21-0. Playing defense, Friedman made an interception in the second quarter, but what really thrilled the crowd was Friedman's uncanny ability as a double threat on offense. Would he run or would he throw? The answer to that question would plague Big Ten opponents for the next two years.

The entire Wisconsin team stopped off at their deceased teammate's hometown on the way back to Madison. Six of the players served as pallbearers.

While the Michigan Band clearly had an enjoyable trip to Illinois, the *Michigan Daily* lashed out after the Wisconsin game. Perhaps the editors, unable or unwilling to criticize the football team, decided to take their frustration out on the band.

> The recent performances of the band become a matter for criticism...In the matter of band etiquette and in general maneuvers...the Varsity fails miserably. This was displayed at Illinois. The Illini band produced inferior music, but its appearance so far surpassed that

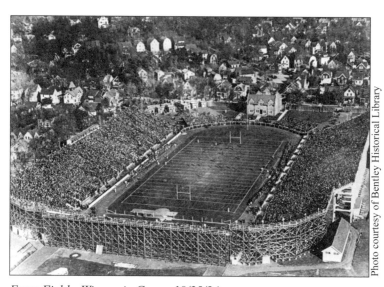

Photo courtesy of Bentley Historical Library

*Ferry Field—Wisconsin Game, 10/25/24*
*45,000 fans in attendance; Michigan 21, Wisconsin 0*

of Michigan's that the effect was almost ludicrous. Of course, their organization is a part of the ROTC and as such has more opportunity for adequate training, but it is also nearly twice as large and as such must be more unwieldy, requiring infinitely more training…the local band can afford to emulate the Illini in effectiveness of drill.

At the Wisconsin game, the band was little better. It presented a ragged appearance and cooperated poorly… there was no explanation of the confusion which resulted between the cheerleaders and the band. In fact the whole performance between halves displayed ignorance…and poor training…If the Varsity band expects to be placed on a solid basis financially it must show that it is worthy of the effort.[216]

## The Minnesota Game

The next game on the schedule was in Minneapolis, where the Michigan football squad would participate in the third dedication of a stadium in this most remarkable season. The new Gopher complex would seat 50,000, and a capacity crowd, the largest ever to see a game in Minnesota, would pack the stands. The town was bedecked in Maroon and Gold. At Thursday night's pep rally, students doused a whole house with oil and set it afire. The topic of conversation was the battle for the Little Brown Jug.

The scene at the train station in Ann Arbor was subdued. Only a few hundred students showed up to cheer the 27 men who would represent Michigan in this contest. Nonetheless, at game time, Hill Auditorium was packed for the grid-graph results.

The game went well for Michigan. Minnesota fumbled a punt in their own territory in the first quarter and the Wolverines recovered. On the next series, the amazing Friedman threw a perfect

---

touchdown strike to the halfback, Bill Herrnstein. The extra point was missed, but in the second quarter, after another 33-yard pass play from Friedman, Michigan faked a field goal at the 5-yard line and scored a touchdown to make it 13 0 at the half. That was the extent of the scoring, and Michigan escaped with a major victory even though Minnesota had 11 first downs to Michigan's four.

Yost took the time after this game to commend the Minnesota community for "the finest sportsmanship we have ever seen." In a letter sent to the Minnesota student newspaper, Yost wrote,

> This letter is sent to you to express to the student body of the University of Minnesota, Michigan's recognition of and appreciation for the royal welcome extended her team last week. In our opinion, the relations between our two universities are the finest existing in the Western Conference.
>
> Minnesota played a hard, clean game. Minnesota's cheering section exhibited the finest sportsmanship we have ever seen. Minnesota welcomed us, did everything possible to make us comfortable, and sent us home with the warmest feelings toward as fine a rival as Michigan has ever known.
>
> It is our sincere and unanimous hope that the relations existing between Minnesota and Michigan may always remain this way and that when Michigan is Minnesota's host, Michigan may equal in hospitality the high mark you have already set.[217]

This victory revived the Wolverine faithful. A large crowd gathered at 6:00 P.M. at the station to welcome the team back to town, but the Wolverine gridders had already arrived on the 4:30 P.M. express. The players had long disappeared into the November evening.

---

[217] Board in Control, Box 6, November 1924 (1)

## The Northwestern Game

The question of who was actually the head coach of Michigan's football squad pervaded this season. There was no official announcement about a transfer of duties, and Yost and Little together guided team practices and appeared along the sidelines during games. One Michigan alum finally composed a poem that was printed before the Northwestern game:

Oh, Mr. Little, Oh Mr. Little,
I congratulate you on your football team,
All the people that are here.
They have come from far and near;
And surely you have shown them some machine.
Oh Mr Yost! Oh, Mr Yost!
It is very nice of me 'bout you to boast
But can't you really guess,
What makes Michigan's success?
Sure its your work Mr Little!
No, its your work Mr. Yost![218]

Whoever was head coach, Michigan remained in the Big Ten title hunt. Chicago and Illinois were undefeated, but they played each other on the same Saturday the Wolverines hosted Northwestern in Ann Arbor. Northwestern was not expected to pose much competition. In fact, they had won their first conference game in two years by beating Indiana the previous week.

Most of the interest in Ann Arbor focused on the former Michigan quarterback, Irvin Uteritz, who was now an assistant coach for the Northwestern Wildcats. Even so, 33,000 fans, the largest number ever for a Michigan-Northwestern game, showed up at Ferry Field.

In the first quarter, Michigan pinned Northwestern deep in their own territory with a punt to the 5-yard line. Northwestern punted on first down, the ball going out of bounds at the Wildcat

---

[218] *Ann Arbor News*, 11/5/24, p 12

24-yard line. Two plays later, Tod Rockwell, back at quarterback, broke loose over left tackle and it was 6-0.

In the second quarter, Friedman threw a perfect 30-yard touchdown strike to Rockwell. The kick was good, and it was 13-0. On the next series, Friedman intercepted a pass at the Northwestern 27-yard line and returned it to the 22. On the very next play, Friedman hit Marion, the fullback, for a touchdown and the score stood, 20-0.

In the third quarter, Friedman threw a 15-yard pass that hit Rockwell in full stride at the Northwestern 23-yard line and the quarterback took it in for the score. The final was 27-0. Amazingly, Michigan had not been scored upon in this season except for the fiasco in Champaign-Urbana.

Chicago and Illinois played to a 21-21 tie in what some claimed to be the greatest game ever played on Stagg Field. Michigan was still not out of the title race.

## The Ohio State Game

Michigan would now travel to Ohio State for the first time since the great dedication game in 1922. Ohio State's huge stadium had not been sold out once since that game, but it would be filled to the rafters again to welcome the Wolverines. Michigan fans bought up 15,000 tickets, but the student contingent was much less than in 1922, perhaps because so many had just gone to the Illinois game.

Michigan practices were held behind closed doors inside Yost Field House as the afternoons darkened early. The *Ann Arbor News* reported that Ohio State had focused on the Michigan game all year.

> According to Michigan scouts who have visited Ohio there is a large white star in the varsity dressing room at Columbus. In the middle of the star is a single word, "Michigan." Every player has to pass the star when he goes out on the field and when he returns after the afternoon practice. And from the time the candidates

start arriving at the clubhouse, Coach Jack Wilce has a man stationed near the door pointing to the star. Here nothing is said. He simply points to the star and this has been going on for several weeks.[219]

Yost wrote to a friend,

We are leaving tonight for Ohio State. Outside of the Illinois game where the team selected for that game blew up, we have played excellent football, not having been scored on by any other university. I am in hopes we can win the Ohio State and Iowa games which will make, as a whole, a very fine season.[220]

The game started badly for the Wolverines. On the third play, Ohio State found a wide open receiver on the Michigan 45-yard line, and he raced the rest of the way for a touchdown. The Buckeyes missed the point after, and it was 6-0. Friedman did most of Michigan's passing, but in the first half receivers dropped ball after ball. In fact, the Wolverines threw 12 passes in this game before one was completed.

At the end of the third quarter, the Wolverines finally put together a drive. Starting at their own 49-yard line, the quarterback Rockwell got loose around end to the OSU 25. Friedman hit Rockwell with a pass to the 17. On a Statue of Liberty play, Rockwell took the ball from Friedman and went around left end to the 6. Two plays later the Wolverines scored, the point was good, and Michigan led, 7-6.

A few plays later, Rockwell intercepted a Buckeye pass and returned it to the Ohio 31. After three plays led to no gain, Rockwell booted a 40-yard field goal, and it was 10-6. Michigan scored a touchdown late in the fourth quarter, missed the extra point, and the final score was 16-6. Michigan had won another game before only the second sold-out crowd in the Buckeye stadium.

---

[219] *Ann Arbor News*, 11/11/24, p 12
[220] Board in Control, Box 6, November 1924 (2)

The same day, Minnesota defeated Illinois in Minneapolis, after Grange suffered a severe shoulder injury that ended his season. The Wolverines were now ahead of Illinois in the standings, and behind only Chicago. The final games of the season would pit Michigan against Iowa in Ann Arbor and Chicago against Wisconsin. A Michigan victory coupled with a Chicago loss would put Michigan back in the Big Ten championship chair.

## The Iowa Game

Now it was Michigan's turn to suffer a team tragedy. Edgar Madsen, a second string end and high school teammate of captain Herb Steger, practiced with the team on Monday. He developed a fever Tuesday morning, was admitted to the health service Wednesday afternoon, and died of lobar pneumonia Thursday night. Needless to say, a somber cloud hung over the team by week's end.

Iowa's football team was given the wildest demonstration anyone could remember before they boarded the eastbound train. Thursday afternoon, they held a spirited workout at Chicago's Grant Park Municipal Stadium (soon to be called Soldier Field), and they proceeded to Ann Arbor on Friday. It would be the first time a Hawkeye team played in Ann Arbor in 22 years.

Weather for this game, played before a Ferry Field capacity crowd of 45,000, was terrible. Hail fell for a time in the first period, and then a freezing rain settled in over the stadium. It was, no doubt, a preoccupied band of Wolverine football players who took the field. A moment of silence was held at halftime for Edgar Madsen, ROTC students fired three volleys, Taps were played, and the flag was lowered to half mast.

Michigan scored first, claiming a safety to make it 2-0, but Iowa completed a touchdown in the first period and a field goal in the last to make the final score 9-2. Michigan attempted 14 passes, completing only two. Iowa used a fierce defensive rush that seemed to throw off Friedman's timing to some degree, but his receivers dropped several passes that many thought should have been caught.

Chicago won the Big Ten title by defeating Wisconsin, and Michigan dropped to fourth place with two losses. In an editorial entitled, "It's All Over Now," the *Daily* wrote,

> While no one would venture to wish continued defeat for Michigan teams, there is in this season's minor reverses a certain value to the student and alumni supporters at least. The test of a good sport is the manner in which he takes defeat. The team, during and after the Illinois and Iowa games, proved themselves in this respect. The rest of the University now has its opportunity to prove that intercollegiate competition is worthwhile, that in victory or defeat there is unity and good sportsmanship.[221]

The annual football banquet was held again at the Union. Sponsored by the Exchange Club of Ann Arbor, Rotary and Kiwanis, it was decided to open the affair to all male students. As a result, 500 Michigan men bought tickets to the event. Not a woman was to be seen. Robert J. Brown, the center, was elected captain for the 1925 team. A pleasant announcement was that Edliff "Butch" Slaughter had been selected for Camp's All-American team at guard. Yost had thus placed a Michigan man on each of Walter Camp's last three All-American first teams.

Curiously, at the end of the 1924 season, not at the beginning, there was an announcement addressing the issue of who was Michigan's head football coach. Under the headline, "Little is Now Head Coach," the *Ann Arbor News* reported on December 16, 1924:

> The future of football at Michigan rests with Coach George Little. Three years ago Fielding Yost secured Little as his assistant, hoping he would prove the very man for the position of head coach.
>
> Yost, who directs all athletics at Michigan, realized he could no longer devote all his time to any one sport and

---

[221] *Michigan Daily*, 11/25/24, p 4

was looking to the future when he selected Little.

Only two defeats in the three years that Little has assisted Yost have convinced the big chief that Little is the man for the job.

While the news has not been heralded from the housetops, Little is now head football coach at Michigan with full authority. While Yost will still assist in an advisory capacity, the future of Michigan on the gridiron is in Little's hands.

Filling the shoes of so great a coach as Yost is some task, but Little is certain to prove equal to it.[222]

As will be seen, this appointment of George Little as head football coach for Michigan would constitute by far the shortest such tenure in Michigan football history. However, Michigan's record books list George Little as the head coach from the beginning of the football season of 1924. The legend subsequently developed that Yost retired before the 1924 season and only returned to mentor the team after the Illinois catastrophe. Little wrote a plaintive note to Yost about this misconception in 1927.

I wish you would tell that publicity man of yours when you see him, not to connect my name only with that Illinois game. I really believe that I did something over there in three years aside from having that team "improperly set" for Red Grange. In his article last Sunday, he tells how you came on the field a few days later to get things straightened out and took over the team which kind of despairs me.[223]

Yost didn't seem to mind having his name separated from the Illinois disaster. When he wrote a review of his last five years of coaching at the end of the 1926 season, he chronicled only 1921,

---

[222] *Ann Arbor News*, 12/16/24, p 12
[223] Board in Control, Box 10, November 1927 (3)

1922, 1923, 1925, and 1926. He skipped 1924 and, by doing so, contributed to the idea that he wasn't coaching the team. Nonetheless, it is clear from the contemporary record that Yost directed the 1924 squad.

What was most significant about the 1924 season was not the games won or lost, but rather the number of people who watched. The demand for seats at Michigan games, home and away, was impossible to satisfy. To better understand the unexpected situation the ticket office faced, one need only look at attendance a few years previous. In 1917, Michigan averaged 6200 fans at each home game; in 1918, a season shortened by the influenza epidemic, 10,000; 1919, 20,000; and in 1920, 18,000. No game was sold out, no requests for tickets were returned, and everyone who wanted could sit between the goals. By 1924, the situation had radically changed and the demand for tickets couldn't be met. No one was happy. Students complained, alumni were furious, and fans and friends of the University were irritated. At the center of the controversy stood Yost, the 42,242 seats of Ferry Field, and the Athletic Department ticket office.

In 1924, the ticket process worked like this: The Athletic Department refused to accept any ticket requests before September 1. Beginning on September 1, the personnel in the office would receive two mail deliveries a day with bags full of ticket requests. They would go through them assigning each a number and this would go on for several days until the ticket allotment was exhausted. Season tickets weren't sold and a person had to submit requests for each game he wanted to see. If, however, the alumni allotment was exhausted on September 1 for a given game, then, of course, any ticket requests that arrived on September 2 would be returned. No one could be sure just when their ticket request would be delivered, so some alumni clubs arranged for an Ann Arbor resident to receive all their ticket requests and then deliver them to the athletic office on the morning of September 1.

Yost was called upon again and again to explain the deplorable situation. The official response went like this: Ferry Field had an official capacity of 42,242 seats. 2500 at midfield were reserved for the visiting team, 2000 for the faculty, 1950 for the "M" club, the President's party and complimentaries, and 574 for the use of the members of the football squad. This totaled 7024 which, subtracted from 42,242, left 35,218. These remaining seats were then divided equally between the alumni and the student body, granting each 17,609 tickets.

This explanation of a physical fact, the capacity of Ferry Field and how it was divided up, satisfied no one. Yost told the Ann Arbor Chamber of Commerce,

> As to ticket distribution the board has done its best to be fair and divide the 42,000 seats equally between the 100,000 persons demanding tickets. Everyone would like the 50-yard line, some have even sent in requests to have a place reserved for them on the 55-yard line and we have done our best to satisfy all.[224]

The *Michigan Daily* presented the student body's position in an editorial on September 23, 1924:

> Every year the student body is confronted with what appears to be an injustice in the distribution of tickets for the major football games of the university. They feel that the Athletic association first considers the public, the alumni and their friends, and gives what is left to students.
>
> This year is not without its difficulty. With no reasonable explanation, the association has decreed that students shall be allowed only one extra ticket…students are not being treated fairly. They are entitled to at least two extra tickets a piece.
>
> The tendency to neglect the student body reflects the

---

[224] *Michigan Daily*, 9/24/24, p 2

spirit in college and university athletics which is most criticized by educational leaders. Too much thought is given to the commercial aspect; too little attention is paid to the promotion of the only worthwhile feature of such contests—a spontaneous student spirit occasioned by a real feeling for the team and school. This can never come while football games are promoted in such a way as to enlarge their possibilities as a spectacle of purely public interest. Students, their family and friends, and the alumni should be the only persons to whom consideration is given in the matter of tickets…

Rumors are prevalent that the Athletic association gives better tickets to outsiders than it does to those connected with the University…Those handling the tickets have a tremendous responsibility and are attempting to do their best. However, they owe the student body a definite explanation of the present intolerable situation.[225]

Among alumni groups, there was much contention over their 17,609-ticket allotment per game. The Athletic association sent out reminder letters to all alumni in August to submit ticket requests by September 1, but there was no attempt to confirm that each request was in fact from an alumnus. Yost felt that all taxpayers in the state of Michigan should have a chance to see Michigan games. Non-alumni did not receive a reminder in the mail, but any requests for tickets they might submit would be processed along with all the alumni requests. So an unknown number of the 17,609 tickets allotted to alumni in fact went to friends and fans of the University who had never attended. This was a source of chronic irritation to alumni. One angry alum wrote Yost that he hadn't been able to get tickets to a game, but his chauffeur had.

A September 1924, letter to Yost from an unhappy alumnus typified the general feeling.

---

[225] *Michigan Daily*, 9/23/24, p 4

I am just in receipt of your check...refunding remittance covering reservation for four seats at the Michigan-Wisconsin game which I sent approximately three weeks ago...Last year the same thing happened under exactly the same circumstances. I am at a loss to understand how alumni can secure seats to the popular games. Last year games to which I was denied seats were witnessed by persons who were not then and had never been connected in any way whatsoever with Michigan nor the schools of the opposing teams...There is something radically wrong with a system that permits such a situation to develop. It is quite certain that the Michigan-Wisconsin game this year will be witnessed by many persons who are not identified in any way with either university and who are therefore not entitled to consideration until alumni...are taken care of.[226]

Over the years, this complaint was stated again and again by irritated alumni, but Yost never wavered from his responses to the disappointed Wolverines.

You will find enclosed an outline of the plan of distribution of tickets . . It is understood that any taxpayers in the state of Michigan can secure tickets from the Alumni allotment. So far as I know, no state supported institution prevents any of its taxpayers from buying tickets for the football games. This is not true at Yale, Harvard, Princeton and other endowed institutions...Shall a rule be enforced that only alumni can buy tickets in the alumni allotment and that he can only buy them for himself or other alumni or alumnae? This rule would never be passed here...In my opinion, there is no chance of having a rule which denies the residents of Michigan the privilege of purchasing tickets to the football games

---

[226] Board in Control, Box 6, September 1924 (1)

of their state university…At the last session of the legislature an appropriation of $10,000,000 was made for the maintenance of this University. So far as I know, there has always been and always will be objections to any plan of distribution from those who are not able to secure tickets under the plan.[227]

In another letter, Yost was even more emphatic,

Can we continue to tell these people that this is their University when we want appropriations from them, and then not provide facilities and opportunities for them to visit the University and see *their* teams in action… Whether it should be or not, you know as well as I do, that the date of a big football game is the occasion on which most of these same citizens are most anxious to come to Ann Arbor. Shall we call these men who make our University possible just "Tom, Dick and Harry" who have no right to be considered in our plan of football ticket distribution? Are we democratic or are we not? Do we practice what we preach when we say that the University of Michigan is a Democratic institution?[228]

Of course, Yost received criticism from both sides. In another 1924 letter, a disappointed fan wrote,

There appears to be considerable criticism throughout the state as to the size of allotment of tickets to Alumni compared with that set aside for the general public of this state. Will you kindly inform me and thousands of other taxpayers why the U. of M. Alumni, many of which were never permanent residents of this state, are given any preferences in allotment of tickets over Michigan taxpayers who are not Alumni. As students, the Alumni are given first consideration in the matter of

---

[227] Board in Control, Box 6, September 1924 (1)
[228] Board in Control, Box 9, May 1927 (4)

securing tickets, which is perfectly just. After being given those advantages as students over taxpayers, I cannot see wherein they are entitled to any more advantages in securing of football tickets over other admirers of our own U. of M. simply because we do not happen to be members of the Alumni.[229]

And then, of course, there were those who got into the stadium, but were unhappy with their seats.

This year I made out my application for football games and had them delivered in person by a messenger from my office at the Athletic Department on the morning of September 1st. I now find that the tickets are in Section 00…I am rather forced to the conclusion that there is some decided favoritism shown in the selection of tickets and that I do not happen to be among the elect.[230]

Yost's responses to these letters were usually measured and patient, but sometimes he, too, would reveal his frustration. To one unhappy alum, Yost wrote, "the problem of ticket distribution is a very difficult one, especially so when 100,000 want the 43,000 tickets that we have."[231] One alum wrote a particularly nasty letter in which he said that Yost and the University would want a contribution from him someday, but he wouldn't be "shelling out another time."[232] Yost replied,

I can readily understand how a man may be disappointed in his allotment of tickets, but I cannot understand how anyone with any sense of justice can write a letter with the spirit in which yours was written…I know you are wrong in your facts and I am just as certain you are rotten in your attitude.[233]

---

[229] Board in Control, Box 6, October 1924 (3)
[230] Board in Control, Box 6, October 1924 (1)
[231] Board in Control, Box 6, October 1924 (3)
[232] Board in Control, Box 6, November 1924 (1)
[233] Board in Control, Box 6, November 1924 (1)

Many more complaints were directed privately to Yost, but one irate law school graduate sent his missive to the *Michigan Daily* in mid-October, and it was published on the front page.

> There is certainly some rottenness somewhere. It is mighty tough to be shut out after you have contributed to make the game possible…I do not know exactly how many persons Michigan stadium accommodates at the present time. I am aware it is a large number…Making allowance for the student body, teaching staff, etc…at a figure of 10,000…I should like to respectfully inquire… where are the other 30,000 tickets?
>
> I should like to respectfully inquire of you and the Michigan authorities how in the name of all that is good and great do you expect a Michigan Alumnus to hereafter subscribe to any Michigan undertaking… Without fear of contradiction and on the facts as I have them, I do not hesitate to state that there is something wrong. Either the Athletic association itself or someone in connection with it is guilty of mismanagement or else there has been somewhere some actual fraud of some kind…
>
> The Michigan university cannot expect help from Michigan Alumni who are practically denied and flatly refused opportunity to use the facilities for which they are asked to pay.
>
> I respectfully request that you give this letter any publicity you see fit…and that the Michigan Union refrain from asking me to contribute…until it and other prominent bodies in connection with the university have undergone an investigation of the football ticket situation at Michigan.[234]

---

[234] *Michigan Daily*, 10/14/24, p 1

The very next day the *Michigan Daily* editors published their solution, reversing their previous position against a new stadium.

> It is obviously impossible to accommodate 50,000 alumni and the general public in 17,000 seats set aside for these classes of people...

> The *Daily* agrees...on the fundamental question involved. As long as it is impossible for the majority of alumni to renew their ties by returning at least once a year for a game little can be expected from that source of University support. And as long as the majority of students are limited to one extra ticket a piece, they can neither help out the alumni nor carry through what is their undeniable right—the privilege of inviting their parents to games. These same parents represent a powerful influence in the affairs of the University...The alumni and taxpayers most interested and influential where the University is concerned are being alienated by a condition which can be remedied.

> The first and only complete remedy is found in a new stadium. The structure is entirely inadequate for the present-day conditions and should be replaced when the project is financially possible. Most people consider that the time has not yet come when a campaign, such as would be essential, is practicable. Nevertheless, a new stadium must be considered.[235]

The *Ann Arbor News* concurred with an editorial of its own.

> The alumnus is not to be blamed for feeling disgruntled over his inability to witness the Wisconsin game, but he is overstepping the bounds of reason when he attacks the athletic association with charges of mismanagement and fraud. The athletic association did not originate the

---

[235] *Michigan Daily*, 10/15/24, p 4

law of supply and demand; it is operating in the fairest
way that it can devise under that law…The situation is
regrettable, but a hundred investigations will not remedy
it. The only solution will be found in hardware stores and
cement plants. The way to make the supply satisfy the
demand is to erect a new stadium.[236]

Of course, the flip side to all these complaints and proposed
solutions was a completely sold out Michigan football season,
both at home and away. In late August, before the requests poured
in, the ticket manager said, "indications are that we will have the
heaviest sales of tickets we have ever known."[237] This prediction
was confirmed when tickets for the home games with Wisconsin
and Iowa were sold out the first week. In 1922, the ticket office
received 320 requests for Wisconsin game tickets on September 1,
but on the same day in 1924, the office was inundated with 11,161
requests for the Badger engagement.

Yost had decided to erect 5000 additional seats in the east end
of Ferry Field, but still thousands upon thousands of ticket requests
—and the enclosed money—were returned to disappointed fans. In
fact, the athletic department estimated that 50,000 ticket requests
were returned for the Wisconsin and Iowa games.

The 1924 season would finally compel Fielding Yost to advocate for a new stadium in Ann Arbor. Michigan had been the best
drawing card in the nation that year, playing before 344,000 fans,
*more than any other school in history*. Ohio State had been unable
to fill its stadium since the dedication game in 1922, but when
Michigan returned in 1924, the place was packed. The same thing
occurred at all the other road games. If Michigan could play before
70,000 fans in Columbus and Champaign-Urbana, why not in
Ann Arbor? After this season of football, the momentum for a new
stadium would be too powerful to stop, and determinedly leading
the charge would be Fielding H. Yost.

---

[236] *Ann Arbor News*, 10/15/24, p 4
[237] Board in Control, Box 6, August 1924 (2)

# Chapter 7

# The Crucial Spring of 1925

In 1924, Yost's thinking about a new stadium had been transformed. In the spring of that year, he submitted a report to the Board in Control of Athletics in which he listed immediate pressing needs for the athletic department. One was the urgency for "increased seating capacity of the football stands,"[238] and another was for repairs to the concrete on the south stand at Ferry Field. There was no call for a new stadium in this report. However, a few months later, at the end of the financially successful football season of 1924, the coach was actively promoting a new stadium. Yost's Michigan football team had played in enough stadium dedication games on foreign fields. Now he wanted one in Ann Arbor.

As would be expected from such a personality, once Yost decided on a course of action, he proceeded quickly and decisively. In letters dated November 12, 1924, after the three stadium dedication games in which Michigan played, but before the sold-out Ohio State game, Yost wrote to several schools that had already built new stadiums.

> We have realized the time is not far distant when we will have to undertake the erection of a new stadium at Michigan and this letter is sent to you in the hope that you will give us an outline of the ways and means through which your own stadium was financed.

---

[238] Board in Control, Box 41, Book #1

Out of your fund of experience, you should be able to give us certain conclusions of great value and, on the other hand, you should be able to point out certain mistakes which you did not foresee when making your own plans.

Was your stadium financed by athletic earnings, by loans or small individual donations? If it was largely financed by small donations, do the donors receive prior rights on ticket purchases?

A detailed letter will be greatly appreciated and if, at some future time, we may go over various points with you personally, your cooperation will undoubtedly prove a great aid to us in the solution of our own problem.[239]

Suddenly, the athletic files of the time became filled with letters about the possibility of a new Michigan stadium.

In 1923, Yost had taken a highly publicized trip to the west coast where he had spoken innumerable times to thousands of high school and college students from Los Angeles to Seattle. He had taken time then to visit both the new Los Angeles Coliseum and the University of California stadium in Berkeley. On January 15, 1925, he wrote the manager of athletics at California asking for their blueprints, saying that Michigan wanted "to provide for at least 75,000 seats in the lower deck," but also "to provide for expansion later by reason of an upper deck."[240]

It was the construction of the Los Angeles Coliseum that most impressed Yost. It was built with a "cut and fill" process by excavating the bowl and throwing the earth up on the sides to constitute a solid foundation for the seats. It was estimated that 300,000 cubic yards of dirt were moved in the building process, but the whole Coliseum was completed for an estimated $800,000, far short of the amounts spent at California, Illinois and Ohio State. Not only was this approach very economical because a huge superstructure

[239] Board in Control, Box 46, folder: stadium seats
[240] Board in Control, Box 6, January 1925 (3)

was unnecessary, the structure would prove to be quite safe. In a game in Michigan's stadium in 1905, a large section of the wooden stands collapsed, injuring several spectators. Yost could never forget this event and the idea that spectators in a large stadium could sit on solid ground appealed to him.

Yost had other ideas for Michigan's stadium. Virtually every stadium built up to that time sported a track circling the football field. This was true at both Ohio State and Illinois as well as at the Los Angeles Coliseum, but Yost wanted a stadium just for football. He opposed a track because he wanted the crowd to be as close to the field as possible.

In a February 1925 letter to a University engineering professor, Yost emphasized this point. Discussing the proposed stadium at the University of Pittsburgh, Yost noted that the first row of seats was 125 feet from the end of the field. He wanted the seats in Michigan's stadium to be 20 feet from the end zone. The front seat on the end would thus be 105 feet closer to the end zone. Pittsburgh was planning sideline seats to be 80 feet away from the playing field, but Yost wanted Michigan's to be 30 feet from the side line.

Yost was not impressed with the elliptical nature of other stadiums either. California and Pittsburgh both had stands that curved away from the field at midfield and also at the ends, placing fans further away from the action. Yost wanted Michigan's stadium to be a rectangle with straight lines on the sides and ends, which would put the stands very close to the field. The engineers supported this concept, saying it would be less expensive to build a stadium with such a configuration.

In another February 1925 letter to an engineering firm, Yost stated that he would propose a stadium to seat 75,000, but, "I have in mind also that the strength and design shall be such that an upper deck of some 40,000 seating capacity can be erected in some future time if the demand warrants it."[241]

When the football season of 1924 began, Yost was still unde-

---

[241] Board in Control, Box 7, February 1925 (1)

cided about the utility of a new stadium in Ann Arbor. However, by November of that year, Yost had become committed to building one. In three more months, by February 1925, Yost had mentally completed the picture of the stadium that the University of Michigan community has celebrated ever since.

On January 14, 1925, Yost spent the day in Ann Arbor with Bernard Green, an alumnus of Michigan and President of Osborn Engineering Company of Cleveland, Ohio. Green's company had built Minnesota's stadium as well as several others, and Yost was impressed with the quality of their work. Green met several of the members of the Board in Control of Athletics and walked through some of the proposed stadium sites with Yost. His company would eventually build Michigan Stadium.

In 1925, Stadium Boulevard did not yet exist, but the route had been proposed and funded by the state to serve as a bypass around central Ann Arbor. Yost felt that if the new stadium were moved from Ferry Field it should lie on this proposed highway. In early January, he asked the engineering school to study the surrounding topography and present site options. He was especially interested in land where the University golf course currently lies and in another parcel that stretched along the proposed Stadium Boulevard between Washtenaw and Packard Roads.

By the end of February 1925, Yost could send his engineers blueprints and pictures of the stadiums at the Universities of Pittsburgh, Minnesota, California and the Los Angeles Coliseum. He also had surveys showing the topography of the land to the south and west of Ferry Field, including the areas where Michigan Stadium and the university golf course now lie. At this early date, Yost favored a new stadium site that would have been on the current golf course grounds, on the south side of Stadium Boulevard.

By this time, Yost also knew how he could accomplish the financing of this new stadium. He was well aware of the trouble the University of Illinois faced in completing their stadium. Pledges were difficult to collect. Also, several hundred thousand dollars were raised from among fraternities, sororities, and other student groups at Illinois, and Yost felt that such a drive would be unpopular in Ann Arbor.

Yost had also witnessed difficulties at his own alma mater, West Virginia, in sustaining a subscription drive for a stadium. A 1923 appeal to graduates of West Virginia lies in Yost's personal files.

> In the 56 years of its existence, the West Virginia University has never appealed to its graduates in a general campaign for funds, whereas it is the history of all our neighboring institutions, state as well as endowed, that their alumni are continually bestowing buildings, endowments, and other material gifts…
>
> A movement was initiated by the Alumni Association for a Stadium which would be the joint gift of devoted graduates and loyal citizens of West Virginia.
>
> The Stadium was designed to be a monument to the pride of West Virginians generally and especially to be a mark of the devotion of the sons and daughters to their Alma Mater…
>
> The facts are these: ONLY 360 OF THE 2900 SUBSCRIPTIONS RECEIVED HAVE COME FROM GRADUATES. MORE THAN 83% OF THE GRADUATES HAVE FAILED TO RESPOND TO THE APPEAL.
>
> Of course there are any number of reasons why these… graduates have not responded. The majority, we imagine, think they are "too hard up," but this will scarcely hold… A great number…have simply been negligent.[242]

Yost sent $100 for this effort, but when a second appeal arrived and asked for more, the coach demurred. Yost was determined not to have to beg for money for a new stadium.

---

[242] Yost papers, Box 2, 1923

In another letter dated February 1925, Yost outlined his financing plan. Yost estimated the new stadium would cost $1,250,000, with $250,000 available from the football seasons of 1925 and 1926. Therefore, $1,000,000 would have to be secured from some other source. Yost made it sound simple:

> If we had a bond issue of $1,000,000, there would be 2000 $500 six per cent bonds to be sold. If we offered these as 20 year registered bonds, the purchaser to have the right to buy two preferred tickets for each game until a certain date, I believe the trouble would not be in selling them but in planning a distribution of these 2000 bonds with this ticket privilege so we would not have any criticism from anyone that they didn't have a chance to buy.[243]

With this proposal, Yost wouldn't have to write any letters begging for contributions. Rather, Wolverine fans would be writing him begging for a chance to buy a bond.

No one: no student, no alumnus, and no friend of the university would be "giving" anything to the athletic department. Rather, the athletic department would sell a bond at a given amount of interest and pay back all the money over time. Since Yost assumed the attraction to a buyer would be preferred access to football tickets, not the interest rate, the rate was set at only three percent interest.

This plan by Yost for stadium fundraising was ingenious, and it proved crucial for defusing the possibility of strong opposition to the idea. After all, the Regents had clearly stated in 1923 that they were opposed to a fundraising scheme for a stadium that would divert funds from other needed campus projects. Students in Ann Arbor faced financial difficulties achieving an education, and Yost quickly rejected the idea of student fundraising for the athletic department. Finally, it had always been a Michigan athletic tradition that no attempt would be made to secure funds from the state, like the school in East Lansing had done for its new stadium.

---

[243] Board in Control, Box 7, February 1925 (1)

Bond purchases would be voluntary, buyers would get football ticket preferences, and the athletic department would pay all the money back so that future contributions to the University would not be hindered. In fact, Yost estimated that the athletic department could realistically pay back 200 bondholders per year, which would then make this money available for other campus projects if donors wished. With the exception of the Big Ten football championships of 1922 and 1923, Yost's innovative approach to stadium financing was most responsible for the great stadium that today graces the corner of Main Street and Stadium Boulevard.

The *Ann Arbor News* trumpeted the new plans. With a headline on the sports page that blared the report of record receipts for the athletic department, the paper related:

> With football receipts totaling nearly $300,000 and with the clearance of debt on the Yost Field House, a new football stadium, costing in the neighborhood of $2,000,000, is the next expenditure planned by the board in control of athletics, providing the sanction of the regents is received.
>
> For the year 7/23 to 7/24, baseball lost $7000, track lost $15,000, basketball lost $3000, and other sports lost $9,000. Only football earned money, clearing about $150,000.
>
> The receipts for the 1924 season totaled $331,641 which allowed all debt to be paid off and left the athletic dept with a considerable surplus.
>
> Two plans have been submitted for a stadium. One would be to increase the present seating capacity of Ferry Field by building concrete stands around the field. This stadium would seat 50,000 people while a new stadium such as is planned would care for 75,000 specatators."[244]

[244] *Ann Arbor News*, 1/27/25, p 12

In an editorial the next day, the *News* was effusive:

> Nothing strengthens school spirit like athletic games…
> Football maintains its lead in popularity, and because the
> demand for seating capacity far exceeds the available seats,
> it is evident the additional space for spectators is needed…
> The amazing fact is revealed that football supports all the
> other sports. Yost Field House was built for indoor sports,
> but the greatest of outdoor college sports has paid for its
> construction…Baseball, basketball, track, and hockey are
> desirable, and football makes them possible…
>
> The students want this stadium. So do the alumni and
> the people of Michigan…There is no reason to expect
> that the Regents will be able—or will desire to—find
> fault with such a palpably sound program.[245]

Yost must have slept very little in February 1925. Letters about
a new stadium were flying every which way. On February 23, Yost
sent a letter to Bernard Green of Osborn Engineering, the company
that would eventually build the stadium. He included topography maps of the area where the University golf course currently
lies, but he also included a section known as the Miller Tract, a
piece of land just east of Main Street and north of the golf course
property, the very land upon which Michigan Stadium now rests.
Ferry Field was laid out on an east-west axis, but Yost was hoping
his new field could be north and south so that the sun would not
be in the players' eyes. Yost wanted to know what Green thought
of the various ravines depicted on the topography maps. If there
was a ravine where a north-south field could be more easily placed,
where would Green put it?

Yost was very specific in these letters to Green. He wrote like
an engineer. He had the height of the ridges measured, he knew
the depth of the ravines, and he worried about water drainage. He
demonstrated a very clear command of the situation.

---

[245] *Ann Arbor News*, 1/28/25, p 4

In March, Yost went to New York City to consult with several companies that had already built stadiums. He spent time with engineers who had built famous racetracks and others who had built the stadiums at Cornell and Brown. He viewed designs and blueprints of stadiums from ancient times to the present, including several in Europe. He sent a long letter to Green from New York with a sketch of a stadium in detail, showing the number of rows, the height from one row to another, the depth of the rows, and the possible points of entry.

In late March, Green wrote back. He had examined the topography maps and preferred a site south of where the current stadium lies, on the golf course property. He suggested a main deck of 80,000 with proper construction so that an upper deck seating about 45,000 could be erected at a future time.

By late March 1925, Yost was prepared to present his stadium proposal to the Board in Control of Athletics. It would be a crucial report that Yost knew would be read by the Regents as well. He emphasized that, "Our responsibilities demand foresight and vision. We must not confine ourselves merely to the problems of Today, but we must face with courage, wisdom and foresight the problems of Tomorrow."[246] He reiterated that "an acute situation"[247] has developed because of the overwhelming demand for football tickets. Ferry Field could now seat 44,924, but that number was hopelessly inadequate.

Yost emphasized that it "is the duty of this Board"[248] to serve those groups making demands on the athletic department. Those groups included "supporters of visiting teams…who expect us to show the same consideration shown in their own states, the steadily increasing student body, the Faculty…, the Alumni, increasing each year at the minimum rate of 2,000, and the citizens and taxpayers of the State of Michigan."[249]

---

[246] Board in Control, Box 48, Minutes, 1910-1927, p. 216 (attachment)
[247] Board in Control, Box 48, Minutes, 1910-1927, p. 216 (attachment)
[248] Board in Control, Box 48, Minutes, 1910-1927, p. 216 (attachment)
[249] Board in Control, Box 48, Minutes, 1910-1927, p. 216 (attachment)

Yost once again made his appeal for the taxpayers. *"This is a State University—not a privately endowed institution.* Ownership of this institution is vested not in our students, faculty and alumni—but in the people whose taxes make it possible."[250] Yost would never tire of making this point.

Yost then listed all the schools that had already built new stadiums around the country, with their capacities. He even included a new stadium "tentatively planned"[251] for the University of Chicago. The implicit statement here was that Michigan was far behind in this parade.

At this point in the report, Yost found it necessary to digress and address the concern about professionalism in athletics. He was only too aware of those who felt there was no place for athletic extravaganzas on scholarly campuses. Critics had claimed that large crowds would corrupt the amateur game, but Yost asserted that if that were going to happen, it surely would have occurred already with the 45,000 that packed Ferry Field. In fact, there was no evidence that sportsmanship had suffered due to the large stadiums at Illinois and Ohio State. Yost turned the argument around. "If there is value in the lessons of sportsmanship our games teach and inculcate, why should they be limited to a few when many might just as well profit from them? The question is not one of size, but of administration. If our program is properly managed, we need not be alarmed by its size."[252]

Next, Yost launched into an extensive discussion of why Ferry Field should be abandoned. First of all, the site was too small for significant expansion. Ferry Field was hemmed in on all sides. Secondly, it was too low to be excavated. Yost was determined to dig a hole. Thirdly, to promote "athletics for all," the land nearest the main campus should be devoted to intramural sports. By building a new stadium elsewhere, prime acreage close to campus could be made available to the general student body. Yost already envisioned

---

[250] Board in Control, Box 48, Minutes, 1910-1927, p. 216 (attachment)
[251] Board in Control, Box 48, Minutes, 1910-1927, p. 216 (attachment)
[252] Board in Control, Box 48, Minutes, 1910-1927, p. 216 (attachment)

Photo courtesy of Bentley Historical Library

*Calisthenics class on Ferry Field*

the giant intramural building that now stands along Hoover Street. Lastly, a new stadium with increased capacity at the Ferry Field site would lead to hopeless traffic congestion on game days.

Yost then presented a most convincing financial argument. This assertion was targeted directly at the expressed sentiments of the Regents: that Ferry Field be refurbished. The north and west stands of Ferry Field were wood. If they were to be replaced with a cement stand to complete a horseshoe configuration, the estimated cost would be $750,000. If this were done, the stadium could still seat only 50,000 spectators, hardly more than could be accommodated now. This expense would not be justified since it wouldn't meet the increasing demand, it wouldn't significantly increase athletic department income, and, lastly, a whole new stadium could probably be built for around $1,000,000.

Then Yost outlined the most desirable site for a new stadium. He related that the athletic department had looked at virtually all available land in the Ann Arbor area, but the site that seemed most preferable was south of the proposed new bypass highway, where the University Golf Course is now located. The new bypass would bring crowds directly to the stadium, both from the east and west, and therefore Ann Arbor's streets would not be clogged. The railway passed right by the site, and new spurs could easily be added.

The stadium itself, Yost wrote, should seat between 70,000 to 75,000, with a design and strength that would allow expansion one day for 30,000 to 40,000 more. He related that much personal study had been done by him and others, and he specifically mentioned the Los Angeles Coliseum, the Rose Bowl and the University of Pennsylvania stadium. He estimated a new stadium, including land acquisition, to cost $1,250,000.

Yost then outlined his novel approach to financing the effort. He reiterated that each bond would come with two preferential seats at football games for 20 years, but no individual would be allowed to purchase more than two bonds. Yost had already decreased the proposed interest rate to five percent. The title to the stadium would be held by the Trustee of the bond issue and when the last bond was paid off, the property would be owned by the University of Michigan.

This most remarkable and cogently argued document was presented by Yost to the Board in Control of Athletics in late March 1925, and approved on motion of "Mr. Yost, seconded by Professor Frayer."[253] The vote was unanimous. The Board of Regents was "respectfully requested to reconsider"[254] its recommendation of 1923—that the stadium remain on Ferry Field. The Michigan alumni association conveniently met in Ann Arbor the same day, and they too endorsed the document.

The Regents were scheduled to meet in late April, so Yost then initiated a personal drive to convince the Regents to build a new stadium. Regent James Murfin was a lawyer and judge in Detroit and was the Regent who sponsored the 1923 resolution. After reading Yost's report, Murfin wrote a letter of warning in early April:

> I have been very happy in my fondness for you to realize that you and I have never seriously disagreed on many substantial questions of policy. I know we are both prompted by the same thought and ideals. This stadium

---

[253] Board in Control, Box 48, Minutes, 1910-1927, p. 216
[254] Board in Control, Box 48, Minutes, 1910-1927, p. 216

problem is genuinely serious…I can see this is going to be a very much controverted question.

I have had many knocks on your proposed plan from faculty men on campus.[255]

In a letter to another Regent, Yost emphasized the need for stadium expansion:

During the last two years I have met with over 200 different groups of citizens of the State of Michigan, in both the Northern and Southern Peninsulas. These groups were composed of Chambers of Commerce, Rotary Clubs, Kiwanis Clubs, Lions Clubs, Fathers and Sons meetings, Superintendents of Schools, State Conventions of Principals and perhaps one-half of these meetings were with high school people where their student bodies were present. The continuous questions asked me are about as follows: "Coach, how can I get a ticket to the football games this fall?? What are you doing to provide seats for us? Do the alumni think they still have a preference for seats when we paid for their education?"[256]

Yost then reiterated that only with football income could the university possibly achieve the goal of "athletics for all," that the stadium could be built without costing the university a dollar, and that expansion of the old stadium would cost far too much for the few new seats that would be created.

Another long letter to a Regent described in detail Yost's proposed financing. After doing the math to show how the bonds would eventually be paid off, Yost asserted that a new stadium was a most important investment in the future of the university.

I cannot understand how anyone can entertain the notion that a plan such as this, that will satisfy thousands of

---

[255] Board in Control, Box 7, April 1925 (2)
[256] Board in Control, Box 7, April 1925 (1)

alumni and taxpayers, and which will develop friends
instead of critics of the University, can in any way interfere
with our chance to receive gifts and appropriations from
these same sources. In fact, I think it is the road to greater
interest, loyalty, and support of our University. I believe
I know the people of Michigan. I know their desire to
come to Ann Arbor at the time of our games…You may
not know how strong this desire is, but those in charge
of football ticket distribution do.[257]

Yost then explained that his proposal was for far more than
just a new stadium:

It includes also the purchase of 100 or more acres of
additional land for use by the boys of today, tomorrow,
in fact, far into the future…It offers an opportunity
for the development of at least 40 acres for Intramural
Athletics, about 80 acres or more for a University Golf
Course, and makes available for use as squash, handball,
and basketball courts other parts of Ferry Field near the
campus [where Yost was already planning to put the
intramural building].[258]

Yost concluded this letter by listing all the stadiums he had personally seen and the various builders with whom he had consulted.

Yost was prodigious and unrelenting in this effort as the April
assembly of the Regents approached. He must have awaited the
meeting with considerable anticipation, but on the day of the
gathering only a few Regents could get to Ann Arbor. The whole
agenda was postponed until the May meeting. This unexpected
delay surely disappointed Yost, and it would have serious implications, but it didn't halt his frenzied work.

In May, Yost wrote another long and detailed letter to Regent
Murfin. The two men were good friends and knew each other well

[257] Board in Control, Box 46, folder: stadium seats
[258] Board in Control, Box 46, folder: stadium seats

for Murfin had served on the Board in Control of Athletics from 1901 to 1918. However, Murfin's solution to a larger stadium was to limit attendance to students and alumni, negating the need for more seats by cutting out the general public. This idea remained especially repugnant to Yost. Yost forwarded to Murfin direct quotes from the University Bulletins of 1921 and 1923, which were distributed to the Michigan state legislature: "To the Members of the Legislature of 1921: The University of Michigan belongs to the people of the state."[259]

From the 1923 Bulletin, Yost found this message addressed to the members of the Legislature:

> We are engaged in a common enterprise. We are endeavoring wisely and economically to conduct the affairs of a great State. Sometimes we forget that first and foremost every one of us is a citizen of Michigan and shares responsibility for everything the state does. The University of Michigan intends to have this point of view. Above all else, it means never to forget that it belongs to the people of Michigan.[260]

Then Yost brought the need for more tickets directly to the Regents.

> Some members of the Board of Regents evidently know what this pressure for tickets is for they have requested as many as sixty tickets for their friends at single football games. Shall we *satisfy this desire* for football tickets and make possible this larger plant and facilities for athletic exercise at our University?[261]

Regent Murfin replied to Yost's long and detailed letter with just three short paragraphs, one being, "You made a mistake when you went in for football instead of the law. As an advocate either orally or in writing you have no equal."[262] Yost had won a crucial vote.

---

[259] Board in Control, Box 7, May 1925 (2)
[260] Board in Control, Box 7, May 1925 (2)
[261] Board in Control, Box 7, May 1925 (2)
[262] Board in Control, Box 7, May 1925 (2)

A front page article in the feature section of the *Michigan Daily* on Sunday, May 10, 1925, afforded Yost the opportunity to present his case to the student body. In a wide-ranging interview, Yost covered all the points he had so eloquently made to the Regents. He pointed out where Ferry Field, the pride of the Wolverines in 1921, now stood. "With the exception of the University of Virginia, which has less than half our enrollment, none of a list of 14 of the largest and most popular universities in the country has so small a stadium seating capacity as we have."

After laying out the proposal for financing the stadium, he stated:

> In other institutions it has been necessary to conduct drives among the students of universities to gather sufficient funds with which to build new stadia. At Illinois, Ohio State and Minnesota, for example, subscriptions amounted to an average of more than $100 per student. The plan of the Athletic Association here does away with any such move, making it unnecessary for students to contribute at all.[263]

Yost then directly addressed the stadium "race" issue that had percolated through the *Michigan Daily* and other newspapers.

> What the universities of Illinois, Ohio, Pennsylvania, California or any other university have done has no bearing on what we may do. Ohio, Illinois, Pennsylvania, and California and many other universities realized that they needed additional seats to meet their needs for their football games, and took steps to get them. We at Michigan see a similar need and are accordingly taking steps to fill it. It is no "race."

> When the Medical School sees that it needs new buildings, it begins proceedings to acquire them. At Michigan we have outgrown the old Medical building, the old

---

[263] *Michigan Daily*, 5/10/25, feature section, p 1

Library, the old hospitals, University Hall, the Museum and many other buildings. Just in the same manner we have outgrown our present accommodations for spectators at football games. Would it not have been absurd to argue against the new hospital, the new Angell Hall, the new Library or the new Medical building on the ground that Michigan should not enter a "building race" since many other universities had put up similar structures? We needed the buildings and got them. We now face the same situation in connection with our football stadium.

Michigan is going forward—not backward. We're not after a new stadium simply because other universities have them. We want it because we need it and because we owe a new stadium to the people who have every right to see Michigan teams in action…

I don't call it a "race." I call it plain, simple justice…[264]

One can only marvel at Yost's incredible energy during these few months. Sometime in the fall of 1924, he determined to build a new stadium in Ann Arbor. Once he made that decision his focus was relentless, his effort endless, and his work prodigious. All Yost needed now was approval from the Regents. The coach was ready to break ground in the summer of 1925 and to open the stadium in the fall of 1926. It wouldn't happen. Yost's feverish activity to build a new stadium would come to a screeching halt in May 1925.

Perhaps one of the most significant factors in this delay was the death of the University's acclaimed leader. President Marion Burton, only 50 years old, a great friend of Yost's who sincerely admired the Michigan athletic program, developed pneumonia in November 1924, and quickly became incapacitated. He clung to life in the President's House for months. Medical reports for a time were positive, but they then turned persistently negative. Finally, in February 1925, this most beloved Michigan President lost his

---

[264] *Michigan Daily*, 5/10/25, feature section, p 1

fight for life. He had only been president since 1920, but perhaps no leader of the university was ever more universally loved. Politicians in Lansing praised his communication skills, faculty loved his collegial nature, students adored his approachability, and the people of Ann Arbor valued his commitment to the community. The athletic department knew it had a safe place in his vision of a university community. Suddenly, irreparably, all that was gone.

The *Daily* grieved, "The University is desolated today because of the demise of a man whose place in our life it will be impossible to fill. We have lost a revered friend and a remarkable administrator. A great man has gone from our midst."[265] Thousands paid their respects at his funeral. The whole student body, according to their college of enrollment, lined the streets from the President's House to Forest Hill cemetery for the funeral procession. Burton had often spoken of how he would love to see a bell tower on campus, and alumni immediately began fundraising plans for a campanile.

Yost had lost a true and dear friend. Though it was never so stated, perhaps this event explained some of Yost's furious activity in the first six months of 1925. Who would be the new president? Would he be friendly to the concept of intercollegiate athletics on campus? What would he think about a proposal to build a massive new stadium? The Regents appointed an interim president and began the search for a new one.

There was much ferment within academia during the 1920s about the proper role of athletic spectacles on campus, and many influential people saw no place for them. Faculty opposition to Yost's grandiose athletic plans always existed on the main campus, symbolized by the fact that all four faculty members on the Board in Control of Athletics voted against naming the field house after Yost. A significant undercurrent of faculty discontent existed because the Board in Control of Athletics had three student members and three alumni members, all beholden to Yost. This combination could always outvote the four faculty representatives.

---

[265] *Michigan Daily*, 2/18/25, p 1

Much of the on-campus opposition coalesced around an assistant professor in the sociology department, Robert C. Angell. He was a formidable antagonist, the grandson of James Burrill Angell, the university's great president from 1871 to 1909. In 1940, Angell would become chairman of Michigan's sociology department. In an article on the front page of the *Ann Arbor News* in December 1924, Angell made his case:

> A sincere attempt to prevent alumni sending athletically capable but intellectually apathetic men to college would help to purify the academic atmosphere. The presence in college of those who have no true interest in intellectual matters, and no desire to have their interest aroused is a great menace to the tone of the institution...
>
> Intercollegiate athletics offer the most serious problem of all. Complete abolition of intercollegiate athletics suggests itself as the quickest solution to the problem. Supporters of this view cite the case of Reed College which was founded in 1910. This institution has not had any intercollegiate teams...and claims to have suffered no ill effects because of it. Indeed the faculty was so pleased with this policy that after a five years' trial it voted unanimously to continue it...
>
> The Purdue committee on improvement of scholastic attainment recently said, "The plain unmistakable truth of the matter is that there is no possible hope of coping with the evils of professionalism and of the unhealthy growth of college athletics unless we remove the cause at its foundation. This cause is principally to be found in the present system of hiring athletic coaches and in placing the principle emphasis upon the winning of games and college championships..."
>
> The same authority favors the abolition of the board in control [of athletics] as well, saying, "It has done in

the way of enlarging the scope of athletic management what no undergraduate board would ever have dreamed of doing...It has built stadiums, coliseums, bowls, it has brought the gate receipts of a team for a season into the hundreds of thousands of dollars..."

Since a single institution such as Michigan cannot well act alone in a matter of this sort, a conference of executives, members of governing boards, and faculty representatives of all the universities in the Western Conference might well be called to agree upon a joint plan of action. It goes without saying that a conference called to better existing conditions would go on record as opposing any enlargement of plant designed to accommodate more spectators...[266]

Angell then concluded his article with what might be the most astonishing statement ever made in Ann Arbor: "As a seat of learning and culture, Michigan has no interest in winning athletic titles."[267]

While Yost fervently worked to promote the stadium, The *Michigan Daily* was strangely quiet. No editorial in 1925 addressed the issue until March 31. A self-appointed group of alumni, some from each university in the Big Ten, met in Chicago and issued a statement critical of the tendency to commercialize sports. The *Daily* followed with an editorial supporting this group:

Their words are interesting chiefly in that they kick the teeth out of the football zealot's supreme argument. The football zealot, when seduced into discussion with one who can see some purpose in a university other than to have the largest and coldest and most wind-swept and most unalterably solid stadium in the world, is apt to say: "But it's a great thing for the university! Advertises,

[266] *Ann Arbor News*, 12/17/24, p 1
[267] *Ann Arbor News*, 12/17/24, p 1

you know! Makes the rich alumni kick in through new museums and things! It SELLS the university to the alumni![268]

The editorial continued that this group of Big Ten alumni sees intercollegiate athletics "as a malignant growth on the firm flesh of education, and one which should be removed by the nearest doctor." If there was a discernible pattern to be detected in this debate at the editorial desks of the *Daily*, it would seem to consist of strong support for a stadium in the fall when students were looking for football tickets, and opposition in the spring when the football craze lay dormant.

Big Ten Commissioner Griffith tried to help Yost with an interview in the *Ann Arbor News*. Griffith related that he doubted if football players would devote more time to Greek verbs if their sport were abolished. He didn't think that those who bought football tickets would necessarily be spending that money on books or art treasures if the game were terminated. He rejected the idea that football was not an appropriate pursuit for universities, but he didn't think it followed that all the students would be in the library Saturday afternoon if no game were offered. Finally, he emphasized that around the conference intra-mural sports had grown with football, and that in 1924, 36,000 men in Big Ten schools were enrolled in physical training classes of one kind or another.

In late April, the *Daily* announced a campus debate to be held at Hill Auditorium over the proposition, "Intercollegiate athletics, in their present form, are objectionable and should be materially modified."[269] It was sponsored by the faculty senate "to provide a means of open discussion on topics of immediate and pressing concern."[270] Dean Edmund Day of the business school would be the moderator, and the advocates on each side would consist of a professor backed by a student member of the debate team.

---

[268] *Michigan Daily*, 3/31/25, p 4
[269] *Michigan Daily*, 4/28/25, p 1
[270] *Michigan Daily*, 4/28/25, p 1

Those arguing against a new stadium received the most press coverage. Professor Thomas H. Reed of the political science department recommended abolishing the position of paid coaches, ending games played by a few "specialists,"[271] and halting the competition in stadium building. The team opposed to the proposition claimed that by watching athletes perform, students are stimulated to become physically active themselves, but little more was reported. The size of the crowd at this debate was not recorded, but it was mentioned that this was the first time anyone could remember an open debate on campus concerning intercollegiate athletics.

Yost clearly misjudged and discounted the depth of faculty opposition to his plan. However, the faculty senate always wielded veto power over recommendations made by the Board in Control of Intercollegiate Athletics to the Regents. Historically, the faculty rarely exercised this power and there is nothing in the Yost papers of the time to suggest that the coach was even remotely concerned about it. Throughout the early months of 1925, Yost's focus was on the need to reverse the Regents' 1923 vote on the stadium proposal, and much of his energy was devoted to that effort. He seems to have overlooked the faculty's ability to thwart his plans.

However, in May 1925, the faculty senate took an unexpected course. When Yost's recommendation to build a new stadium was placed before them, the faculty mustered some opposition. Rather than endorse the report, the senate voted to study the situation. "In an effort to acquaint itself with athletic conditions at Michigan, the senate requests the President to appoint a committee of five to investigate university athletics and report its findings to the university senate."[272]

This request blindsided Yost and brought all his efforts to a halt. Dean Alfred H. Lloyd of the graduate school had been named acting President and he quickly appointed a committee to be chaired by Dean Edmund Day of the business school [moderator of the recent campus debate], Professor Ralph Aigler of the law school,

---

[271] *Michigan Daily*, 4/29/25, p 1
[272] *Ann Arbor News*, 5/12/25, p 1

who chaired the Board in Control of Intercollegiate Athletics, Dean of Students Joseph A. Bursley, Professor Alfred Lovell of the engineering school and Professor Arthur E. Boak of the history department. The committee would report directly to the faculty senate, but no date was set for the report's completion.

Yost had hoped the Regents would reverse their position on a new stadium at their May meeting and thereby allow him to proceed with groundbreaking in the summer of 1925. Under his plan, there would be a new stadium in Ann Arbor for the 1926 season. This possibility was now lost. The Regents would not act on the stadium proposal until the report of the faculty committee was complete.

Acting President Lloyd was quick to issue an explanation.

> Michigan's study of athletics will be a positive rather than a negative one. The word 'investigate' carries with it the idea of suspicion. There is not the slightest idea of suspicion of anything wrong in the athletic department of the university. There is a lack of equipment for intramural athletics and this will be one of the fields the study will enter.[273]

Robert C. Angell celebrated the delay in a letter to the *Daily*.

> Though I despair that those of us who oppose enlarging the intercollegiate athletic plant will be able to accomplish much in the face of student and alumni sentiment, yet I wish to make one public attempt…to help avert what many consider a grave mistake…I am confident that there are a majority of the faculty and a large number of the more intelligent alumni who, though silent, are opposed to a larger stadium…

> What will a larger stadium mean? It will mean greater Roman holidays than we have now…The players themselves will be forced into an even more rigorous

---

[273] *Ann Arbor News*, 5/13/25, p 1

training…These men will think and act football the year round. Oh, yes, they will "get by" in their work in one way or another; they have to. But they will not develop any real breadth of mind…

But, after all, the players are but a drop in the bucket of university life. What of the rest? They will talk football at every meal for two months instead of at every other meal. They will spend more afternoons watching football practice than they do now…Literary students will, if possible, do even less weekend work during the fall.[274]

Professor Angell really irritated Coach Yost. In a letter to a newspaper editor, dated the very next day, Yost pointed out:

This same Robert C. Angell is a former member of the Varsity Tennis Team. He played with racquets and tennis balls purchased by the Athletic Association. He played on tennis courts built and maintained by the Athletic Association. He went on out-of-town trips and had all his expenses paid by the Athletic Association. He wears the "M" Hat and "M" Sweater awards he received from the Athletic Association. The money for all these items was taken from the earnings made by these horrible football men.[275]

Further opposition surfaced in an article written by H. G. Salsinger, the regular sportswriter for the *Detroit News*. In his column on May 20, 1925, Salsinger pointed out that the University was itself running a deficit:

Some of those opposed to the plans refer to the recently published financial condition of the University of Michigan. It became known several weeks ago that Michigan was $200,000 in debt…Michigan went $200,000 in debt while saving every dollar possible.

[274] *Michigan Daily*, 5/14/25, p 4
[275] Board in Control, Box 7, May 1925 (2)

Building repairs, sadly needed, were neglected because the University did not believe it could afford to spend the money. Salaries of instructors that should have been increased were overlooked. The faculty at Michigan is much underpaid...

While Michigan went $200,000 in debt, the gate receipts at her football games were nearly twice the sum of her indebtedness. This money, taken in at the gates, was used for varsity sports and for the new Yost Field House...

While Michigan cannot make necessary repairs to her buildings and while her instructors cannot get much needed increases in salaries and while she cannot engage additional instructors, she talks of a million dollar stadium for football. True, not a dollar of the money necessary to build this stadium will come out of the taxpayers' pockets; not a dollar will come from a university fund, but the fact that Michigan had a deficit of $200,000 on the educational side...is bound to be linked with the fact that Michigan gathered in more than $300,000 at football last autumn...Technically, there is no connection between the two, morally they are handcuffed...

Quite a number of people will refuse to divorce the two factions. The Yost plans separate Michigan from sport. They create a gulf between the two...It is doubtful if the majority will view the matter just as Yost views it...There will be the cry of "a million for the body and not a dollar for the mind..."

In a number of letters protesting against the plans the moral issue is set forth. Several correspondents complain that sport is being made the paramount issue and education is becoming annually more remote in the general scheme of the university...Instead of being devoted to the cause of education, the university is becoming devoted to the cause of promoting sport spectacles and annually raising them in importance and grandeur.

There is also Yost's plan of intra-mural sports for all. It has been one of Yost's favorite subjects for a number of years and he plans, with the building of the stadium, to add 50 tennis courts, hand ball, squash and racquet courts and an 18-hole golf course...

The undergraduates will say that if Michigan could not afford to build the various courts in the financially fat seasons of recent years then the chance of having them put through with the added expense of the stadium...is even more remote.[276]

Yost knew that such an article could not be ignored, and he responded the very next day with a five-page personal letter to Salsinger. He related that he had never heard anyone propose before that athletic department earnings should be used to pay salaries of instructors or professors or maintain university buildings. He pointed out that,

Until the last three years, there has not been much profit annually in our intercollegiate athletic program. Football is the only game that has ever shown a profit...

The profits of the last three years have been due largely to the fact that we played twice at Ohio State in their large stadium, which they built and paid for; once in the Illinois stadium which they built and paid for; once in the new Minnesota stadium; and the further fact that we had a game with the United States Marines at which we took in about $75,000 all of which came to us...

Your suggestion that some might claim that there was a "million for the body and not a dollar for the mind," would hardly be true in face of the fact that the State of

---

Michigan at the last three sessions of the Legislature has given to the University of Michigan around $28,000,000 to build its buildings and pay its professors and instructors. The last session added $700,000 annually to the University budget for increase of salaries, so I cannot understand how anyone would claim, with these facts, that there was not " a dollar for the mind…"[277]

Salsinger was not dissuaded. In an immediate response, he wrote to Yost that "ever since the stadium was proposed I have received letters arguing against it. I have also had visits from a number of men (I presume they all attended Michigan) protesting against the plan."[278] Salsinger went on to say that he was "personally opposed to the stadium" and listed his reasons:

I am opposed to the finance plan because it may involve serious difficulty in future years…Should the public lose its taste for football, or should a number of losing teams at Michigan kill patronage, then the plan will be seriously hampered…

I am opposed to the stadium because it endangers football. It makes too much of a spectacle…It is out of proportion with the general scheme of things…

I am opposed to the stadium plan because if attendance falls off on account of losing teams, something may be done to remedy that and the means used will not be what you or I regard as in keeping with the amateur spirit or the amateur law…

I am opposed to the stadium plan because it will arouse a certain element against football, an element that may gather enough strength in the next five or ten years to cut down the game or cut it out entirely…[279]

[277] Board in Control, Box 7, May 1925 (1)
[278] Board in Control, Box 7, May 1925 (1)
[279] Board in Control, Box 7, May 1925 (1)

So it was that Fielding H. Yost's careful plans for a new stadium in Ann Arbor came to a halt in the late spring of 1925. Yost's efforts had propelled the issue before the University community, the press, and the people of the state, but had yet to be given approval to proceed. The faculty senate had appointed the Day Committee to "investigate" the athletic department, but no future date was given for a final report. The University itself was being guided by an interim president, and nothing was yet known about who the new president would be. Clearly, there could be no groundbreaking for a new stadium in the summer of 1925 with a dedication game in the fall of 1926.

Yost did, however, win one victory of significance in May 1925. The Regents gathered in Ann Arbor late in the month and rescinded their stadium resolution of 1923, passing a motion to "formally re-consider its action with respect to the building of a large stadium, thus opening the question for further consideration by all the various interests involved."[280]

With this event, the struggle for a new stadium was put on hold until the report of the Day committee. What was there for Yost to do? As it turns out, Yost had a football team to coach. George Little, officially presented as the new Michigan head football coach in December 1924, had already departed Ann Arbor for a new job as athletic director and football coach at Wisconsin. There was no one on the staff who could lead the team other than Yost. It may have been with some relief that the old coach abandoned the stadium wars in the summer of 1925 and turned his focus to the coming Michigan football season. The Wolverines would feature Benny Friedman behind center and a gangly sophomore end from Muskegon by the name of Oosterbaan.

---

[280] Proc of the Board of Regents, September 1923-June 1926, p 614

# Chapter 8

# 1925: "The Greatest Football Team I Ever Saw"

Fielding Yost had finally and officially turned the reins of the Michigan football team over to his primary assistant, George Little, in December 1924. Two years previously, Little had been offered the job of head football coach at Wisconsin, but he had refused the opportunity when Yost intimated that he would one day be Michigan's head coach.

In early 1925, Wisconsin renewed its pursuit of Little. It had been a miserable year in Madison. The Badgers had tied Minnesota and Chicago, but they had lost every other Big Ten contest and had been clobbered by Notre Dame. Unhappy alumni wanted someone who could turn the program around, and George Little remained their primary target. To sweeten the deal, Wisconsin, in January 1925, offered Little not only the position of head football coach, but also that of athletic director.

Little was very flattered. At the age of 35, he would be one of the youngest persons in the country to direct an athletic program at a major university. With rumors swirling around the Ann Arbor campus, Little considered his options. Yost made clear his willingness to match any salary offer made by Wisconsin for head football coach, but Michigan had an athletic director, and Yost wasn't about to vacate that position.

By the end of January, Little announced that he was accepting the Wisconsin position and would assume his duties there on April 1, 1925. In Michigan's long and gloried football history, Little would be the head coach for the shortest time. He had officially assumed the duties at Michigan in mid-December 1924, and would only occupy that position for three and a half months.

Michigan fans watched the unfolding events with some trepidation. Little had arrived in Ann Arbor as Yost's chief assistant in July 1922, and Michigan had won two Big Ten championships since that time. As would be expected, there were those who claimed that Yost's recent success was based on the brilliance of his assistant.

The two men admired each other very much. Yost released an official statement:

> All Michigan men will regret to see George Little leave us. I lose a very capable assistant director and football coach. Little has made himself so useful that his place will be very hard to fill. He is a tireless worker and at no time, day or night, could he be found thinking of anything but Michigan's athletic program. Michigan's loss is Wisconsin's gain. Every Michigan man wishes George success. It will take long thought and careful planning to fill the gap he leaves.[281]

Little replied,

> I consider it a great honor to have been selected by the authorities of the University of Wisconsin as director of intercollegiate athletics…Naturally I leave Michigan with a feeling of regret, for my past three years under Mr. Yost could not have been more pleasant. In addition to learning some of the greatest underlying principles of sportsmanship, fair play, and Mr. Yost's own deep seated ideals, I have made a friend whom I respect and love.[282]

---

[281] *Michigan Daily*, 1/23/25, p 1
[282] *Michigan Daily*, 1/23/25, p 1

Yost was left without a head coach at a difficult time. He thought he had solved a problem that now landed in his lap again. He had other capable assistants, but he had spent almost three years grooming Little for the job, and there was no obvious candidate for head coach.

Little's resignation came at the very beginning of Yost's strenuous effort in the spring of 1925 to build a new stadium in Ann Arbor. He was occupied as well with other problems as athletic director. He had just hired Matt Mann to coach the swim team and was in the middle of a search for a wrestling coach that would eventually bring the legendary Cliff Keen to Ann Arbor. He was negotiating to purchase the Weinberg ice coliseum so that students would have a place to skate and the new hockey team would have a home. He was pressing forward with plans to enlarge the university's intramural plant to include more tennis courts and perhaps a new intramural building for indoor sports. He already had a very busy agenda without resuming the football coaching responsibilities.

He wrote to a friend:

> George has left us and from now on will be a "friendly enemy." For the present our policy for coaching next year has not been settled. It will depend on the personnel we are able to secure. Rest assured that we will consider everything very carefully and try to do what is for the best interests of Michigan.[283]

By the middle of March, Yost had considered "everything very carefully" and placed himself back in the role of Michigan head coach. He aggressively pursued Harry Kipke, who had been an assistant coach at Missouri the previous year, and signed him as a Michigan assistant by early April. All his other assistants were former Michigan football players and included Frank Cappon, who shared backfield duties with Kipke, and Tad Weiman and Jack Blott, who coached the line. Yost arranged for the Michigan coaching

---

[283] Board in Control, January 1925 (2)

staff to host the Princeton football staff during spring practice in Ann Arbor and returned the favor by going to New Jersey for the Tiger's spring work-outs. He wrote a personal letter of invitation to the candidates for the 1925 team:

> We all mean business—and we must remember that Ohio, Illinois, Wisconsin, Minnesota and the Navy also mean business. They're working hard—we've got to work harder…Get out your calendar. Put a big circle around April 21. That's that day you are to report at Ferry Field, in uniform, ready for business.
>
> You don't need to promise you'll be there…I know you will be on hand *if you are a real Michigan man*—and that is the only kind we want.[284]

Two new rule changes were put in place for 1925. The previous year's experiment of kicking off from the 50-yard line was deemed a major mistake. Too many balls sailed out of the endzone. The kick-off was put back at the 40, and teams were allowed to use a kicking tee. Secondly, the penalty for clipping, an act judged particularly dangerous, was increased to 25 yards from 15.

The *Ann Arbor News* celebrated the opening of fall practice in September 1925:

> It was a gray haired, agile veteran that watched his twenty-fifth squad tear up the historic turf in the opening sprints. Only the smile, that has defied the years and the buffeting of defeats and the heartbreak of the game, and the fine dark eyes today are the same as that of the young man. Perhaps the spirit, masked by the more serious development of the veteran, also is the same.[285]

Yost took the team indoors to the field house for the first two days of practice because of unrelenting rain, but the minute the team practiced outdoors, large anticipating crowds appeared. There

---

[284] Board in Control, Box 7, March 1925 (3)
[285] *Ann Arbor News*, 9/15/25, p 12

were high hopes for this Michigan squad with Benny Friedman back at quarterback and a veteran line mostly in place. A young sophomore end, Bennie Oosterbaan, was noticed for his ability, but he wasn't playing with the first string initially so the famous combination of "Benny-to-Bennie" had yet to be discovered.

By September 23, the large crowds of spectators were overflowing onto the field and hampering practice. In exasperation, Yost locked the gates to Ferry Field in mid-week. He then announced that a full scrimmage open to the public would be played on Saturday, September 26, but that students had to understand the serious nature of the preparation at this late date and keep off the field.

## The Michigan State College Game

Michigan's first game in the fall would be against the traditional opponent in East Lansing, but no longer would this rival be the Michigan Agricultural College. In May 1925, the little school had announced that it was changing its name. Now it would be called Michigan State College. The school had diversified considerably in recent years, and many degrees were given in disciplines other than agriculture. Engineering graduates, particularly, had expressed their unhappiness at the declaration of "Michigan Agricultural College" on their degrees. After much debate and soul-searching, the school declared the seventieth anniversary of the founding of the college, May, 13, 1925, a holiday and announced the name change to the world. The college president predicted that student enrollment would reach 3,000 within a few years.

Yost generally paid no attention to this contest. In the previous three years, he had gone on scouting trips when Michigan took on the team from East Lansing, but perhaps he had a premonition that games with "Michigan State" would take on a new intensity. Or maybe the very close call the previous year had grabbed his attention.

For whatever reason, Yost stayed in town and personally directed his team for this opening game. The final scrimmage on Wednesday saw the varsity handily defeat the freshmen, 19-0. The crowd in attendance was the first to publicly see Benny Friedman and Bennie Oosterbaan in action together since the sophomore end was playing more and more often with the first string. Perhaps the audience could sense the legend to be created by these two great players.

On game day, the *Michigan Daily* had a lead editorial with enhanced bold type:

> Welcome, Michigan State—for the first time we welcome you under your new name. This will be our twentieth meeting on the football field. We expect a hard game, hard and clean, and we hope that the spirit of sportsmanship which has existed in the past between Michigan's two great educational institutions will always continue.[286]

Michigan State had defeated Adrian, 16-0, the previous week. The team came to Ann Arbor with a delegation of 6,000 fans and many of the same players who had given Michigan so much trouble the year before. It was announced that the game would be broadcast by two Detroit radio stations and one in Lansing.

Michigan handily defeated Michigan State in this first contest played under the names we know today, 39-0. It was the largest crowd ever to witness a season opener in Ann Arbor: 30,000 fans. Quarterback Benny Friedman showed "uncanny ability in running,"[287] scoring once on a 65-yard dash. He thrilled the crowd with some beautiful passes that again and again struck the receivers in full stride. Bennie Oosterbaan, a sophomore, did not start this game for Michigan, but before it was over, he had caught two touchdown passes, one a spectacular one-handed grab, and Yost would start him ever after. The Benny-to-Bennie show had opened to rave reviews.

Michigan had a very attractive home schedule for the rest of the season. The Wolverines would host Indiana, Ohio State, and Minnesota from the Big Ten, and Yost had scheduled a much an-

---

[286] *Michigan Daily*, 10/3/25, p 4
[287] *Michigan Daily*, 10/4/25, p 1

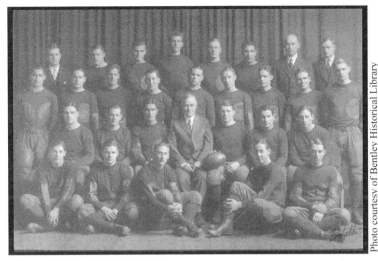

**The University of Michigan Football Team of 1925**
**This team won a Big Ten title for Michigan,**
**the third in four glorious years**

*Row 4: Donaldson (student manager), Weber, S. Babcock, Gabel,*
*Stammon, Dade, Coach Wieman, Hoyt (trainer)*

*Row 3: Flora, Gregory, Thisted, R. Babcock, Dewey, Molenda, Fuller,*
*Grube, Oosterbaan*

*Row 2: Hawkins, Lovette, Friedman, Coach Yost, Captain Brown,*
*Baer, Edwards*

*Row 1: Puckelwartz, Miller, Parker, Gilbert, Herrnstein*

ticipated intersectional game with Navy. Demand for tickets was beyond anyone's wildest imagination. Michigan's publicity director wrote to Yost in late August:

> Ticket applications have Harry [the ticket office director] running in circles already. He is working about 12 hours a day on them. I'll bet we could sell 75,000 seats for the Navy game before September 1st. This is sure to be the greatest season ever from an attendance standpoint.[288]

For the first time in Michigan football history, eager fans began lining up outside the ticket office at 4:30 A.M. on September 1,

---

[288] Board in Control, July, 1925 (2)

the first day game tickets were sold. The panicked office opened at 8:00 A.M. before a huge crowd on State Street, and within one hour the whole allotment for the Navy game was gone. Within three hours, the Ohio State game was sold out. Yost was astonished, but couldn't have been more pleased. Within days, he initiated plans to build more bleacher seats in the east end of the stadium so that he could eke out a few more seats on Ferry Field.

## The Indiana Game

The next Saturday saw the Indiana Hoosiers arrive in Ann Arbor. Not only had Indiana never beaten a Michigan team, they had never scored on the Wolverines. In four previous contests, Michigan had scored a total of 156 points to 0 for the team from Bloomington. This game would not alter the pattern.

Friedman did almost everything. He completed 11 out of 24 passes against the outmanned Hoosiers, five of them for touchdowns. In the first period, he returned a punt 55 yards for a touchdown, and before it was over, he had kicked eight points after touchdowns. Oosterbaan, starting for the first time, caught two touchdown passes. Yost played substitutes for much of the second half, and Michigan won handily, 63-0. The *Ann Arbor News* sports reporter gushingly declared "Friedman the best passer Michigan ever had and Oosterbaan the best receiver."[289]

## The Wisconsin Game

The Wolverines now hit the road for the first time, and the game to be played was the much anticipated contest in Madison, Wisconsin. George Little had arrived the previous spring to much fanfare and had worked hard to put a competitive Badger contingent on the field. Almost immediately upon his arrival, Little had hired two former Wolverine players as assistant coaches: Irv Uteritz and Butch Slaughter. Yost would not only be competing against his former assistant, but also against two star Wolverine players.

[289] *Ann Arbor News*, 10/12/25, p 12

Yost closed practices for the week and conducted many of them inside the field house. Little had added 10,000 temporary seats to increase Camp Randall stadium's capacity to 42,000, but even so, the Wisconsin athletic department announced early in the week that the game was sold out. It would be the largest crowd to ever see a game in Madison.

Of course, Little had coached Friedman the previous year and took some credit for bringing him off the bench after the Illinois fiasco. He knew very well the ability of the Michigan passing attack and spent much time emphasizing the fundamentals of pass defense in preparation. The Badgers had two great outings before the Michigan game, defeating Ames 30-0 and Franklin, 35-0. Wisconsin had never defeated a Yost-coached team, and Badgers everywhere were desperate for a victory.

The Wolverines left Ann Arbor Thursday night. A huge crowd collected outside the Union and escorted the team, led by the marching band, to the Michigan Central station. The cheerleaders astounded everyone by completing a series of cartwheels across the tops of the Pullman cars, and there was much singing of "The Victors." Finally, at 10:30 P.M., the coaches cleared the crowd out of the square so the team could get some sleep.

This game was Wisconsin's homecoming and the *Ann Arbor News* reported that:

> Madison is in an uproar. Wisconsin supporters are strong in their belief that Little has a team which will accomplish a feat no other Wisconsin team has been able to since Yost took up the coaching reins at Michigan—namely to trim the Wolverines…if Wisconsin doesn't win Saturday, Madison will be enveloped in gloom…The town is football mad.[290]

Yost spent much time thinking over strategy for this crucial contest. He had taught Little everything about football that his

---

[290] *Ann Arbor News*, 10/16/25, p 12

greater experience could impart. Uteritz and Slaughter had played a combination of six years for him. These Badger coaches would know every move he would be expected to make. So how did Yost approach this game? He decided to do what he had never done before. He spent hours pouring over his old play books to find formations he hadn't used in years. He was particularly attracted to a pass play he had last used against Cornell in 1916, long before any of Wisconsin's Wolverine coaching contingent had been in Ann Arbor. His team practiced it to perfection all week behind the walls of the field house.

He then told Benny Friedman that no matter where the players ended up on the field, this was to be the first play Michigan would execute in the game. Friedman was surprised because it was a passing play; Yost never passed early in a game, especially if the offense was in Michigan territory. Yost said it didn't matter if they were on the Michigan 20-yard line or the Wisconsin 30, he wanted Friedman to quickly bring the team to the line of scrimmage and execute the play. Yost knew his protégés knew everything about his usual game plan, so he determined to bring a different one to Madison.

The Regents had finally voted to give the band 50 cents per student from university fees, so the marching band had plenty of travel money. The band led the Michigan contingent through the streets of Madison, including a rousing rendition of "The Victors" around Capitol Square. The drum major took the band onto Camp Randall, and to the joy of 3000 traveling Wolverines, he executed a perfect throw of the baton "over and far above the goal post."[291]

The whole stadium now witnessed a Yost no one had ever seen before. Michigan won the toss and elected to receive. The opening kick-off was returned to the Michigan 34-yard line. Lining the offense up very quickly, Friedman perfectly executed Yost's passing play from the 1916 playbook. The halfback, Bruce Gregory, was wide open in the flat and took it all the way for the score.

---

[291] *Michigan Daily*, 10/18/25, p 1

There must have been some incredulous looks on the Wisconsin sideline.

Wisconsin elected to kick off again and sailed a beautiful, high kick to Friedman at the 10-yard line. Friedman, much like Red Grange according to the *Daily*, snaked his way through the whole Wisconsin defense for another score. Not even a minute had expired and Michigan was ahead, 14-0. Little had learned from the Michigan fiasco in Champaign-Urbana the year before, however, and, after this explosion of points, he elected to receive the next kick-off. Nonetheless, this game was over. Friedman threw a touchdown pass to Oosterbaan in the second quarter and the final was 21-0.

The *Ann Arbor News* celebrated,

> Coach Yost was probably the happiest man in Madison Saturday night. Yost wanted to win the game and when his charges were victorious, a smile spread over his features and it never left. Yost showed Michigan fans that Michigan can still play football, even though Little did go to Wisconsin.[292]

Nonetheless, Coach Little would greatly please the Wisconsin alumni eventually because this Badger team would go undefeated except for this contest.

## The Illinois Game

The next game on the schedule would be filled with revenge. When Yost made up the home football schedule for 1925, he quickly lined up Ohio State, Minnesota and Navy for appearances in Ann Arbor. With those three teams, he already had a great home schedule. Yost loved the rivalry with Illinois and wanted to keep it alive, but he didn't feel that he needed the Illini in Ann Arbor, too. Discussing the situation with Illinois Coach Zuppke, Yost agreed to return to Champaign-Urbana in 1925 and have Illinois come

---

[292] *Ann Arbor News*, 10/19/25, p 12

north to bolster Michigan's 1926 home schedule. Grange would be a senior so Michigan's legendary nemesis would still be wearing the orange and blue.

In a letter written to the team in late July 1925, Yost encouraged his stalwarts to stay in shape and to remember that, "We are returning to the Illinois Stadium October 24th—is there anything else necessary to be said—*GET READY FOR RED!*"[293]

Once again, Yost conducted secret practices, many of them within the field house. The Michigan team had only four days of practice since they didn't get back from Madison until late Sunday night and had to leave for Illinois Thursday night. The *Daily* stated the obvious, "the problem of stopping Grange is the one that demands considerable attention."[294] Illinois had just lost to Iowa, 12-10, but Grange had run for 231 yards in 31 carries and returned a kick-off for a touchdown. A scout for Pennsylvania, the team Illinois would play after Michigan, said, "Grange is without a doubt the fastest, shiftiest back I've ever seen. His change of pace is nothing short of marvelous."[295] Illinois decided to welcome Michigan back by making it homecoming again.

A rumor swept the Ann Arbor campus on Wednesday that Grange had broken his leg in practice, but it was quickly squelched. Thursday night the team left in buses for Milan where they would catch the overnight train to Champaign. A large press corps badgered Yost for a prediction before he boarded, but Yost only smiled and said, "The outcome of the Michigan-Wisconsin game and the Illinois-Iowa game have very little, if anything, to do with the outcome of the Michigan-Illinois game."[296]

The day before this historic clash, the *Daily* ran an editorial:

Last year, thousands of Michigan students, alumni and friends traveled hundreds of miles to the Illinois Memorial Stadium to see a football game. It was a great

[293] Board in Control, Box 7, July 1925 (3)
[294] *Michigan Daily*, 10/21/25, p 6
[295] *Michigan Daily*, 10/21/25, p 6
[296] *Michigan Daily*, 10/22/25, p 6

game, perhaps the most talked of game of the present collegiate generation, and the fact that Michigan lost the game was counterbalanced by the increased display of spirit and sportsmanship on the part of her supporters.

Today and tomorrow thousands more will travel toward Urbana…Of the thousands who will make the trip, only a small percentage will be students of the University—but it seems inevitable that students who are making football trips be continually placed under the stern, disapproving gaze of the prudish old-maid type of person who expects the student to become a veritable criminal while on a football trip…

Of course, the student becomes loud, boisterous, while on football trips, naturally some of them act as they wouldn't act at home, but, after all, the only time when we ever really have our "rah-rah college boys" in this day is when they take these weekend trips to distant stadiums, and there is no sound reason why we should not allow them to "rah-rah" themselves hoarse if they so desire…

Michigan may emerge from Saturday's contest at either end of the score, but regardless of the outcome, it is well to remember that Michigan is older in years, richer in tradition, and superior in athletic accomplishments to any and all of our Conference rivals, and that the world expects us to display a finer and higher type of spirit and sportsmanship…Whether we win or lose, we can still afford to maintain that spirit which so befits "The Champions of the West."[297]

Railroad officials stated that the crowd being transported to Champaign-Urbana for this game would break all records. Every available Pullman car in the country was engaged for the weekend. Twenty-nine special trains would be chartered: two of fourteen cars

---

[297] *Michigan Daily*, 10/23/25, p 4

each from Ann Arbor; three from Detroit; four from St. Louis; one from Kansas City; and nineteen from Chicago. The Michigan Band was enjoying its new budget and piled into one of the Ann Arbor trains for the trip.

It was a misty, soggy day that greeted the crowd in Champaign-Urbana. Illinois repeated its stunt of the year before and took the field without socks. This time Yost ignored the event. Michigan won the toss, and no doubt with the previous year's fiasco in mind, elected to take the opening kick-off.

This game was a war. Neither team substituted once. The 22 men who took the field for the opening kick-off played every down, offense and defense, start to finish. Michigan penetrated to the Illinois 15-yard line in the second quarter, and the multi-talented Friedman kicked a field goal for a 3-0 lead.

Grange could not break loose. Oosterbaan performed masterfully on defense, stopping all the sweeps to the sophomore's side, either by downing Grange himself or turning him back toward other defenders. Grange went around left end in the first quarter for his longest gain of the day, 15 yards, but he ended the game with 65 yards on 25 carries. Most importantly, perhaps, Michigan intercepted Illinois eight times. Bo Molenda, the fullback on offense, had four steals and the phenomenal Oosterbaan had two. The wet weather also hampered Michigan's passing game as Friedman only completed two of 12 and had two intercepted by Grange. In the fourth quarter of this titanic struggle, the players were so covered with mud that spectators couldn't tell which team was which, but, in the end, Michigan took an epic 3-0 victory to the locker room.

Grange wrote in his autobiography,

> The Michigan battle of 1925 was an especially tough one for me personally. Because of what I had done to them the previous season, I was a marked man. The entire Wolverine defense was geared to stop me and they did

a good job with the aid of a sloppy turf. I particularly remember Benny Friedman, Michigan's great quarterback [Friedman played safety on defense], sticking to me the entire afternoon like flypaper.[298]

Grange also much admired the work of Michigan's center, captain Bob Brown, that day. "Brown was a wild man…His was the greatest performance at center that I ever hope to see. He is the only center that I have ever seen who came out from his position to get opposing backs on end runs."[299]

This supreme effort by Michigan's defense is best appreciated when one realizes that Grange ran for 231 yards against Iowa the week before. The week after this Michigan game, Illinois traveled to Philadelphia to take on eastern power Penn. In that legendary game, Grange single-handedly destroyed the Quakers, running for 363 yards and cementing his reputation as perhaps the greatest back to ever play the college game.

Surprisingly enough, there was little taunting over this satisfying victory. Yost insisted that Michigan be gracious in both victory and defeat, and these two historic games against the Illini would symbolize that spirit. The *Ann Arbor News* said only that Yost deserved much credit "for avenging last year's nightmare."[300]

George Little sent a telegram from Madison, "Congratulations to you, the team, and the staff for the splendid Illinois victory. Red is stopped and everyone in Madison knows why. The team left a great impression here because of their splendid ability and smart game."[301] Yost replied, "Thanks for your telegram of October 26th and the spirit which prompted you to send it. The results of the Illinois game Saturday were very satisfying in that we won and that Michigan stopped the "Red Head" cold."[302]

---

[298] **The Red Grange Story**, University of Illinois Press, 1993, p 70
[299] *Michigan Daily*, 12/2/26, p 6
[300] *Ann Arbor News*, 10/27/25, p 12
[301] Board in Control, Box 7, October 1925 (1)
[302] Board in Control, Box 7, October 1925 (1)

## The Navy Game

Michigan could finally return for a game in Ann Arbor, but there would be no rest for the weary. The midshipmen of Annapolis would play their first game ever in the Midwest, and the Wolverines had to be ready for the challenge. Nonetheless, a very satisfied football coach had his team atop the Big Ten at this point in the season with a 3-0 mark.

The *Daily* reported that Yost had his charges doing kicking and passing drills on Ferry Field until it was too dark to see the ball.

> No matter how far advanced a Michigan team may be, the coach continues to work on fundamental blocking and tackling, which probably is more responsible for the phenomenal success of most Yost elevens than any other single factor. Yost still says, "Give me 10 good blockers and a dummy can carry the ball!"[303]

Navy brought a respected squad to Ann Arbor. They had been unscored upon in their first three games, handily defeating William and Mary, Marquette and Washington College by a combined score of 81-0. In the week before their trip to Ann Arbor, they had tied perennial power, Princeton, 10-10. Yost squeezed 2200 more seats onto Ferry Field for the largest official crowd ever to assemble in Ann Arbor for a game, 48,000. Yost loved the Boy Scouts and made plans for 600 of them to be ushers for the game, some from as far away as Illinois and Wisconsin.

The *Daily* editorialized on page one about a never-ending event before a big game, "The Annual Drunk:"

> Football weekends, with Ann Arbor filled to overflowing with alumni and visitors, as well as students and supporters of the visiting team, have been characterized by those who know conditions as they are and who are not afraid to face the facts as "annual drunks." Even in a center of learning, the mistaken impression still exists

---

[303] *Michigan Daily*, 10/28/25, p 6

that a football victory should be celebrated with over-indulgence in intoxicating liquors and a defeat forgotten by the same process.

Liquor is the most detrimental force with which the University has to contend in conducting football weekends…Games at Ferry Field are frequently marred by the disturbance caused when men under the influence of liquor are removed from the stands. Endless trouble has been caused when Saturday night parties…have been reduced to mere drunken brawls. The evil is readily seen; the remedy cannot be found until the students themselves take the proper stand in the matter…When a student of the University errs, he does not suffer alone…he drags his…University to disgrace with him.[304]

It was a beautiful, crystal clear, autumn Ann Arbor football Saturday, and the Midshipmen disintegrated. Yost would later say this was the greatest game he ever saw a Michigan team play which, considering his 25-year legacy in Ann Arbor, was quite the statement.

Michigan's fullback, Bo Molenda, scored first on a 22-yard run. On the next series, Navy was stuck deep in their own territory. On second down, they punted, but it was blocked and recovered by them on the 1-yard line. They still had a third down, so they punted again, but it was a poor effort and Michigan returned it to the Navy 14. Michigan got to the three yard line before being stopped on downs, but Navy punted on first down, had it blocked, and this time Michigan recovered it for a touchdown, and it was 14-0 at the end of the first quarter.

In the second quarter, Friedman threw a 25-yard pass to the Navy 18-yard line and followed immediately with a touchdown strike to the fullback. In the third, Friedman hit Oosterbaan for a touchdown and then on the next series found Oosterbaan at the

---

[304] *Michigan Daily*, 10/30/25, p 1

Navy 1-yard line. The fullback got the touchdown on the next down, and Michigan led, 35-0. In the fourth quarter, Michigan substitutes scored three more times, and Navy was demolished, 54-0.

Yost wrote a friend after this game:

> I have never seen a more absolutely perfect football game than the Michigan-Navy game. It was remarkable; in fact, wonderful. I do not know that the team will ever play another game like it. I should hardly expect it to do so for this game was so nearly perfect as regards generalship, judgment, and technique.[305]

Years later, Friedman would reminisce about this clash with Navy. Yost loved a counter play he used at Michigan his whole career, one he affectionately called "old 83." Friedman remembered the call in the Navy game:

> The old man's philosophy of football was very simple. It was, "Barnum was right." He believed there was a sucker to be found on every team and he used to capitalize on it in many instances…I'll never forget the first time we called "old 83" against Navy in 1925.

> It's a Yost invention and just about the most famous of sucker plays. When I lateraled the ball to Bill Hernstein, he was away for a touchdown without any opponent in the vicinity. I looked over at the old man, and he was standing there on the sideline with his head thrown back and laughing hilariously.

> That was the type of play that gave him a kick. He believed, not in power, but in finesse, passing, faking people out of position.[306]

A kind of euphoria known to every football fan took over in Ann Arbor. The *Ann Arbor News* trumpeted, "Michigan has one

---

[305] Board in Control, Box 7, November 1925 (1)
[306] Board in Control, Box 45, scrapbook

of the greatest teams in the country today."[307] The *Daily* reprinted a whole article from the *New York Times*:

> The Michigan eleven is not only one of the greatest teams of the year, but one of the greatest machines ever assembled on the collegiate gridiron. They marched down the field with every manner of attack at their command and that takes in practically every manner of attack ever invented by football genius. The passing was a marvel of coordination, the plunging was powerful, the flank movements were flashy, but greatest of all was the conceal-ment of every intention. Yost has the greatest team of the year. The power and versatility…of that Michigan team against a very good Navy eleven proved that Yost has one of the greatest teams that ever wore the Maize and Blue, and that, admittedly, is a very generous rating.[308]

Yost greeted these accolades in the time-honored fashion, "When a team begins to feel too sure before a football game, that is the time for it to stop and pinch itself."[309] Even so, Michigan had yet to be scored upon in 1925. This was truly an awesome Yost juggernaut, one that clearly had a great chance to win the national title.

## The Northwestern Game

Fans noted almost as an afterthought that the Wolverines were next slated to play the hapless Northwestern Wildcats at Grant Park Stadium, soon to be re-named Soldier Field, in Chicago.

The *Ann Arbor News* characterized the attitude on Michigan's campus: "Northwestern, to be met this Saturday, should fall easy prey to the Yostmen, but beyond the Northwestern game, Yost faces two menaces in Ohio State and Minnesota."[310] The Wildcats had lost to Chicago and Tulane and had barely squeaked by Indiana.

[307] *Ann Arbor News*, 11/2/25, p12
[308] *Michigan Daily*, 11/5/25, p 6
[309] *Michigan Daily*, 11/4/25, p 6
[310] *Ann Arbor News*, 11/2/25, p 12

They would get no respect from delirious maize and blue fans, but the *News* ominously noted one strength the team had: "In Lewis, Northwestern has a deadly goal kicker."[311]

Grant Park Stadium was sold out. Michigan left Ann Arbor Thursday night and showed up at the lakeside stadium for a practice session Friday afternoon. The playing field was 20 feet below ground level, and there was no grass and no drainage. It had been raining Friday morning and the Michigan players found themselves ankle deep in a thick, mucky "gumbo."[312] It was a quagmire. Nonetheless, the *Ann Arbor News* reported that, "Yost was optimistic. 'My boys will win,' was his prediction on the eve of the game. Northwestern agreed with Yost."[313]

The game would be a Wolverine nightmare. It started raining early Saturday morning and it quickly became a deluge. By game time, the gridiron was covered with water. Yost scanned the field and said he didn't see how a game could be played. The referees agreed that the weather conditions were the worst they had ever seen, but the game was on, and the scoring was over quickly.

Northwestern was stopped on their first possession, but they punted deep into Michigan territory. The ball landed with a splat on the Michigan 4-yard line. Friedman sucked the ball out of the mud, but he was hit almost instantly and fumbled. The ball flew up and into the hands of a Northwestern player who was then clobbered by his own teammate because the uniforms were already so muddy no one could tell who was who. The Wildcats had the ball at the Michigan four, but three plays into the line netted nothing. Their great kicker booted the slimy ball through the uprights for a 3-0 lead, and the game was virtually over. The *Daily* told the sad story:

> With the mud almost ankle deep, with a steady, driving rain pouring relentlessly upon the already sogged field, and with a sharp wind blowing from Lake Michigan across the gridiron, both teams found it utterly impossible

[311] *Ann Arbor News*, 11/3/25, p 12
[312] *Ann Arbor News*, 11/7/25, p 12
[313] *Ann Arbor News*, 11/7/25, p 12

to carry on any semblance of a football attack and the contest resolved itself into a punting and fumbling duel, the like of which has rarely been seen on any collegiate gridiron…Skidding and slipping in the slime and slush, kicking at every opportunity, and fumbling the mud-caked, elusive ball repeatedly, neither the Wolverines nor the Wildcats could approximate anything that might be termed an attack.[314]

There was only one pass thrown in the game, an incomplete effort by Friedman. In fact, there was only one first down in the game, that by Michigan on a 14-yard run. Northwestern played nine men on the line of scrimmage most of the game, and the Michigan offense was swallowed by the mud and slime. Friedman complained after the game that he couldn't throw the ball because his hands were so cold that he couldn't feel it. Michigan's center concurred. He had to look at the ball to hike it because he couldn't feel it with his hands.

The sports writer for the *Ann Arbor News* noted, "Yost was a heartbroken man Saturday night."[315] The old coach was quoted as saying, "Never before in my 30 years of coaching have I seen a field so unsuitable for football…It was inhuman to ask a team to play on such a field."[316] The editors at the *News* couldn't quite disguise their disappointment.

For years Northwestern has had a great swimming team. We don't know how many of the varsity aquatic stars play football, but we imagine that there were several on the team, judging from the fondness which the purple team displayed for the mud…After the first few plays of the game it was hard to distinguish between the players. It was not a football game, and we would hate to tell you what it was…[317]

[314] *Michigan Daily*, 11/8/25, p 1
[315] *Ann Arbor News*, 11/9/25, p 12
[316] *Ann Arbor News*, 11/9/25, p 12
[317] *Ann Arbor News*, 11/11/25, p 12

The gridmire news from Chicago last Saturday came as a surprise and a shock to Michigan. It scarcely was believable that this magnificent eleven which had swept all foes before it, had been downed by one of its least formidable antagonists...Michigan will not cry over spilt milk—or mud...Football could not be played at Chicago last Saturday, but the contest will have to be called a football game...

One wonders how soon it will be before the great architects of this nation will be able to produce a stadium with a glass roof which will keep bad weather out and let good weather in...We don't let [weather] in on our drama, our concerts, our basketball and other amusement activities. Why, then, permit it to be a factor in football...especially when Big Ten championships are at stake?

Northwestern has beaten Michigan. But that will not stop that wonderful football machine composed of Yostmen. You may put a good man down in the mud, but you can't keep him down."[318]

Upon arriving in Ann Arbor, Yost unhappily reported that practically all the equipment the Michigan players wore in the game was ruined. Only the oilskinned pants were salvageable. Leather head gear and shoulder pads were so shrunk by the time the team got home, Yost said they wouldn't fit a high school team. Nonetheless, there could be no more lamenting over this disastrous encounter. Ohio State was due in Ann Arbor.

## The Ohio State Game

As always, the Buckeyes were eager for this game. News reports out of Columbus related that, incredibly, the Ohio State coach had hurried his players back out of the locker room following their game with Indiana on Saturday to put them through a scrimmage

[318] *Ann Arbor News*, 11/10/25, p 4

in preparation for the clash with the Wolverines. The *Ann Arbor News* declared the coming contest, "perhaps the most traditional and bitter gridiron rivalry in the Midwest."[319]

Needless to say, there would be another capacity crowd on Ferry Field. Fourteen special trains would bring the fans to Ann Arbor, and students set up a special reception table at the depot to meet them all.

The *Michigan Daily* ran an editorial that reflected the student distress over the lack of good seats in the stadium.

> Do you realize there are many thousands of poor hungry students right here in Ann Arbor who sit far from the game, that only by the aid of field glasses can they keep in touch with the contest…
>
> You, who come from Detroit and Saline and Lansing, who are lucky enough never to have any connection at all with the University, and therefore are able to get seats in the south stands…You, stranger, are indeed lucky.
>
> The Lord knows the Athletic Association needs the money. They have but one wee field house, two gyms, and an administration building. Is that fair? Can you expect them to turn out good teams with this equipment? Bring anyone, everyone, from far and near, just as long as they have the money—Fill all the good seats—To hell with the students![320]

Friday night a pep rally was held in Hill Auditorium. Yost told the enthusiastic crowd that the Navy game was the greatest he had ever seen a Michigan team play. He skipped the Northwestern debacle. Professor Thomas Reed of the political science department took the stage last and admonished men who took their girlfriends to football games. "I have small respect for a male student that goes to a football game with a young woman. He can't yell to the

---

[319] *Ann Arbor News*, 11/11/25, p 12
[320] *Michigan Daily*, 11/14/25, p 4

full power of his lungs with a girl at his side—and he's not there to hold hands all afternoon."[321]

Ohio State brought 8300 fans, the largest visiting crowd to ever see a game in Ann Arbor. They also showcased their 134-piece band. It was to no avail, as the Wolverines dominated this game. Ohio State never crossed midfield and only got one first down. Nonetheless, Michigan's offense sputtered as Buckeye defenders put great pressure on Friedman.

Michigan recovered a blocked punt on the Buckeye one yard line in the first quarter, but it took them four downs to punch the ball over for a 7-0 lead. Friedman booted a 33-yard field goal in the second period, and the Wolverines won the game, 10-0.

## The Minnesota Game

Now it all came down to the final game on Ferry Field. Michigan, Northwestern and Wisconsin each had one loss in the conference, but Michigan had played six conference games while the Wildcats and Badgers only played four. Minnesota was undefeated in the conference and had plastered Iowa, 33-0, while Michigan was taming the Buckeyes. So the Big Ten title would be decided in the final game between Michigan and the Gophers.

The weather took a decidedly bad turn in the week before this late November contest. Yost took the team inside the field house and banned spectators from practice. Crews were employed to remove the snow from Ferry Field so that a dry field might be ready for the game. Minnesota had a great running game, but Michigan had one of the best lines on defense that Yost had ever put together. It was expected to be a classic contest.

A pep rally was scheduled for Hill Auditorium again, but the Dean of Students surprised everyone and refused the request to use the building. Apparently some wayward Michigan students had caused some damage and turmoil at the theatre on State Street after the Ohio State rally. The Dean was determined that such unbecom-

---

[321] *Michigan Daily*, 11/14/25, p 1

ing rowdiness not be repeated. The students were in a quandary, but Yost and the athletic department then offered the field house as the site for the gathering. On Friday night, the marching band in full regalia led a jubilant crowd down State Street from the Union.

If there was a single pep rally that one might wish to go back in time to see, perhaps this was it. Yost Field House was packed with several thousand enthusiastic students, but the old coach led off this gathering in a curious way. Perhaps the Northwestern fiasco was foremost in his mind.

Fielding Yost was a very sought-after speaker at this point in his life, especially for audiences of young high school and college men. One of his constant themes was the importance of being a good loser, and in one of his speeches he expanded on this concept:

> I believe if you have the spirit of a good loser, that is the surest thing to make a good winner. What do you do in defeat? Do you curl up and quit and offer an alibi? It is not expected that any normal human being should be happy as the result of being a loser, nor do we understand by a good loser one who is contented with defeat. *Not how you feel in defeat, but how you act counts.* Do you go off with head up, unafraid, facing the future? That is the question. I do not suppose there are many who feel defeat more keenly than I do. Never yet have I enjoyed one. There is a great value in being a good loser and manfully meeting adversity, for misfortune comes to all of us at some time in our lives. What a monotonous world this would be if we had fair weather all the time and nothing ever occurred to try our souls. Under such a system we could never find out what kind of moral courage we have, nor, in fact, could moral courage be developed under such conditions. It is not intended that we should win all the time…we must be prepared to face difficulties and adversity.[322]

---

[322] Yost papers, Box 7, scrapbook

To begin this pep rally before a Big Ten championship football game, Yost had an undergraduate read a favorite poem the old coach had often quoted since the catastrophic Wolverine defeat at the hands of Grange and the Illini:

Dear lord, in the battle that goes on through life,
I ask but a field that is fair,
A chance that is equal with all in the strife,
A courage to strive and to dare;
And if I should win, let it be by the code
With my faith and my honor held high;
And if I should lose, let me stand by the road,
And cheer as the winners go by.

And Lord, may my shouts be ungrudging and clear,
A tribute that comes from the heart,
And let me not cherish a snarl or a sneer
Or play any sniveling part;
Let me say, "There they ride, on whom are laurels bestowed,
Since they played the game better than I."
Let me stand with a smile by the side of the road
And cheer as the winners go by.

So grant me to conquer, if conquer I can,
By proving my worth in the fray,
But teach me to lose like a regular man,
And not like a craven, I pray.
Let me take off my hat to the warrior who strode
To victory splendid and high,
Yea, teach me to stand by the side of the road
And cheer as the winners go by.[323]

After this intriguing beginning, Yost warmed up his audience. He said again that the Navy game was the best he had ever seen a Michigan team play. He brought out the Little Brown Jug for the

---

screaming crowd; the coveted trophy was now covered with a new coat of paint such that the maize and blue and maroon and gold truly gleamed.

Dan McGugin, the Vanderbilt coach, was in town for this contest. He took the podium and told the cheering students that Yost had "the greatest imagination, the greatest fertility, the greatest capability for teaching the game"[324] of all the men in the coaching ranks today. Charles Baird, the man who originally hired Yost at Michigan and the alumnus who donated the carillon for Burton Tower, next took the stage. He had been football manager for the Michigan team from 1893 to 1895, and he told of the very first Michigan-Minnesota contest that he had been privileged to witness as a college freshman in 1892. If one were to make a list of the great events Yost Field House has hosted, this magical evening would surely be included.

Three thousand Minnesota fans crowded five special trains from Minneapolis. The Golden Gopher football team was greeted upon arrival in Ann Arbor with 1200 telegrams from students back home, urging them on to victory. The game, however, was no real contest. Yost's great 1925 team destroyed the Gophers in this conference championship game.

Michigan maintained a 14-0 lead at halftime. In the third period, Friedman faked a field goal and threw a touchdown pass to Oosterbaan. In the fourth quarter, an intercepted pass was returned 65 yards for another Wolverine score. Friedman found Oosterbaan one more time in the endzone, and this remarkable twosome fittingly ended the scoring for this great team. Michigan walked off the field with a 35-0 victory and another Big Ten title, the third in a remarkable four years.

Minnesota's powerful running game achieved only three first downs, and the offense crossed midfield just twice. Michigan intercepted four Gopher passes and Friedman had a great day, completing seven of 15 passes for 135 yards. It would be the first

---

[324] *Michigan Daily*, 11/22/25, p 4

time since 1910 that no team had crossed Michigan's goal in a season. Benny Friedman would finish the campaign as the Big Ten scoring leader with 52 points: four touchdowns, two field goals, and 22 points after.

Yost was elated. "In all my experience, I never saw a team perform as well as Michigan did Saturday. And in all the lines that I have ever seen, the Michigan forward wall Saturday was the strongest."[325]

The triumphant *Daily* could find no fault.

> Confronted by one of the best teams in the country, Michigan yesterday battled her way to the Conference football championship for the third time in four years. Scored upon, but with her goal uncrossed, a team which in every way is as good, if not better, than the old "point-a-minute" teams has overcome the nation's best that Michigan might continue to rule the West.
>
> Too much credit cannot be given to the men who make up that team…especially this is true of the linemen, who throughout the season have presented one of the most impregnable walls known to football history.
>
> And Yost, the "grand old man of football," has again demonstrated that the "Old Guard" is often far ahead of the younger generation by adopting a style of play hitherto unknown; and bewildering all opposition with his brain-children. Yesterday's game closed Yost's twenty-fifth year as Michigan's gridiron mentor. Few men are able to point to a quarter-century filled with such achievement and progress.
>
> Yost is still the "old man," the "grand old man," and he continues to uphold Michigan's banner as "Champions of the West."[326]

[327] *Ann Arbor News*, 11/23/25, p 12
[326] *Michigan Daily*, 11/22/25, p 4

The remarkable 1925 season commemorated Yost's 25th year at the helm of Michigan's football program. The tradition he established in that quarter century of gridiron success would be the foundation for all else that followed. Michigan today has the winningest program in American college football, has the most Big Ten football titles of any conference school (despite being out of the league for 12 years), and routinely fills Michigan Stadium on Saturdays with the largest crowd to watch a football game anywhere in America. It all began with Yost. At this point in his career, he had one of the best coaching records in America: 163 wins, 30 defeats, and 10 ties. He had guided undefeated teams in 1901, 1902, 1903, 1904, 1910, 1918, 1922, and 1923. He had produced 13 All-American football players, more than any other coach in the land. It was the perfect ending to this quarter century of coaching excellence to have Yost himself designate his 1925 team the best he had ever mentored.

The football banquet at the Union was a wonderful Wolverine celebration. After announcing that the team had elected Benny Friedman captain for 1926, Yost delivered an ebullient address to this great Wolverine team.

> You are members of the greatest team I ever coached; in fact, you are the greatest football team I ever saw in action. I am making this statement cognizant of the wonderful record of the 1901 team and the point-a-minute teams that followed.
>
> Let me tell you why I am proud of you. Facts—facts—there are hundreds of facts sticking out from every angle no matter which way you examine the record. You accumulated a total of 227 points and held your opponents to 3. You kept your goal line from being crossed for a touchdown the whole season long. This, in itself, is a record when strength of opposition is considered that cannot be claimed by any other team in

America this season. No major team in years has made such a remarkable defensive record—and that against the strongest kind of opposition.

Three of you—Friedman, Oosterbaan, and Molenda— are among the five leading point-makers in the Big Ten. Friedman stands first; Oosterbaan is third and Molenda is fifth. Each of you three made more points than Red Grange…

In the six hardest games, only 12 first downs were made against you by rushing and 8 by passing. During the last three games, Northwestern did not make a first down; Ohio made none by rushing and only one by a pass, and Minnesota made but 3…In other words, during the last three games, only four first downs were made by rushing and passing combined. This is the most remarkable defensive record ever made in football.

I am proud to have coached you. I am proud to say that every last one of you played the game from the start to finish like a man and a sportsman. You were undaunted the one time when the scoreboard showed you had lost and you were generous the seven times you overwhelmed your opposition. You were great in victory and great in defeat.[327]

Michigan's "Grand Old Man" had been fully rewarded. Walter Camp, the originator of the "All-American" team, had died in early 1925, but the *New York Sun* newspaper took over naming a squad, and Michigan fans were delighted when both Friedman and Oosterbaan were placed on the first team. The sports writer for the *Detroit Free Press* named his All-American team: the whole Michigan line plus Friedman.

Of course, this greatest of all Michigan teams packed Ferry Field with exuberant Wolverines. Illinois, with the great Grange, would

---

[327] Board in Control, Box 41, #1

claim the national attendance title in 1925 with 380,000 spectators, but Michigan would be second with 355,000, 10,000 more than the previous year. Throughout the fall of 1925, Yost coached his football team and avoided the stadium controversy.

He did participate in the very first of a series of "Michigan Radio Night" programs broadcast by WJR

*Photo courtesy of Bentley Historical Library*

*Yost and his two All-Americans in 1925—(l) Oosterbaan, (r) Friedman*

in Detroit. The initial program featured the University president with a welcoming comment, the director of the new University Hospital telling of Michigan's medical services, a representative of the alumni association appealing for membership, and, finally, Yost, who, in the middle of this frantic football season, agreed to talk about ticket distribution. For this Wolverine audience, the coach detailed how the allotment of alumni tickets was determined for the Navy game, about the great numbers of applications, far more than could be filled, and of the "shuffling and drawing" method employed to determine who got tickets and who didn't.

With fevered fall football enthusiasm once more spreading through Ann Arbor, the *Daily* became a determined stadium advocate. An editorial published in mid-October titled, "The Stadium:

What Are The Objections?" contained none of the misgivings expressed in the spring of 1925.

> If the students want it, and there can be no doubt on that score, and if there is no good and sane reason why they should not have it (and as yet none has been advanced), the more efficiently our athletic system can satisfy their desires, the better for all concerned. And there is no reason why this should not be extended to include alumni and the people of the state.

> One finds it hard to understand how a stadium of 75,000 seats, or even 125,000, will have a more detrimental effect on the student body than one of 45,000…A stadium twice or thrice the size of the present one will not in any way effect student attendance or interest…the scholarship of the athlete surely will not deteriorate because the number of spectators has been increased by 40 or 50 thousands…

> It makes little difference whether a team's supporters number one thousand or one hundred thousand, hero worship is bound to find its place in the hearts of a certain percentage.

> Objection is made to the fact that a larger stadium will make of the game "a great public spectacle." Is there some rule of rhetoric that says that a football game does not become "a great public spectacle" until the attendance reaches a mark over and above 45,000? Is there any justification for statements to the effect that an athletic contest that is witnessed by 100,000 people is any more harmful than one at which less than half that number are present? As a matter of fact, when we consider the conditions at the University, a stadium twice the size of the present one would, in all probability, make things infinitely better. With almost 10,000 students wanting to attend, and usu-

ally wanting to bring one or more guests, with a large part of our more than 60,000 alumni begging for seats, with thousands upon thousands of people in this and nearby states trying to get accommodations for every big game every year, and with an increasing number of supporters following the teams of our opponents to Ann Arbor, we can hardly find any outstanding evil in attempting to satisfy their desires to see Michigan in action…

If there are any definite objections against the construction of a new and more adequate stadium, students, faculty and administrative officers would be glad to hear them…[328]

This effort was quickly followed by another editorial just five days later.

The Athletic Association has announced that more than $100,000 had been returned to prospective purchasers of tickets for the Navy game —and yet the game is two weeks away…

Those who oppose a new stadium have a powerful argument to face in those figures. The students have their seats—the return of this money will not send any undergraduates back to their studies, but it will deprive thousands of Michigan's loyal alumni and their friends from seeing their team in action. Just how hard such a blow is to the alumnus who wants to see Michigan play cannot be appreciated without reading the letters they send to the Athletic association, all begging for tickets and demanding a new stadium, capable of seating all of Michigan's sons and daughters who still have the desire to watch the school's team play at Ann Arbor.

All the tickets for the Navy game were sold out in one

---

[328] *Michigan Daily*, 10/13/25, p 4

hour; more than $40,000 has already been returned on tickets for the Ohio State game, which is still a month away. The Minnesota game will be sold out long before the two teams meet on Ferry Field. The present supply of tickets does not begin to satisfy the demand. In justice to men and women who have been students at Michigan, the proposed new stadium, recommended by the Board in Control of Athletics, is apparently a necessity. What are the objections?[329]

The controversy then took a leap forward when sociology professor and stadium nemesis, Robert Angell, was seen applying for extra tickets for the Navy game. Professor Allen Sherzer of the mechanical engineering department wrote a letter to the *Daily* that was featured with a big boxed headline in late October:

The "semi-fanatical" outbursts of Robert Angell require a response. First of all, he does not speak for the faculty, but, rather, for himself, and what the writer believes to be an "insignificant" group. Secondly, Angell himself has been seen at football games, not only taking the place of another, but also contributing himself to what he has called "demoralization of the University."

Thirdly, there is no proof that enlarging a stadium leads to diminished academic focus or performance on the part of a university. The two can readily exist side-by-side and without detriment as has been amply exhibited at Harvard, Yale, Stanford, Ohio State, and Illinois.[330]

Professor Sherzer, in true engineering fashion, then presented a numerical table showing that Michigan, in 1925, had far more alumni than any other school in the country. Michigan's graduates numbered 68,000, exceeding Harvard's 39,000, Princeton's 14,000, and even Illinois' 34,000, Illinois being the next largest

[329] *Michigan Daily*, 10/18/25, p 4
[330] *Michigan Daily*, 10/31/25, p 4

group in the Big Ten. Professor Sherzer then divided the number of stadium seats each school maintained by the number of alumni to show that Michigan provided 0.7 seats per alumnus, the poorest number by far. Illinois boasted 2.2, Wisconsin, 4.5, and even Harvard had 1.1.

Sherzer pointed out that if Michigan were to come up to the "average" of the rest, the university would need a stadium seating 92,000 to 135,000. Michigan must remember that "we have a large family and it takes room to accommodate them."[331]

This letter would not go unanswered. Many faculty members agreed with Angell. W. W. Sleator, Professor of Physics, defined the academic controversy by writing a reply two days later:

> The University is responsible to the people of the state. It will be faithless to its trust if it provides ignorant or incompetent teachers, or if it tolerates indifference, laziness, or dissipation among its students. But it can never fail by not increasing its stadium. It could not fail by abolishing competitive athletics altogether…it could be argued that the University, though under no obligation in the matter, might profitably and properly enlarge the stadium…if there is any profit, we should be ashamed to take it. I do not believe that the University has the right to exploit the members of the football squad, nor the students interested in the spectacle, for the sake of any advantages the games may bring. Will any administrator of the University admit that we depend upon football to secure the needed support and interest of the University? —that our scholarship, our teaching, our investigations are not good enough to do it? If we do, then either the University deserves no support, or else alumni support is worthless.

We have, I know, gone so far in providing public holidays

---

that it is difficult not to go further. By building our present stands, and compelling our students to maintain the present football machine, we have, I am sorry to say, tacitly assumed the obligation which does not really exist.

We have done wrong. It is fundamentally impossible that a college or class should be represented by its athletic team. The football team is, from the athletic point of view, almost the least representative, or most misrepresentative, group of men we could pick out. Their training contributes almost nothing to the physical education of the student body. Also the control of the football situation means the control of a great deal of money…

I think absolutely no provision should be made —perhaps none need be made—for public attendance of contests. Students…might reasonably contribute money enough to build some stands if they wanted them. I think that the demand for a larger stadium has become ridiculous.[332]

Into the middle of this boiling controversy stepped the new University of Michigan President. The Regents had announced in the summer of 1925 that they had selected a new president, Clarence Cook Little, the former president of the University of Maine. At 37, Little would be the youngest leader the university had ever selected. Yost knew virtually nothing about him when the announcement of his appointment was made, but an alumnus informed the coach that Little had been an athlete in college at Harvard, one year winning the intercollegiate shotput competition.

Little's inauguration was set for November 2, 1925, and thus it occurred in the middle of Michigan's run for the football championship and the very day after physics professor Sleator's letter was published in the *Daily*. One of the primary questions on campus was this: where would the new President stand in the roiling debate over intercollegiate athletics? Clearly, Little was aware of this, for a

---

very significant portion of his inaugural address was focused on the issue. His comments couldn't have come at a more critical time. No doubt all the faculty members of the Day Committee, actively debating the stadium issue, were in attendance.

> Few of us who really think the matter through carefully will, I think, deny the great value of athletics in teaching lessons of self-control, judgment, rapidity of thought, power of decision, team play, good sportsmanship, and other most essential traits.

> Many of us, however, are aware of certain unpleasant sentiments within us, when we consider the great business organizations which have grown up in almost all American universities to handle the hundreds of thousands of dollars paid by spectators for the privilege of witnessing the various forms of contests. Let us for a moment try to analyze the situation by asking and attempting to answer certain questions.

> The first question to be asked is whether "earning power" is one of the chief objections to intercollegiate athletics and, if so, why?

> A moment's thought shows that "earning power," or amount of money received from the public, is a very real factor in shaping a great deal of adverse faculty and alumni opinion. Thus, we find no very great faculty opposition to intercollegiate rowing which has, for colleges involved, practically no earning power. On the other hand, football with a tremendous earning ability is accursed.

> Why is this attitude so general among faculties?

> I think that several elements are involved. First, organized athletics make no financial contribution to academic expenses. It shows little interest in academic excellence,

but much and most effective interest in maintaining the minimum eligibility requirements. Second, the salaries of coaches, paid largely from the receipts from athletics, appear large to the faculty member who considers the relative length and expense of his own period of training compared with those of the average coach. Both of these things trace back to a feeling akin to jealousy. A man, who for years has been begging for a $5000 piece of equipment with which to conduct some experiment dear to his heart, cannot but become slightly green when the receipts from a single football game total, let us say, twenty times that amount. In such situations as this, there is a constant pull away from the rational and toward the emotional treatment of the problem.

The second matter of inquiry is on the ground of the amount of publicity. Does this produce adverse sentiment and, if so, why...?

Once again I believe that a very human jealousy is involved. For some nineteen year old youngster, blessed with a powerful physique, a clear eye, speed and courage, to receive public recognition far surpassing that given to the discovery of fossil eggs thus proving that certain dinosaurs were oviparous, is, to certain minds, anathema. As an after thought the cry is raised that it is bad for the boy—it supersaturates his ego until he crystallizes conceit. This at times is certainly true. The publicity of athletic success is an acid test for young students – the weak dissolve, the strong remain…Moreover, for conceit producers, we should have to eliminate clubs, fraternities, class officers, honorary societies, student dramatics, debating and, finally, even Phi Beta Kappa itself, if we are to spare our college youth from temptation rather than to teach them to overcome it.

The third matter of importance is attendance at intercollegiate contests. Does large attendance arouse resentment and, if so, why?

There is no doubt that in many cases the crowds which attend athletic contests have a very great influence in creating antagonism toward the game which brings them. Two main reasons seem to be involved, first, the old jealousy again. Eighty thousand watch a football game and less than five hundred attend a lecture by the world's greatest living authority on the origin of atolls. It is not right; it is not just; but it is human nature.

The second reason is given as the waste of time for thousands of students involved in the attendance at a football game and in their journeys and discussion both [before and after games]. This objection does not seem to me to be particularly serious. A counter question might be pertinent. Will the critics guarantee that the mental energy and physical powers of the thousands of individuals in question will be better employed if football and all that goes with it be wiped out? I believe that they cannot do so. In a day of the highly explosive mixture of youth, gasoline and liquor borne swiftly on balloon tires to remote retreats…Youth might be doing—and possibly would be doing—infinitely worse things than watching open-mouthed and open-hearted the fortunes and misfortunes of their college teams…

In general and in particular I am in favor of intercollegiate athletics. They bring us into contact with our neighbors—they build loyalties and character. They are in my opinion quite as valuable for women as for men. They contain too many deep personal memories of friendship otherwise missed and of examples of courage otherwise unrecognized, for me to turn traitor to them now.[333]

---

[333] *Michigan Daily*, 11/3/25, p 10

One can only imagine, somewhere in the shadows of Hill Auditorium that day, Fielding H. Yost listening most attentively to these words, a slight smile gradually shaping his beaming countenance as his hopes were realized. The old coach couldn't have asked for a more ringing endorsement of Michigan's athletic endeavors from this new, young university president.

However, one other issue complicated the stadium picture in 1925. Red Grange, the great Illinois back, played his last game for the Illini in November before the largest football crowd ever to assemble in the Midwest—85,000—in Columbus. Illinois won the game, but Grange shocked the college football world by declaring immediately afterwards that he would be joining the professional ranks.

The National Football League had only been in existence five years and had struggled to survive every season. Playing for money was anathema to the amateur purists and, to them, destroyed the value of the game. No longer would loyalty to school and love of the game dominate, but rather money would put the players on the field. Grange fueled the controversy by making the comment that college had prepared him for nothing else, that playing football "was the business he knows best."[334]

Grange's defection poured gasoline on the burning campus football debate. Now it seemed only too obvious that colleges were becoming nothing more than training grounds for mercenaries. Where would all this end? Most damning, Grange was a senior at Illinois, but he left the university before completing his degree requirements. He didn't seem to even care about his degree.

The *Ann Arbor News* initially took a restrained position.

> Everybody owes it to himself in this world to make the most of his opportunities, and it seems that Red Grange's natural aptitude in a certain field of endeavor has presented him with an opportunity to assure him a comfortable livelihood. It is not likely he will devote his life to the game, but simply make use of the professional

---

[334] *Ann Arbor News*, 11/23/25, p 12

contract to set him on his feet, financially speaking. It will be an honest way of getting a start in life. At least, he will be far above a shyster lawyer or a quack medic, or some other kind of crook..."

Grange must choose a path upon which to walk, or run, through the world, and it is his privilege to choose that one upon which his progress may be the most rapid. He has given his best for his college, and now he must be thinking of Grange; and when he decided to sign a contract it was his own business..."[335]

However, this philosophical position evaporated when the *News* editors learned that an agent had offered a professional contract to Michigan's own Benny Friedman.

We were inclined to take a somewhat charitable view of the proceedings which made Red Grange of Illinois a professional football player...

But now, professionalism, apparently all swelled up over its own importance, and seeming to regard the college as a training school for its recruits, has stretched forth a pecuniary hand and tried to transfer one Benny Friedman from his regular stamping ground, Ferry Field, to the pastures green where money talks. And this is a decidedly different story. We could view with complacency the deal with Red Grange, but the attempt to allure our own Benny with filthy lucre is going a step too far...

Captain Friedman is still busy acquiring an education. Professional football would deprive him of the opportunity to round out his scholastic career. If professionalism got Friedman, the argument, now rather weak, against intercollegiate football would be greatly strengthened. Because professionalism would be weakening the cause of education.

> Furthermore, Friedman has still a year ahead of him as an amateur gladiator, and he is entitled to the new opportunity that has been offered him by virtue of the captaincy of the varsity eleven…
>
> Now, it is perfectly apparent that professional football needs to be sat on. It needs to be shown its place, and its place is one in which it will not be able to interfere with intercollegiate sports or with the college education of any youth in the land.[336]

Michigan fans of today can well understand the consternation that briefly swept the Wolverine community. Now that Grange had left school early to play professional football, would Friedman follow suit? There was a collective sigh of relief when Friedman declined the offer. "I'll turn the telegram over to the 'Old Man,'" he said. "I think he can answer it more pointedly than I can."[337] With obvious satisfaction, President Little commented, "Friedman has too good a head to accept such an offer."[338]

By mid-December, Big Ten Commissioner Griffith was ready to pronounce the end of professional football.

> Football will never become decadent through its spoliation by professionalism. Through greed and avarice they lost their chance. Most of the professional teams throughout the country were broke this year. Their managers grasped at the opportunity to build up the game professionally by obtaining college stars. They played them to extinction because of their greed for gate receipts. Everybody saw through the idea. The games were not sport, they were 'hippodromed' contests played simply for the money that the promoters would get out of them.
>
> Almost over night, sentiment changed…I saw sentiment

---

[336] *Ann Arbor News*, 11/30/25, p 4
[337] *Ann Arbor News*, 11/25/25, p 10
[338] *Michigan Daily*, 11/26/25, p 1

for professional football sprout, loom, wither, and now I believe it has died.[339]

However, the future of professional sports was more accurately assessed when it was announced in mid-December that Grange had garnered the unbelievable sum of $400,000 since leaving school: $100,000 for playing football for one month and $300,000 for a proposed movie contract. He went home for Christmas and bought his father a car.

One more controversy would envelope the Ann Arbor football scene. The *New York Sun* named an All-American team and invited them all to a banquet in New York. Friedman and Oosterbaan, the pride of the Wolverines, were more than happy to accept.

The *Daily* was disgusted:

> Two Michigan men will attend such a banquet in New York; their football work has kept them from their studies all fall, and now that the season is over and their minds are free to start on a semester's school work, they have been invited out of town on a trip that will take an entire weekend. One is inclined to wonder what the New York newspaper thinks a university is for.
>
> While the two men so honored are highly deserving of all praise that they may receive on their work as members of the champion Wolverines, it seems a trifle too much that they should be asked to leave the University for an extended trip. This new idea should be discouraged at once, and the papers responsible for such action made to realize that college football players are also college students and that the football season occupies all the time they can afford to spend on the sport.[340]

The All-Americans heard quite a banquet speech in New York. The specter of Red Grange hung over the whole event. Edward

[339] *Michigan Daily*, 12/18/25, p 1
[340] *Michigan Daily*, 12/2/25, p 4

K. Hall, chairman of the intercollegiate rules committee, used the occasion, amazingly enough, to attack special recognition for individual players. "We don't want individual stars in football. We will have them, but that is not what we are striving for. What we want is team players playing a team game." After excoriating newspaper men for adulating individual stars, Hall said that comparing a player "with all the heroes of history…that is very much to the detriment of said heroes and it is overplaying the game." In closing, Mr. Hall expressed his hope that "this is the last dinner for an All-American team that will ever be held in America."[341]

The *New York Sun* then proceeded to give expensive gold watches to all the invited players, which was too much for the National Collegiate Athletic Association. The organization passed an emergency resolution to "combat a tendency to overemphasize and professionalize" college football. The resolution had five key proposals: limit pre-season training, limit the number of intercollegiate contests in a season, limit the number of games played in non-college owned stadiums, abolish any athletic scholarships, and encourage campus intramural games. These steps were taken because,

> Intercollegiate football has become so popular and commercialized so seriously as to affect the chief educational purpose of colleges; that history and experience teach that healthful, recreational competitive sports die when inflicted with professionalism; that promoters of professional football have this fall for the first time induced undergraduates to leave college; and that the *New York Sun* on December 5 banqueted a group of prominent undergraduate football players and presented to each of them a present of such great value that the acceptance of it as a prize by a winning athlete would have professionalized him.[342]

[341] *Michigan Daily*, 12/9/25, p 1
[342] *Michigan Daily*, 12/16/25, p 1

So it was in this very steamy college football environment that Fielding H. Yost laid down his coaching mantle and rejoined the battle for Michigan Stadium. Of course, the spectacular success of the 1925 football team, bringing another Big Ten championship to Ann Arbor, poured fuel on the stadium fire. Nonetheless, the Day Committee, the faculty group reviewing the matter, had issued no report and there was no idea as to when it might be forthcoming. Even so, as soon as the football season was over, Yost began accepting speaking engagements, and at each one he promoted the need for a new stadium in Ann Arbor.

Was the old coach indefatigable in this effort? Do Michigan fans enjoy this greatest of all stadiums today because of Yost? Here is an example of Yost's speaking schedule in mid-December 1925: Monday night he spoke to the Detroit Alumni Club; Tuesday night to the Saginaw High School players banquet; Wednesday afternoon to the Normal football squad recognition banquet in Ypsilanti; Wednesday night to the Ann Arbor Chamber of Commerce; and Thursday night to the annual Detroit Hi-Y banquet. This schedule does not represent an aberration, but rather the man's usual speaking engagements when the football pads were put away.

In late 1925, though, Yost didn't provide his popular address about the value of participating in sports. He had a special message for the Michigan community: a new stadium is needed in Ann Arbor. The *Ann Arbor News* provided extensive coverage of his address to the Saginaw gathering:

> You cannot sell one seat to three or four persons. There are only 47,000 seats available. This is twice as great a number as were available four years ago and yet is woefully insufficient.

> No one realizes the necessity for an adequate stadium more than does the Board in Control of Athletics, I can assure you. This board has already approved general plans for a new stadium, and the purchase of 120 additional acres of land. On a part of this land, the new stadium will

be located, and on the other part, an 18-hole University golf course…

When confronted with situations similar to the one that now confronts Michigan—though by no means so pressing—Ohio State University constructed a stadium of 75,000 seats. The University of Illinois put up a 75,000 seat stadium, Yale University arranged to take care of 80,000, Pennsylvania, 80,000, California, 80,000 and so on through the list. Yale has had a stadium seating 80,000 for the past 15 years. Can any one truthfully say that these great universities have in any way been harmed by the crowds attending their games?

Other departments at the University have expanded. The old medical building, the old library, the hospitals, University Hall, the museum, the engineering shops, the school of education quarters, the accommodations for the school of agriculture, and many other facilities have proved inadequate. In turn each of the above needs was met by the construction of a new building. Would it not have been absurd to argue against any of these buildings on the ground that Michigan should not enter a "building race" with other universities that were putting up similar structures?

In the construction of this new stadium and expansion program, the Board in Control of Athletics plans to provide funds entirely out of athletic earnings. This is in keeping with Michigan's past in the development of her athletic facilities. No other university in America has found it possible to finance its athletic program entirely out of its athletic earnings.

Just a short time ago I spent a day or two at Illinois during the campaign for funds for the new Illinois stadium. I saw the student body subscribe over a million dollars of this amount, which was thereupon matched by the alumni. A year later, I spent two days in Minneapolis and saw the students of the University of Minnesota subscribe three quarters of a million dollars for a new stadium, which amount was matched by alumni of Minnesota. Similar plans of financing have been effected at most all the other universities where new stadiums have been built.

Yet in face of the fact that no donations are asked from alumni or students of Michigan, we find opposition to the building of a new stadium. These plans are not "Yost" plans, but are plans of the University of Michigan, and for the use of students, alumni and friends of the University of Michigan. If the stadium is not desired by these interests, so far as I am concerned that ends it. However, these are my views regarding the situation. I cannot help but feel that there are others who share these views.[343]

The *Daily* provided immediate support:

Coach Fielding H. Yost, who knows football and who knows conditions at Michigan far better than most of those who are loudest in their criticism of his plans for Michigan athletics, once more delivered a plain, common sense, review of the stadium question…

Coach Yost was directing Michigan football aspirants for several years before most Michigan undergraduates were born…and there is no reason for believing that he is now bent on taking the University that he loves down the wrong road.

There was an undertone of disappointment when the coach spoke of the time he visited the University of Illinois and watched the student body there subscribe more than a million dollars for an Illini stadium—of the time he visited Minneapolis and saw loyal Minnesota men give

[343] *Ann Arbor News*, 12/9/25, p 12

three quarters of a million dollars that they might have a stadium…In both cases the student funds were matched by alumni subscriptions, and today the stadia stand as monuments to the spirit of those universities.

At Michigan, no such campaign is being considered. Michigan men, who are wont to criticize the Athletic association when they fail to get 50-yard line seats, are not being asked to contribute a single penny for a new stadium…Yost would give to Michigan an athletic plant that would compare favorably with those purchased with such sacrifice at other schools—and yet his plans are the object of scathing criticism from persons who have made a superficial study of stadium problems…

The new stadium is not planned for the benefit of Fielding H. Yost. It is designed for the good of Michigan students, thousands of alumni who are unable to see their team play, friends and parents of students, for whom it is becoming impossible to obtain seats, and the citizens of the state, who are showing a growing interest…Yost's plans have made a stadium seating 75,000 of these people possible, with no sacrifice on the part of the students, no expenditure of money by the University itself. What more could be asked of an Athletic association?

Yost has said all that there is to say. There is no apparent solution to the problem of ticket distribution other than the erection of a stadium in keeping with Michigan's growth.[344]

So Yost once again became the primary advocate for a new stadium. Resolutions in support from alumni groups began to pour into the university Regents, but the faculty's Day committee remained silent. When would they make their report and what would they say?

___

[344] *Michigan Daily*, 12/9/25, p 4

# Chapter 9

# The Day Committee Report

Coach Yost didn't stay in Ann Arbor in January 1926. Anyone who has spent a January in Ann Arbor knows the logic behind that decision. Yost teamed up with his dear friend, Dan McGugin, and went to Florida to evaluate the booming real estate market. The two men were especially interested in a newly platted project that would soon be on a rail line. The proposed name of the place was Naples and Yost eventually bought some property there.

So Yost was not in town when the *Michigan Daily* published a screaming headline on January 19, 1926: "University Senate Favors Stadium." The article went on to say:

> Unanimous approval of a new stadium, seating at least 60,000 persons, was expressed by the University Senate last night, following the reading of the report by the special committee to consider the athletic situation. The committee endorsed the project, "provided the larger stadium is properly located, built with the utmost economy and subsequently filled under a system of ticket distribution which offers substantial guarantee as to the character of the crowd."[345]

Two telegrams in the athletic files profile the excitement engendered by this event. An assistant football coach, Tad Wieman, wired Yost: "Presented splendid report unanimously approved by Senate stop Approves all essential features of your plans including stadium."[346] Another telegram was sent to Yost by his wife: "Understand lengthy report on athletic situation Senate committee tonight stop Unanimous for stadium of 60 thousand stop *Detroit News* man just told me congratulations will send clippings tomorrow."[347] Wieman then wrote to Big Ten Commissioner Griffith,

> This report was very thoroughgoing, the significance of which I am sure will be very far reaching. So far as I know, this is the first time that any official university faculty body has gone on record with a definite commendment [sic] acknowledging physical education in all of its phases, including intercollegiate athletics, to be a definite, accepted part of general education. These fundamental principles are made the foundation of the report...most of all I am delighted with the principle established.[348]

As one might expect from the University of Michigan community, this would not be a report simply adulating football and the need for a huge arena to cheer on the boys. Rather, this would be an in depth and serious look at physical education in general, its proper role on campus, and the need to involve all students in regular, appropriate physical activity. While Yost would have some points of contention with this report, not the least of which would be the actual seating capacity of the proposed stadium, it nonetheless represented a great victory for his philosophy concerning the proper role of physical education and "athletics for all." It would be the first report ever produced by a university "acknowledging physical education in all its phases, including intercollegiate athletics, to be a definite, accepted part of general education." This report, written by representatives of the faculty of the University of Michigan at a crucial time for intercollegiate athletics, would

---

[346] Board in Control, Box 7, January 1926 (1)
[347] Board in Control, Box 7, January 1926 (1)
[348] Board in Control, Box 7, January 1926 (1)

have a broad impact across the nation. Above all others, the influence of Fielding H. Yost, in his roles as lawyer, coach and physical education advocate, would be seen throughout the Day report. It represented a great victory for much that he had argued for since becoming athletic director in 1921.

The faculty representatives making up the committee included Dean Edmund Day of the School of Business Administration, the chairman and for whom the report was named, Professor Ralph W. Aigler of the Law School, Joseph A. Bursley, Dean of Students, Alfred H. Lovell, Professor of Electrical Engineering, and A. E. Boak, Professor of Ancient History. This august group initiated their report by adopting a tenet Yost had been preaching for years:

> Physical education is a phase of general education. Bodily development has significance and value primarily as it is associated with corresponding growth of mind and character. In so far as physical health and strength, and accompanying habits of physical exercise and exertion, make possible a fuller realization of other capacities—be they mental, moral, or spiritual—the development of a sound and disciplined body becomes an integral part of any comprehensive educational program…

> To argue that the college is essentially an "educational" organization and hence concerned only with the scholarly interests of its students is to give "education" too confined a meaning. After all, the function of the undergraduate American college is to educate for life, not for the practice of this or that trade or profession. Education for life is not to be had exclusively from books and teachers…

> It is not enough for the student to acquire a store of learning, a quickened imagination, a deepened appreciation of the treasures of art; ideals of personal conduct must be elevated and strengthened, the will must be tried, bodily health must be preserved and developed,

healthful habits must be cultivated and established—the whole man must be coordinated and disciplined. There must be provision furthermore for wise relaxation and wholesome recreation and play…

The fundamental question is: to what extent do athletics as conducted at the University now form a valuable part, and to what extent may they be made to form a more valuable part, of a comprehensive program of education for life?[349]

The committee then proceeded to examine physical education as it was then constituted at Michigan. All men were required to fulfill one year of physical education classes. Women had to complete two. Intramural sports were voluntary, but it was estimated that about 75 percent of male students participated in one sport or another during the school year. The overwhelming problem with both the compulsory physical education classes and the intramural program was the lack of facilities and staff. It was felt that, "in general, the facilities for women are distinctly less satisfactory than those for men."[350]

A long discussion of intercollegiate athletics then ensued. At the time, Michigan had 10 officially recognized varsity sports: football, baseball, basketball, track, cross-country, tennis, swimming, hockey, golf, and wrestling. It was estimated that about 1000 men participated in one sport or another, comprising about 10 percent of the student body. Yost Field House solved most of the facility problems for the intercollegiate programs. Unlike the intramural programs where facilities were recognized to be severely lacking, the committee could find only one problem of "plant and equipment" for the intercollegiate program: the football stadium.

But before the committee proceeded to discuss the stadium situation, it was felt that another question first had to be answered. "Are intercollegiate athletics to be regarded as a desirable element in

---

[349] *Michigan Alumnus*, supplement, 1/30/26
[350] *Michigan Alumnus*, supplement, 1/30/26

the general athletic program?" While the affirmative was answered in three parts, the faculty committee gave free reign to its concerns. They wrote that, firstly:

> The direct training afforded by intercollegiate athletics appears to be valuable. Physical development; special skills; courage and stamina; and sustained effort are some of the more important results to be had from intercollegiate athletics by those who are able to take part…

Secondly:

> Intercollegiate athletics may be advocated…because of their influence upon the general system of competitive sport at the University. The Varsity squad constitutes the "honors group" in this particular line of undergraduate endeavor. There is substantial good to be had from the general desire among the students to work up in any line of physical education or intramural sport until they can make the "Varsity."

But the committee had some worries:

> The danger of the present situation is that the connections between intercollegiate and intramural sport will not be sufficiently close. It is important to keep wide open all the avenues through which students may move from the lower levels of physical endeavor into the higher.

Thirdly:

> Intercollegiate athletics may be supported…on the ground that they engender and give play to certain enthusiasms and loyalties which are valuable to alumni and students…Intercollegiate contests are among the few occasions at which the entire student body comes together. The sense of common interest which animates the crowd at a football game plays a part in the

development of common loyalties. There is no reason to believe that enthusiasms developed in connection with the support of athletic teams interfere seriously with the development of enthusiasms for other University interests and organizations.

But there were some concerns here, too:

The danger lies in the appearance of a kind of college spirit that is little more than vociferous support of athletic teams. There is more danger of this sort of development among the alumni than among the undergraduates. One of the most serious difficulties in intercollegiate football at the present time is the insistence of the alumni upon *winning* teams. Efforts must be made to keep alumni opinion essentially sane and conservative in matters of athletic policy.[351]

Thus, the Day committee outlined the positive aspects of intercollegiate athletics. However, there were some definite evils that had to be confronted, and the committee expanded upon them.

Excessive and unwise publicity is a general evil. Here the newspaper press is probably more responsible than any of those immediately in charge of athletics. Undue emphasis upon intercollegiate sport is a serious failing among both undergraduates and alumni; it is difficult to retain a rational set of academic values on the eve of important intercollegiate contests…

The aggrandizement of the individual player has been carried to most unfortunate extremes in the case of our football stars. If there is any sport in which the individual should be rarely singled out for praise it is football, for in no other sport does success depend so completely upon the coordinated effort of all members of the team; yet the spotlight of newspaper publicity is commonly centered

---

[351] *Michigan Alumnus*, supplement, 1/30/26

on the man who makes the pass or receives it, or the man who happens to carry the ball in some open play. The inevitable result appears in the almost irresistible temptation offered football stars to join professional teams at extraordinary salaries. Still another evil which seems to be at its worst in football is the pre-eminence of the coach. Football teams are referred to as if they were the personal possession of the head of the coaching staff…[no doubt a swipe at the tendency to call the Michigan team the Yostmen].

Unless the evils can be largely eradicated, intercollegiate football will not stand the test of time…

As matters now stand, intercollegiate athletics may be said to exist "in excess."[352]

To eliminate some of these problems, the committee suggested that the schools in the conference agree to limit the amount of practice time athletes must devote, limit the number of competitions, reduce the length of schedules, and restrict the functions and activities of the professional coaches.

The committee then, finally, addressed the question for which everyone was waiting. What about a new stadium? On this issue, the committee adopted Yost's recommendations. Ferry Field was simply inadequate. Drainage was terrible and an expensive aboveground structure would be needed. Besides, Ferry Field was close to the campus and shouldn't be devoted to "a structure used but a few times a year."[353]

A new location for a stadium was not a problem. There were several appropriate tracts in the Ann Arbor area. However, "in general design and type of construction, any new stadium should represent the utmost simplicity. No attempt should be made to give it the form of a monument or memorial."[354] Football, said the

---

[352] *Michigan Alumnus*, supplement, 1/30/26
[353] *Michigan Alumnus*, supplement, 1/30/26
[354] *Michigan Alumnus*, supplement, 1/30/26

Michigan faculty, had enough of an aura on its own. The game didn't need to have the war dead wrapped around it. Again, Yost's influence was evident: "If the site upon which the stadium is built is so selected and graded that the structure lies largely below the ground, the minimum requirements of general appearance can be met without heavy outlay."[355] The committee then inserted a statement in opposition to selling bonds "carrying the privilege of preferred football ticket application."[356] The faculty felt the athletic department budget could by itself build such a stadium. This represented, of course, a complete misunderstanding of the necessary funding. Yost would ignore the suggestion.

The committee then proceeded with a long discussion of the need to restrict attendance at the games. This assertion, too, would be a jab at Yost's insistence that tickets be available to everyone. The faculty didn't endorse that idea. The University "is an institution of higher learning, not a purveyor of popular entertainment."[357] The faculty felt there should be appropriate

> attempts to control the character of the crowd…Spectators, whether they be college men or not, who are guilty of poor sportsmanship or disorderliness, constitute a liability…Displays of the right sort of college spirit are the saving feature of popular attendance at intercollegiate contests. In the interest of right-spirited sport, crowds at football games should be primarily crowds of college men and women.[358]

The committee then entered the minefield of ticket distribution. Tickets should be preferentially given to students and alumni. Any left over could be distributed to citizens of the state. Keeping all this in mind, much of which Yost would ignore, the faculty committee finally got to the critical paragraph:

---

[355] *Michigan Alumnus*, supplement, 1/30/26
[356] *Michigan Alumnus*, supplement, 1/30/26
[357] *Michigan Alumnus*, supplement, 1/30/26
[358] *Michigan Alumnus*, supplement, 1/30/26

Given a wise distribution of tickets…the committee is…
not opposed to the construction of a stadium with 60,000
seating capacity, provided the stadium is properly located,
built with the utmost economy, and subsequently filled
under a system of ticket distribution which offers substantial guarantees as to the character of the crowd.[359]

Thus, the faculty of the University of Michigan finally gave a
less than ringing endorsement for a new stadium.

The Day committee had a few other demands to make upon
the stadium proponents. Construction of a new stadium was to be
coupled with the development of satisfactory facilities for required
physical education and intramural sports. It was the emphatic recommendation of the committee that, "if and when a new stadium
is constructed there be built concurrently a minor-sports building
for the accommodation of indoor intramural athletics among the
general student body." The committee wanted physical education
requirements to be increased to two years for men and perhaps
eventually to three years for all students. In what constituted perhaps the greatest victory for Yost's personal philosophy, the faculty
committee emphatically stated that, "physical training should
constitute an integral part of collegiate education."

Finally, the faculty committee had one last recommendation to
make, one aimed squarely at Michigan's very popular head football
coach. The committee insisted on changing the composition of the
Board in Control of Intercollegiate Athletics.

It is of the utmost importance that…the administration
of athletic affairs be in the hands of well-informed, far-
visioned educators. There is just one place in which to
center responsibility for athletic policy and that is the
place in which is centered responsibility for educational
policy. No other position can possibly be taken if it be
granted that athletics find their real justification in general

---

[359] *Michigan Alumnus*, supplement, 1/30/26

physical education, and physical education is regarded as a phase of education as a whole. Athletics cannot remain a thing apart. There must be no state within the state; no athletic system independent of the educational system. The control of athletics must be made subordinate to the control of education.[360]

The University of Michigan Board in Control of Intercollegiate Athletics consisted of Yost, three student members, three alumni members, and four faculty. Yost essentially controlled this group because students and alumni almost always voted with him. Faculty sentiment didn't matter, as was seen previously when all four faculty representatives voted against naming the new field house after Yost. The Day committee wanted that changed. Their proposal was to increase faculty representation on the committee to a total of eight, which would give them one more vote than Yost and his contingent. While this suggestion would be the one Yost would resist the most, the body of the report gave him two great victories: a green light for a new stadium, and formal recognition by the faculty that physical education belonged in the curriculum.

Now that the Day report had been unanimously adopted by the faculty senate, there was only one obstacle left before planning for the construction of Michigan Stadium could commence in earnest. The Regents had to approve the report. The report had been completed in time for the late January meeting of the Regents, but the body had briefly discussed it and deferred action to February. According to the *Daily*, it was to be a "special order of business"[361] for the February meeting, but when the end of February rolled around, discussion was again deferred to March. In March, a quorum was not present so the Regents put the issue off once more until April. Yost indicated his disappointment to Bernard Green, the president of Osborn engineering, the Cleveland-based company he favored to build the stadium:

---

[360] *Michigan Alumnus*, supplement, 1/30/26
[361] *Michigan Daily*, 2/9/26, p 1

The Board of Regents met yesterday and again adjourned without taking any action in regard to the stadium, so it is a question now of waiting another month or more to know just what the Board in Control of Athletics will be permitted to do in regard to stadium construction.[362]

The item that seemed to be holding up approval was the proposal to change the membership of the Board in Control. Yost was fighting to retain his dominance. He suggested dropping one student from the board and adding a faculty member. Yost claimed this would give faculty control of the Board if he were truly considered a faculty member, as he had an appointment in the School of Education. Thus, there would be three alumni, two students, five faculty and Yost. So, technically, there would be six "faculty" votes out of 11, but obviously this arrangement would leave Yost in power as the tie-breaker. The Board of Regents Chairman, James O. Murfin, a dear friend of Yost, informed the coach in mid-April that the faculty would never accept such a proposal.

The issue of the Board's membership would represent the only significant defeat for Yost as a result of the Day report. Yost would get the stadium he wanted, and he would receive an official faculty endorsement of his philosophy concerning the importance of physical education. He would eventually ignore completely the faculty's suggestions about the size of the stadium, the financing of its construction, and the ticket distribution, but he would be forced to make a concession over the composition of the Board in Control.

On April 22, 1926, the Regents finally approved the faculty report including the recommendation for a new stadium in Ann Arbor. However, the Regents directed that the Board in Control of Intercollegiate Athletics be re-constituted on May 1, 1926, to consist of two student members, three alumni, and nine faculty, two of whom were to be the President of the university and Yost as the athletic director. The other seven faculty representatives were

[362] Board in Control, Box 8, February 1926 (2)

to be appointed by the President. Thus, the President and the appointed faculty members would always be able to outvote Yost, the students, and the alumni.

However, Yost did not come away from this historic meeting of the Regents empty handed. First, the Regents made it clear that the change in governance of the Board in Control was not because of any malfeasance.

> The Board in Control of Intercollegiate Athletics as it is now constituted has functioned well and splendidly for years. We have heard no criticism of this group or of this system nor is any pointed out in the report in question. Their work has been peculiarly constructive and their affairs have been handled with the keenest appreciation of the best ideals of intercollegiate sport. Our wonderful athletic facilities and athletic plant, as evidenced by our many tennis courts, playing fields, buildings, etc. stand as a perpetual monument to the constructive, unselfish work of the members of the Board in Control of Inter-collegiate Athletics.[363]

There was to be no suggestion by the Regents that Yost's past leadership was being admonished in any way. Secondly, Yost won two major concessions from the Regents about the specifics of the stadium project.

> With respect to the stadium discussion the Board of Regents can see no reason for necessarily confining the seating capacity to sixty thousand, in fact, in our opinion, a stadium of seventy thousand would not be objectionable. On the other hand, we share the common belief that, in view of the many other needs of the University, the stadium construction should be handled, to use the common phrase, "as not to overdo it." With these comments we are entirely content to leave the details of this

---

[363] Regents, 1926 (Proceedings of the Board of Regents, 9/23-6/26, pp. 868-871)

problem to the present Board in Control of Intercollegiate Athletics and its successor in office, believing that
from their knowledge, experience and study, and from
the agitation and discussion which has taken place on
the subject, they are fully capable and qualified to handle
this matter in a way that will produce the greatest good
to the greatest number with the least friction.[364]

So at the end of this crucial meeting, Yost held two great victories in his grasp. First, the Regents agreed to increase the capacity
of the stadium to 70,000, negating the 60,000 proposed by the
faculty. Secondly, they directed that the Board in Control of Intercollegiate Athletics be solely in charge of building the stadium.
Several faculty members had suggested that the Board in Control
should have to return to the faculty senate for approval once the
stadium design was completed. The Regents gave the Board in
Control full jurisdiction over stadium construction. Yost now had
the approval he needed, and he was more than ready to proceed
with the building of Michigan Stadium.

The *Michigan Daily's* headline blared, "Stadium Approved."[365]
An editorial the next day celebrated that:

What was made possible by the action of the Regents…
was the erection of a stadium, outside of the area of
Ferry Field, capable of seating those who have every
right to watch Michigan teams play football—students,
parents, faculty, alumni, and the friends of the University
throughout the state. And Ferry Field, which is closer
to the campus, has been made available for use in
the development of intramural work, which was
enthusiastically approved in the Regents' report.

It has been a long struggle, with the obvious deficiencies of
the present plant at Ferry Field becoming more apparent
each year. It has been settled, after long consideration, in

[364] Regents, 1926 (Proceedings of the Board of Regents, 9/23-6/26, pp. 868-871
[365] *Michigan Daily*, 4/23/26, p 1

> a manner that cannot be opposed by those who desire
> to see Michigan growing, in the development of clean
> sport, both intercollegiate and intramural…
>
> The *Daily* congratulates all those who contributed to the
> happy culmination of the question, and joins the Regents
> in their expression of confidence in Michigan's athletic
> board in control.[366]

Yost would have to suffer one last bureaucratic indignity before
he could commence with his plans for the stadium. Two days after
the Regents' action approving the stadium, President Little appointed the new faculty members for the Board in Control. Among
them was Yost's primary nemesis, Dr. Robert Angell of the sociology
department, who had led the campus opposition to a new stadium.
Dr. Little supported his action by saying that Angell,

> combines with youth a practical knowledge of athletics
> and a willingness to criticize openly what he believes
> to be the inherent weaknesses in over-emphasizing any
> one phase of the athletic program. His active interest,
> his energetic thought and his disregard of popularity in
> stating his beliefs in connection with the athletic situation
> should help the board.[367]

Yost complained to his dear friend, Regent Murfin, about this
unexpected event.

> I cannot understand why it is necessary to punish me by
> adding to the membership of the Board, and especially
> one Bob Angell, whose whole attitude seems to be to
> oppose anything as it is or as it should be…There is a
> great chance to do something worthwhile, but it seems
> just one continuous fight after another and one seriously
> wonders if it is all worthwhile.[368]

---

[366] *Michigan Daily*, 4/24/26, p 4
[367] *Michigan Daily*, 4/25/26, p 1
[368] Board in Control, Box 8, May 1926 (2)

Murfin responded immediately:

> If I had my Bible in hand I would quote with accuracy
> a paragraph to the effect that man who is born of
> woman comes into a world of trouble. That also goes
> for a director of intercollegiate athletics working with a
> jealous faculty.
>
> You know as well as I do that the present set-up of the
> Board in Control is not what I wanted, but it was the best
> I could get. I was and am convinced by compromising
> on this basis we are going to get better cooperation in
> our four year course in physical education and in our
> intramural program. The appointment of Bob Angell was
> deliberately done after Dr. Little conferred with me on
> the subject. We both felt to put him on the inside where
> he could learn what he was talking about would prove
> sufficiently educational to ultimately make him a booster
> instead of a knocker…Frankly I have been counting on
> you, Aigler, Duffy and Little to run this entire program in
> a way that will be satisfactory to everybody and as long as
> you four are alive if a Board of forty were created no harm
> would be done except to make you added trouble.[369]

From that point on, Yost never looked back. In a letter dated
April 28, 1926, six days after the Regents approved the project, Yost
made arrangements to meet in Ann Arbor with Bernard Green,
President of Osborn Engineering. Yost was still planning a stadium
to be built south of what is now Stadium Boulevard, bounded on
the west by Main Street, but he also wanted Green to look at a parcel
of land known as the "Miller tract," located just north of Stadium,
also bounded on the west by Main Street. In October 1925, the
athletic department had purchased the property for $18,000.

Ultimately, Green seemed to favor the Miller tract because a
ravine ran through the property from east to west. A remnant of this

---

[369] Board in Control, Box 8, May 1926 (2)

ravine can still be appreciated, no doubt, with the dip that Main Street takes right in front of the Michigan Stadium press box. With a deep ravine running through the property, less dirt would need to be removed and a lower cost could be achieved. Indeed, this would be the land upon which Michigan Stadium stands today.

An initial meeting of the newly constituted Board in Control of Athletics was held on May 3, 1926. Yost wrote Green the next day that, "much discussion was had…There was quite a controversy over the proposed site. One suggested that we go a mile or two out South State Street, which is impossible…Also, much discussion was given to parking space."[370] Yost had no worries about the parking problems. "In my opinion, parking will largely take care of itself. When we have any games here now men, women, and boys stand along our streets trying to get people to park in their driveways and yards at an average of about 50 cents."[371] Yost was right once again. Parking for football games in Ann Arbor hasn't changed in 80 years, except for the price.

At a meeting on May 12, 1926, the Board in Control finalized the site. A report prepared by Yost stated:

> Of the dozen or more sites that have been considered in respect of the new stadium for one reason or another all but three have been eliminated. The ones still under consideration are: 1. The so-called Miller Tract along Main Street, north of the Ann Arbor Golf Club (the Ann Arbor Golf Club was where the University course now lies). 2. A tract about one-quarter of a mile south of the Ann Arbor Golf Club property and about one-third of the way from Main Street to State Street…3. The Ann Arbor Golf Club grounds.[372]

Opposition to a stadium on the golf grounds was strong from those who used the course, and Yost deferred to them since he

---

[370] Board in Control, Box 8, May 1926 (3)
[371] Board in Control, Box 8, May 1926 (3)
[372] Board in Control, Box 46, Folder Misc Stadium

already had plans to purchase the property for the university. The Miller tract seemed most attractive because it would be much closer to campus and an easy distance to walk. Students, faculty, and townspeople would have no need to drive, and neighborhood parking could easily accommodate those coming from out of town. A stadium farther out would tempt everyone to drive, thereby leading to much more congestion and the necessity for extensive parking areas. Yost finalized his recommendation:

> It has already been agreed by all persons studying the matter that the new stadium should be located off Ferry Field and that the new site should be selected with special reference to economies of construction, accessibility to the main arteries of transport and vehicular travel and favorable drainage levels and surface contours. With these considerations in mind the site that stands out in my mind as being the most desirable is the one just north and east of the intersection of the new M-17 highway [Stadium Boulevard] and South Main Street [the Miller tract].[373]

So now that a site had been selected, what would the stadium look like? A formal idea was presented in the *Michigan Daily* on January 13, 1926, by Professor Clarence Johnston of the engineering school, a faculty representative on the Board in Control. No doubt he had entertained several discussions with Yost about the form Michigan Stadium should assume. An accompanying drawing published that day looks nearly identical to the stadium that graces Ann Arbor today. Professor Johnston wrote:

> The topography of the country about Ann Arbor is favorable to the construction of such stadia as may be found in California or the one completed last year for the University of Pittsburgh. The advantages of the simple type, concrete resting on earth, are many.

---

[373] Board in Control, Box 46, folder: stadium seats

1. It is important that any structure be designed and built so that it might be easily modified to meet the needs and desires of those who follow us. A stadium without a gallery [second deck] may be extended by providing new seating areas on the same slopes...This means simply an extension of the original plan. If a gallery's built in connection with the first construction, those who follow us have but little opportunity for making extensions or other modifications.

2. Many people are attracted to football games because they like to see the great audience. For this reason spectators should be able to see the entire audience from any place in the stadium. A gallery makes this impossible...[also] columns must be provided...and each column is a serious handicap to many spectators.

3. A stadium supported on the earth is safe. It never falls. Any elevated structure requires inspection with the lapse of years.

4. Congestion develops where crowds from a gallery join those from lower levels. This should be avoided.

5. The cost of maintenance is reduced by eliminating the gallery.

6. The cost is much lessened by the adoption of a simple design.[374]

This remarkable conception of Michigan Stadium, published before the Day report was issued and more than three months before Regent approval, has withstood the test of time. When Michigan Stadium was enlarged in 1949, Professor Johnston's proposal was followed. New seating was provided simply by extending the slope of the original plan. And who would not agree with his vision of

---

each spectator being "able to see the entire audience from any place in the stadium?" What makes Michigan Stadium so unique is the incredible vista of the whole arena that greets every spectator passing through any portal. The wonderful color and celebration of Michigan football bursts upon the entering fan all at once. Little did he know, too, that the stadium he conceived would be the perfect configuration for "the wave," the favorite mode of mass expression adopted by Michigan Stadium patrons.

Fielding H. Yost now had an immense project before him. Someone had to hire an engineering firm, find an excavator, decide on the type of cement, raise the funds, and keep the whole endeavor progressing so that the structure would be ready for the 1927 season. But Yost was still the Michigan head football coach, and another great season, the last on Ferry Field, was imminent. Friedman and Oosterbaan would be back, and many a team around the Midwest wanted another shot at those two, let alone at their legendary head coach. Could the old coach build a stadium *and* bring another Big Ten football championship to Ann Arbor?

# Chapter 10

# The Last Year for Ferry Field and Michigan's Grand Old Man

Coach Yost had a full schedule in the summer of 1926. Not only did he have a football team to coach, but he also had a whole stadium to build. Nonetheless, Yost was approached by a producer from Hollywood who was planning to make a football movie called, "The Quarterback." The film moguls wanted authentic football scenes and proposed hiring Yost as an on-site technical advisor for the then astonishing sum of $3000. The film was to be shot in New York State, and either the intrigue or the money—perhaps both—induced Yost to accept.

Upon arriving at the site, Yost immediately released all the actors who had been hired to make up the teams and advertised for experienced football men. In a short time, he had accumulated a cast of former college players who knew the game and could play without needing fundamental direction. He was determined to produce authentic football footage. Initially, Yost was to be engaged for two weeks, but the production stretched over a much longer time. With all his responsibilities persisting in Ann Arbor, he spent the summer traveling back and forth. At one point, he wrote in exasperation to a friend,

> I will have to go back to New York to finish it, having just received word that they are ready to "shoot." They change their minds every other day about what they want

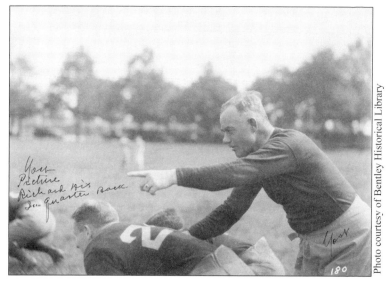

*Yost directing players on the movie set of "The Quarterback," Summer 1926*

done, when they want it done, how they want it done and where they want it done...[375]

Nonetheless, Yost seemed to enjoy the experience, and when the summer was over, he eagerly anticipated the release of the film.

The Michigan student council spent the spring and summer of 1926 trying to decide what to do about the football cheering section. It was felt that, compared to other schools, Wolverine students weren't very synchronized, didn't seem to be as loud, and lacked an essential intensity. The result of this self-examination was a proposal for a new cheering section of 1200 male upperclassmen, which the athletic department agreed to seat between the 25- and 45-yard lines in the south stands. Once enrolled in the section, a male student would present himself to Moe's Sport Shop where, for one dollar, he would receive a cape, a hat, and a megaphone of either maize or blue.

---

[375] Board in Control, Box 8, August 1926 (2)

Fifteen minutes before each home game, students enrolled in the section will go directly to Yost Field House where they will don their uniforms…and rehearse old and new yells to be used in that game. The 1200 students will then parade onto the field in snakedance fashion, and after circling the gridiron, will disperse and fill the reserved section in the south stand.

The section will consist of a huge block "M," 500 students forming the letter of maize and 700 composing the blue background. Students enrolled in the section will be required to wear uniforms at every home game…

No women or anyone other than men students will be permitted to sit in the permanent section…[376]

A *Daily* editorial hoped for game day improvement.

The single material advantage of enlisting in the permanent section is the assurance of a seat at every home game near midfield. After that, it becomes a question of moral obligation. Have students of the University enough interest in systematized cheering at Ferry Field—the impotency of which has been the wonder of many an outsider—to make personal sacrifices for its betterment? Will 1200 of them register for the section, purchase outfits which must be worn at every home game, parade onto the field and scramble into the section?…Michigan spirit will have a chance to manifest itself as it never has before next fall.[377]

The Michigan Band added to the new enthusiasm by announcing that members would start practicing earlier than ever so that they could be on the field for the first home game. Always in the past, the marching band had skipped the first home game and had taken the field only for the second one.

---

[376] *Michigan Daily*, 5/27/26, p 3
[377] *Michigan Daily*, 5/27/26, p 4

Yost had finally revamped the process for ticket applications. Since the old system operated simply on a first-come, first-serve basis starting September 1, many Wolverine faithful in the western part of the state were denied tickets if their mailed request failed to arrive in a timely fashion. Since so many games had been sold out on the very first day, applications arriving on September 2 or September 3 were returned. So for 1926, any and all ticket applications were allowed between August 20 and August 31. They piled up at the athletic department in one huge bin. The mayor of Ann Arbor then had the honored privilege of drawing applications by lottery on September 2. This must have taken all day.

On September 3, Harry Tillotson, ticket manager, announced that the Wisconsin game had been oversold by 11,000, the Minnesota game by 10,000, and the Illinois game by 9000. Within days, the athletic department had returned an estimated $100,000 for unavailable tickets. Mr. Tillotson became known by chagrined alumni as "refund Harry," among other derogatives. Wrote the *Ann Arbor News*:

> Tillotson is receiving several choice letters each day now from alumni and other ticket applicants whose money was returned on the sell-out games. After reading some of the letters, one can learn just what a nice fellow Tillotson is. Cries of thief, robber and blackguard are mild compared to some of the expletives used in the missives.[378]

Veterans of the great 1925 football squad assembled in Ann Arbor the middle of September. Once again, Michigan students crowded the sidelines and spilled over on to the field as Yost put his charges through practices. There was much reason for optimism with two All-Americans returning, a situation that had never occurred before at Michigan. In fact, the whole backfield was intact once Bo Molenda, the fullback, successfully completed an English requirement over the summer and was thus eligible to play. New men would be required on the line, but Yost loved mentoring those

---

[378] *Ann Arbor News*, 9/24/26, p12

players who would fight it out in the trenches. Students were greeted early in the practice sessions by Yost in uniform, working assiduously with the center prospects. The *Ann Arbor News* sportswriter proclaimed a different Yost.

> Coach Yost appears to be the happiest man in the world. Either the coach is rather pleased with his squad this year or else the realization of the stadium project has put him in a happy frame of mind. Yost has been out with the players every day and appears to be in the best of humor. In previous years it has been different. Yost formerly surveyed his squad with a critical eye. Condemnation was more prevalent than words of praise. Anyway, the coach seems pleased this year and his optimism is shared by other members of the staff.[379]

Benny Friedman had been asked to write an article on football strategy for a popular magazine for boys that was published at the beginning of the 1926 football season. His comments illustrate much about football philosophy 80 years ago and how offensive thinking has changed.

> Play for position and look over the defense. Kick on the first down when you're within 20 yards of your own goal. Don't chance a fumble. Kick! From the 20 to the 40 yard line, get your running ends loose. Don't take a chance with forward passes here, or anything else that might go wrong. It won't hurt to kick on the second down.
>
> Between the 40 yard lines, try to score…From the opponent's 40 yard line to his goal is scoring territory. Use everything you've got in this territory.
>
> Look the defense over. If one of the ends has a habit of smashing in, try a reverse end run, or a trick play around his wing. Watch the defensive halfbacks. Perhaps one of them can be easily led out of position…

[379] *Ann Arbor News*, 9/24/26, p 12

Remember how much time is left to play. Know the ability of your teammates. Believe in your plays. Above all, remember the two big principles—play for position and look over the defense.[380]

The only rule change instituted for the 1926 football season was designed to discourage passing. Much debate had occurred over the tendency of some teams to forget the running game and constantly pass. Yost liked the passing game and spoke strongly against any attempts to suppress it, but the Rules Committee was receptive to the idea of reform. The new rule provided that a team that threw two incomplete passes in a series of downs would be penalized five yards. Thus, an incomplete pass on first down and another on second or third down would incur the penalty. Yost thought it was all foolishness. In his opinion, the yards to be gained by passing would not be discouraged by a five-yard penalty.

## The Oklahoma A&M Game

Michigan's first game was against Oklahoma A&M, a team that traveled 1700 miles for this contest in Ann Arbor. Coached by a former Michigan All-American, John Maulbetsch, the Oklahomans created quite a stir by exiting the Ann Arbor train station adorned in identical white cowboy hats.

Friedman performed brilliantly in dismantling this team, playing at quarterback, at safety, and fielding all the punts. Interestingly, Michigan was penalized four times for throwing two incompletions in the same series. Yost would not be intimidated by this new rule. Michigan won handily, 42-3, but Yost showed his experimentation with the new players on the line by using six tackles and seven guards before it was all over.

---

[380] *Michigan Daily*, 9/28/26, p 15

## The Michigan State College Game

The next game on the schedule was the annual tussle with Michigan State College. The crowd was expected to approach 40,000, close to the largest to ever see a Michigan-MSC contest. It would be the inaugural game for the new Wolverine student cheering section.

Michigan won handily, 55-3. Credit was largely due to Friedman. He gained 216 yards through the line and on punt returns. When the State defenders zeroed in on Friedman in the backfield, Yost turned the passing over to the halfback who then threw passes to Friedman, one for a touchdown. On defense, Friedman made several crucial open field tackles. The *Daily* stated the obvious: "His brilliant running, his uncanny forward passing, and his handling of the team make him Michigan's strongest source of scoring power."[381]

Criticism of the quiescent Michigan crowd is not just a modern phenomenon. The *Daily* editors indicated their exasperation after this game.

> The cheering is to be delegated to a specific group of approximately 900 students while the rest of the crowd behaves after the fashion of the mythical gentlemen in the general store—they "sit and think."
>
> The men in the section last Saturday filled their part of the program with an enthusiasm that fully justified the belief of the students who originated the plan, that such a section would help Michigan's cheering. But the rest of the spectators were either overcome by admiration of the section, or else struck dumb by the score, for they maintained a silence that even touchdowns could not disturb.[382]

[381] *Michigan Daily*, 10/10/26, p 7
[382] *Michigan Daily*, 10/13/26, p 4

## The First Minnesota Game

The Minnesota Gophers would now travel to Ann Arbor for the first of two games to be played with Michigan in 1926. Michigan hadn't scheduled the same team twice in one season since splitting a pair with Cornell in 1894, and wouldn't ever do it again. How did it come about in 1926? Minnesota and Michigan had, to some degree, different problems. Minneapolis was a long trip by train, and many Big Ten schools were not interested in making the expedition. Illinois had played Minnesota regularly, but Illinois' coach, Bob Zuppke, was still angered by the injury to Grange that occurred in the 1924 game, and he refused to put the Gophers back on the schedule. Minnesota often had strong 11s so other Big Ten teams preferred to avoid them, but their eagerness to stay out of Minneapolis was nothing compared to the enthusiasm with which some schools kept Michigan off their schedule.

When the Big Ten schools met at the end of 1925 to set the schedules for the next year, Minnesota could only get three Big Ten games. No school would schedule a fourth even though four games with conference opponents were required by the Big Ten. The Gophers had games with Iowa, Wisconsin, and Michigan, but they couldn't entice anyone else. Chicago wasn't interested. Ohio State said it was too far. Northwestern, Indiana, and Purdue refused to pick up the challenge. Michigan had already scheduled Illinois, Wisconsin, Ohio State and Minnesota, but a bemused Yost watched the proceedings for a while, and when Northwestern and Indiana balked at playing Michigan, Yost offered to play the Gophers twice. Northwestern and Indiana promptly scheduled two games against each other as well, and the Big Ten scheduling problems were then solved for another year. So Minnesota would provide the opposition for Michigan's first and last Big Ten contests in 1926.

Yost promptly closed down his team's practices; he even went so far as to post assistant managers at the field gates to shoo away eager spectators. The day before the contest, the J. L. Hudson Company of Detroit took out a half page advertisement in the

*Michigan Daily* congratulating Coach Yost for his quarter century of service to the University of Michigan community.

> Your friends are mindful, Mr. Yost, of the fact that it is twenty-five years ago this fall since you came to the campus of our beloved University of Michigan. Football history, fame and success have been written large since then as proof of your capable leadership.
>
> But great as have been your achievements in the realm of the gridiron, it is your influence in the lives of Michigan men, your ideals of ethics in sportsmanship, and your contributions to intercollegiate athletics that have won for you the admiration and friendship of millions.[383]

Michigan effectively throttled the Gophers in this initial meeting for a 20-0 victory. Friedman completed five of 14 passes for 164 yards, while Minnesota could only manage one completion the whole game. Michigan's third touchdown clinched this game and was the result of classic deception by Yost. In the two previous games, both scouted by Minnesota, the halfback, George Rich, took the ball from center on several occasions and pitched it to Friedman, who threw the ball downfield. In this game, however, the other halfback circled around behind Friedman, grabbed the ball from his outstretched passing arm, and followed a wall of blockers past all the surprised Minnesotans for a 42-yard touchdown scamper.

At this point in the season, Yost's charges had scored 117 points to 6 for the opposition. Michigan's goal line hadn't been crossed since 1924.

## The Illinois Game

Illinois and Zuppke were next due in Ann Arbor for the first time since 1922. Illinois boasted a replacement for Red Grange at halfback by the name of Frosty Peters. Peters had transferred from Montana State where, on its freshman team, he had converted 17

---

dropkick field goals in one game, accounting for 51 of his team's 64 points. Such prowess worried the Michigan camp since the previous year's game had been a very close Michigan victory, 3-0. Zuppke, however, had complained all week about the injuries his team had suffered, which prompted the *Ann Arbor News* to sarcastically suggest the Illini would show up in an ambulance train.

Yost cautioned Michigan adherents who already considered their team invincible.

> When one looks at the Michigan football schedule for 1926, he will readily realize that it was not arranged for the purpose of winning a Conference championship. Last Saturday we played Minnesota, tomorrow we meet Illinois and then follow with the U.S. Navy, Wisconsin, Ohio State, and a return engagement with Minnesota.
>
> The schedule has been arranged to have high class games and strong opposition, where one's mettle is tested— games in which all are interested.[384]

Every inch of Ferry Field was filled with 48,000 fans for this October encounter. The ticket office was mobbed with requests and estimated that 50,000 people were turned away. According to the *Ann Arbor News*, the ticket manager had only one mantra: "Yes, we have no tickets."[385]

The *Daily* called the contest "one of the greatest ever staged on Ferry Field."[386] Late in the second quarter, the game was scoreless with the two teams engaged in a classic punting dual. Finally, Louis Gilbert, Michigan's 157-pound halfback and punter, dropped a perfect ball that was downed at the Illinois one-foot line. Illinois punted out to their own 40-yard line, but Gilbert, also one of Michigan's punt returners, ran the ball back to the 25. Friedman then threw a 15-yard pass to the talented Gilbert, but the offense

---

[384] *Ann Arbor News*, 10/22/26, p 14
[385] *Ann Arbor News*, 10/21/26, p 14
[386] *Michigan Daily*, 10/24/26, p 1

stalled, and just before the half, Friedman kicked a 15-yard field goal for a 3-0 lead.

At the beginning of the fourth quarter, Friedman kicked another field goal to make it 6-0. Finally, late in the fourth quarter, Michigan put the game out of reach by intercepting a pass at the Illinois 23. A perfect throw from Friedman to Oosterbaan took the ball to the two. From there, the fullback took it over for the score, and the final was 13-0. Illinois's heralded halfback, Frosty Peters, was throttled most of the game and missed three field goal attempts. Michigan's goal line remained untouched.

Football euphoria once more swept the Ann Arbor campus. Yost, the genius, had again put an awesome contingent on the gridiron. The next game was the return engagement with Navy, this time in Baltimore.

## The Navy Game

A pleased Yost gave the football team Monday off after the challenging Illinois contest. Thus, Tuesday and Wednesday were the only practice days. Yost closed the sessions while assistants dealt with pestering sportswriters crammed at the gates to the field. The team had no practice Thursday because they were scheduled to leave Ann Arbor at 3:00 P.M., bound for Washington, D.C., where they were expected to arrive Friday morning.

Yost made an exception to his usual travel procedures and allowed an enterprising *Michigan Daily* reporter to join the team for this trip. The reporter's accounts give a vivid impression of what it must have been like to shepherd a young band of Wolverine players across a third of a continent.

The budding journalist initially wrote that the environment was just like a student train except that, with the coaches around, "the fire axe remains in its proper place and the Pullman towels are stolen by the half dozen instead of the gross."[387] At one point, "several of the players were seen studying diligently, but upon closer observa-

---

[387] *Michigan Daily*, 10/29/26, p 7

tion we found they were just trying to create an impression."[388] One player was reading "Madame X" and another perusing a pamphlet entitled, "Artist and Models." More observations followed:

> During the short stop over at Detroit, Bennie Oosterbaan spent his time making the acquaintance of the cigar counter attendant. She was a rare pulchritude, with a figure of the Russian design. We were unable to detect the conversation, but, whatever it was, the woman professed keen interest in the garrulous college boy. In more than one way, Oosterbaan is fast regaining his all-American form.
>
> Bo Molenda felt out of place on the train today and insisted that he be allowed to have a workout in the car. On one line plunge down the aisle, he made nine seats. On another occasion he was stopped for no gain when Flora pushed his suitcase out into the aisle…Molenda was penalized two seats on the play for swearing. Wieman ruled that the train was in motion and advanced the ball in Molenda's favor…The practice was brought to an abrupt end when Mr. Pullman rose in anger and shouted impetuously, "Say, what do you think this is—a fraternity house party?"
>
> Then dinner was announced: With Molenda leading the interference, Oosterbaan, Flora, and Weber were the outstanding men in the rush that followed. Oosterbaan exchanged three or four plates before he found one of the right proportion, apologizing for his actions by saying, "I always play for big steaks."[389]

Yost had arranged for the Michigan football team to meet the President of the United States, Calvin Coolidge, on Friday morning. The *Daily* recorded:

---

[388] *Michigan Daily*, 10/29/26, p 7
[389] *Michigan Daily*, 10/29/26, p 7

The major part of an hour was spent in discussing the various ways of shaking hands with the President and what would be appropriate to ask Calvin in the short interview. Truskowski brought his political science text and read a short sketch on the powers of the President. Oosterbaan failed to see where that could be of any interest to the President and said that he would ask Cal if those fish stories of his were true…Molenda said he would ask Cal to speak at his graduation, but he would set no definite date.[390]

At one point, the players got a bit rambunctious, so Yost had to take action:

Coach Yost segregated the Wolverines, putting the high strung halfbacks and ends in the rear car and all the linemen in the first coach. The linemen claimed the right to be called high strung, but Yost settled the dispute by sitting with the backfield men.[391]

Perhaps Yost's greatest achievement was not the Big Ten titles or the building of Michigan Stadium. Maybe it was chaperoning these "Champions of the West" on road trips. Possibly this bit of journalism explains why Minnesota had trouble enticing coaches to make the long trip to Minneapolis.

In any case, Michigan's football team was met at 7:00 A.M. Friday morning at Washington DC's Union Station by the local alumni club, which sponsored an expansive breakfast. The team then spent three hours touring sights in Washington before heading to the White House for its meeting with the President. However, President Coolidge was occupied and the players were kept waiting for an hour before they were whisked through in record time. One of the Wolverines described Coolidge, quickly shaking hands as the players passed, as resembling a "railroad semaphore,"[392] pumping

[390] *Michigan Daily*, 10/29/26, p 7
[391] *Michigan Daily*, 10/30/26, p 6
[392] *Michigan Daily*, 10/30/26, p 1

his hand up and down. Despite the preparation en route, no one was allowed to ask the President a single question.

After this encounter at the White House, the team was taken back to Union Station from where it caught a train to Baltimore. On arrival, the players were taken to the municipal stadium for a light work-out and a reminder that there was still a football game to be played.

The team had been invited to spend Friday night as guests of the Naval Academy so they were then bussed from Baltimore to Annapolis. They arrived at Bancroft Hall, then the world's largest dormitory, to a thundering cheer from the assembled Midshipmen. However, not all the cadets were present. As the Michigan buses snaked their way around the Academy campus, the Michigan players noted that the Navy team, ominously, was under lights, still practicing.

Perhaps only then did this great Michigan team focus on the game at hand. Navy was undefeated and had beaten Drake, Purdue, Colgate, and Princeton. Navy's coach issued this defiant statement: "The Naval Academy is going into the Michigan game to win and we will be disappointed if we should lose by a single point. We will not be satisfied with a 'moral victory.'"[393] Needless to say, the academy team had been deeply embarrassed by the defeat in Ann Arbor the year before. While Michigan was traveling this time, the Midshipmen were vigorously preparing.

Michigan's much anticipated return to the East Coast, after an absence of many years, was celebrated with a national banquet for alumni in Philadelphia on the Friday night before the game. Special trains had been chartered from Detroit, Ann Arbor, Chicago, Minneapolis, Cleveland, Toledo and Pittsburgh. Thousands attended. Alumni present represented 50 consecutive graduating classes from 1875 to 1925, with the oldest from the class of 1862. The famous "locomotive" cheer and the song, "I Want to Go Back to Michigan," united all the attendees who came from virtually every state in the

---

[393] *Ann Arbor News*, 10/30/26, p 12

union. The throng was addressed by President Little and also the President of the Alumni Association, who said:

> While Michigan is not one of the 13 colonies of this nation, it is the pioneer in many of the great movements of this country. We are particularly proud of the fact that our University was the pioneer in admitting women to co-educational rank among its students. Today they are found pursuing every avenue of study at the University.[394]

On Saturday, before the game, the Jewish Athletic Association of Baltimore had arranged to honor Friedman. As the Michigan Band played "The Victors," the president of the association crossed the field and "presented Friedman with a bronze bass relief of a football player in a charging position."[395]

This event was undoubtedly the highlight of the day for Michigan's quarterback as this disappointing game would prevent another Michigan national championship. Navy completely shut down the Wolverines. Oosterbaan was harassed all over the field, and Friedman was put under fierce pressure in the backfield. To make matters worse, Friedman wrenched his knee in the second quarter. While he was able to return to the game, his mobility was clearly impaired. Michigan completed only six of 29 pass attempts.

On offense, Navy running backs shredded the Michigan line. Even so, it was 0-0 at the half, but Navy got a field goal in the third quarter to make it 3-0. In the fourth, the Midshipmen intercepted Friedman at the 50-yard line and launched a brutal running attack that ripped through the Michigan defense to the goal for a 10-0 lead. It was the first time a team had crossed the Wolverine goal line since the last game of 1924, and it was also the first time Michigan had been held scoreless since the 0-0 tie at the Vanderbilt stadium dedication game.

Jubilant Middies ran wild over the playing field after the game.

[394] *Ann Arbor News*, 10/30/26, p 1
[395] *Michigan Daily*, 10/30/26, p 1

They ripped up both goalposts and carried them over to the Michigan stands where they sang their song of victory.

No doubt the Wolverines had a much quieter trip back to Michigan. The *Daily*'s correspondent sent no reports about the train ride home, but once back in Ann Arbor he filed a final dispatch:

> The Wolverines practiced two days, Tuesday and Wednesday, in which they prepared for the Navy attack. Thursday we were riding a freight to Washington, and on Friday afternoon the men were sent through a public exhibition in Municipal Stadium. Neither the coaches nor the players were prepared for a real game…
>
> Too much sightseeing? Decidedly, too much! The Michigan football team was taken on a sightseeing tour, one of the minor attractions being the Michigan-Navy football game…[396]

The *Ann Arbor News* took a more philosophical approach.

> There is something almost awe-inspiring about a dignified defeat…It's a great team, the kind of team that should represent Michigan—one that plays clean and fairly, putting its soul into the game, accepting victory with a smile and defeat with a grin. Here's hoping that Michigan will always have such teams—teams that win most of the time, but can lose without a whimper when fate is unkind.[397]

## The Wisconsin Game

A grim group of Wolverines set to work on Monday. Michigan was undefeated in the Big Ten, but had Wisconsin in Ann Arbor and trips to Ohio State and Minneapolis ahead of them. Practices were closed. Yost shook up his line after the defeat, starting a new tackle and guard. Very uncharacteristically for him in the middle

---

[396] *Michigan Daily*, 11/2/26, p 7
[397] *Ann Arbor News*, 11/2/26, p 4

of a season, he also pulled his starting center and tried new men at that crucial position. Michigan's line had not prevented the fierce rush put on Friedman, nor had it stopped the Navy running game. It had failed on both sides of the ball.

Ohio State was undefeated, and had arranged an open date before the Michigan game. Rumor swept the Ann Arbor campus that the whole Buckeye team was coming up to scout the game with Wisconsin. The *Daily* wrote that it showed "how anxious they are down there to see a real football game."[398] However, the next question raised was how in the world they had gotten tickets, since the Wisconsin game had been sold out for two months, and the ticket office had turned away thousands of unhappy Michigan fans. The athletic department finally had to issue a statement that there was no truth to the claim that the entire Buckeye team was coming. Ohio State was sending only their head coach and two assistants.

Wisconsin and Coach Little were returning to Ann Arbor for the first time since Little had taken over the Badger football program. Unfortunately for him, the Badgers ran into a hornet's nest of angry Wolverines. Friedman had recovered from his knee injury and played a great game, completing nine of 17 passes for 157 yards. Michigan won easily, 37-0. The home team had 17 first downs and 315 total yards on offense, while the Badgers could manage only three first downs and 63 total yards. It was the last chance for the school in Madison. They would never defeat a Yost-coached team.

This game was the last one to be played on Ferry Field. The stadium had been the home of the Wolverines since 1906, but there was no official recognition of this historic event that day. The hole was already being dug for the new stadium on the hill to the southwest, and Michigan fans filed out of the old stadium with little nostalgia. They were ready for a modern arena in Ann Arbor.

The editors at the *Daily* revealed little affection for Ferry Field, mostly because students were always in the endzone seats. In a column entitled, "Farewell East Stands," they wrote:

---

[398] *Michigan Daily*, 11/4/26, p 4

It was with a feeling of deep regret that we left the dear
old East stands for the last time yesterday. As we looked
back over the years spent in that memory-filled place, it
is with a catch in our throat. We can still picture that
game back in 1925 when the ball was punted back to the
fence at our end of the field, and a Michigan player came
down to carry it back. What a thrill it was to actually see
one of the members of our team in action![399]

They further noted that if the athletic department would
provide them with a plan for the new stadium, the *Daily* would
determine ahead of time just where the poorest seats were so the
athletic department would know where to put the student body.

## The Ohio State Game

Now the Wolverines would travel to Columbus. It was the 23rd
time the two teams had played and the ninth time the two coaches
had faced each other. Ohio State's captain, Marty Karow, was from
Cleveland, and his high school team had once played against Ben
Friedman's team, so the two captains were facing each other for
the fourth time. Ohio State had proclaimed the day Homecoming
and fitted the great horseshoe with temporary seats to attract the
largest crowd ever to see a game in America, 90,000. If all this was
not enough, both Michigan and Ohio State were undefeated in the
Big Ten. The game could well be for the championship.

Yost put his team through a grueling week of practices on Ferry
Field. The old coach was particularly irritated by two pictures in the
*Detroit Free Press* following the Wisconsin game. The photographs
were of two of the Michigan touchdowns, but in each case, two
Wisconsin defenders were shown still standing when the goal was
crossed. Yost wanted to know who had missed their blocks and how
it had happened that these opponents were left upright.

Several hundred students crowded the train station to send off

[399] *Michigan Daily*, 11/7/26, p 4

the 35 players who would represent Michigan in this legendary clash. Arriving in Columbus, the Wolverine contingent "found a city which has gone football mad,[400] all Ohio being wild with aspirations to eliminate the Wolverines from the conference championship race."[401] "Anyone that has been in town for half an hour cannot help but be inspired with the enthusiasm which pervades the entire city and which will be appeased only by Wolverine blood."[402] There were no accommodations anywhere in Columbus, and thousands of fans slept in their cars overnight. All who witnessed this event felt there was more enthusiasm and more anticipation than for the dedication game in 1922.

Before an official crowd of 90,411, the Buckeyes sent their fans into a frenzy by taking a 10-0 lead in the first quarter. However, the second quarter was all Michigan's. Friedman threw a perfect 33-yard strike to Oosterbaan to put the ball at the OSU 12. Faking a field goal, Friedman found Oosterbaan again, who then made a spectacular catch for the touchdown. Late in the second quarter, Yost confounded the crowd by reversing the Benny-to-Bennie combination. Oosterbaan threw a perfect strike to Freidman that gained 20 yards and set up a field goal attempt with 30 seconds left in the half. Friedman, from an awkward angle, connected on a 43-yard effort, and this historic contest was tied.

Late in the third quarter, Michigan got the break they needed. The Buckeyes fumbled on the 6-yard line, and Michigan recovered. Three running plays netted only four yards, but on fourth down Friedman passed to his halfback for the touchdown. Friedman drilled the point after for a 17-10 lead.

Ohio State, however, was not to be denied. Late in the fourth quarter, the Buckeyes launched a drive from their own 31-yard line. Everyone who witnessed this 69-yard effort said it was an awesome performance. Pounding the Michigan line again and again, the Buckeyes finally scored with three minutes left to make it 17-16.

[400] *Ann Arbor News*, 11/12/26, p12
[401] *Michigan Daily*, 11/13/26, p 1
[402] *Ann Arbor News*, 11/12/26, p12

However, breaking the hearts of the home crowd, OSU's drop kick specialist missed the extra point.

Incredible as it may seem to the modern fan, Yost elected to kick off to the scarlet and gray after this score. The final frantic Buckeye drive was stopped when Friedman intercepted a pass at the Michigan 38-yard line. Yost would never lose in Ohio State's great stadium.

The *Daily* proclaimed the heroes.

> The two Bennies unquestionably played the best games of their careers. Oosterbaan was every place Saturday; on the offense he ran with the ball, threw forward passes and was a mighty figure on the receiving end. Defensively, he was stronger than he has ever been…

> Friedman is the hero of the battle. As one coach put it, "There was only one point difference between the two teams, and that difference is personified in Friedman. Friedman never had better accuracy in his passing, two of his passes ending in Michigan touchdowns. He place kicked for the extra point after each touchdown and made the greatest individual play of the game when he place kicked from the 43 yard line to tie the score at the end of the first half."

> Friedman also was on the receiving end of all the OSU punts—and their punt coverage was incredible. It seemed that when the ball came down, the whole OSU team was there to greet it.[403]

---

[403] *Michigan Daily*, 11/16/26, p 7

## The Second Minnesota Game

There was only one game remaining between Michigan and its fourth Big Ten championship in the five-year span that led to the building of Michigan Stadium. Since losing to Michigan, the Minnesota Golden Gophers had beaten Wisconsin, 16-10, Iowa, 41-0, Wabash, 76-0, and Butler, 81-0. This group that had been shunned by the other Big Ten teams could capture a share of the conference championship by defeating the Wolverines.

Michigan, on the other hand, had just played a very grueling road game against their primary rival and had to travel another 800 miles from Ann Arbor for this contest. Team practices were rugged all week. On Wednesday, Friedman, the quarterback, spent the whole session fielding punts and then placekicking field goals from every angle from 15 to 45 yards. The same day, Yost had the whole team practice scooping up fumbles and running with the ball.

Extra seats had been added to Minnesota's new stadium to bring capacity to 58,500. Minneapolis had never seen such a gathering. Tickets for the game, which had a face value of $2.50, were being scalped "by the yard:" $10 for the 10-yard line, $50 for the 50.

Three days of rain, freezing temperatures, and two inches of snow turned the Big Ten's most northern gridiron into a skating rink. The field had been covered with three feet of straw earlier in the week, and Yost had actually joined the workmen in removing it Friday afternoon. The university employed 100 men to clear snow from the stadium seats. A high of 25 degrees was expected for the game.

On this icy but clear day, Minnesota launched a 70-yard drive in the second quarter for a score, but they missed the point after. Michigan's offense just could not get started. Friedman had a terrible day at quarterback, completing just two of 11 attempts and throwing three interceptions, but again and again the Wolverine defense kept Minnesota from adding to their six points. Finally, in the fourth quarter, with Minnesota driving once again, a pitched ball was fumbled at the Michigan 40-yard line. Oosterbaan scooped up the loose pigskin and scooted 60 yards untouched for the touchdown. Friedman, now in a position similar to his Buckeye opponent the week before, coolly walked out and drilled the extra point for a 7-6 lead. A final, furious Minnesota drive was thwarted at the Michigan 25-yard line when Friedman pulled down an interception.

Yost and Michigan had done it again. Another Big Ten title would reside in Ann Arbor, the fourth in five glorious years. For the only time in its colorful history, the Little Brown Jug had been won twice in the same year. No one knew it at the time, but as Fielding Yost victoriously walked off this frozen field in Minneapolis, it would be the last time this legend would coach a Michigan 11.

The returning team was mobbed at the train station, but this time the celebrating students crashed the movie theatre on State Street, and the resulting melee was only broken up when the Ann Arbor police appeared with tear gas. The movie soon to be at the theatre was, "The Quarterback, officially dedicated to America's most beloved gridiron Coach, Michigan's Fielding H. Yost, who personally supervised and directed."[404]

Basking in the glory of this victory, the *Detroit Free Press* gave all honors to Yost.

> Some college activity must take first place, and we are glad that for a brief period each fall, football holds that place of honor. We can think of no activity more worthy of precedence. The ideals of manhood and sportsmanship it instills extend far beyond the membership of the teams and squads. They permeate whole student bodies and make for standards of sportsmanship and honor which are as valuable a part of a college man's education as any book learning. At Ann Arbor the influence of Mr. Yost for good is absolutely invaluable. We do not hesitate to say that he is today the biggest single moral force on

---

[404] *Ann Arbor News*, 11/21/26 p 3

campus and is one of the university's big assets. He has given many a blundering boy new conceptions of the meaning of manhood and, consequently, a timely boost along the way he ought to go.[405]

A few days later, the team met and elected Bennie Oosterbaan captain for 1927. Unbelievable as it may seem, Oosterbaan had played on the 1925 and 1926 football teams, the 1926 basketball team, and the 1926 baseball team. All had won Big Ten championships. The 1927 basketball team would also win the title with Oosterbaan named to the all-Conference first team. A more remarkable athlete has probably never resided in Ann Arbor.

The *Michigan Daily* celebrated the "last pass" from Benny-to-Bennie, the captain of the 1926 team giving the "baton of leadership"[406] to the captain of 1927. The great Friedman would make everybody's All-American team. He had several offers to leave school and play professional ball as Grange had done the year before, but he couldn't be tempted. "Break faith with the Old Man and with Michigan? Never. Whatever I accomplished as a football player, I owe to the Old Man."[407] He went on to say that his greatest regret upon graduating from Michigan would be parting with Coach Yost. (After he graduated, Friedman did play professionally. He was recognized as the NFL's first great passing quarterback, leading the league in touchdown passes for four consecutive years, from 1927 to 1930. His career total of 66 touchdown passes would be an NFL record until later surpassed in 1944. In 1928, he led the league in both rushing and passing for touchdowns, a feat never duplicated.) Yost, for his part, would say that Friedman was the best quarterback he had ever seen play the game: "I have never seen a better man under fire or a better field general than Friedman."[408]

Big Ten attendance in 1926 broke all records. Michigan again led the conference with the largest number of spectators at all

[405] *Ann Arbor News*, 11/21/26, p 4
[406] *Michigan Daily*, 11/24/26, p 7
[407] *Ann Arbor News*, 11/25/26, p 1
[408] Board in Control, Box 41, Articles by Fielding H. Yost, Book #4, interview by Grantland Rice

304 • THE BIG HOUSE

games, nearly 400,000. But the Wolverines didn't lead in home attendance; Chicago did, with 235,000 fans, and Illinois was second, with 225,000. Yost found this reality most intolerable, and he was now about to remedy it.

Could the "Grand Old Man" win a Big Ten title *and* build America's greatest stadium? No doubt he could. And he did.

# Chapter 11

# "Your Stadium is Certainly a Masterpiece"

Fielding H. Yost would now apply all the experience he gained in building the field house to the stadium project. Within a few days of Regent approval for the stadium, Yost obtained the necessary assertion from the state that income from the stadium bonds would be tax free to the holder. This would be true, said Michigan's attorney general, if title to the bonds was held by the Board in Control of Athletics and conveyed to the Board of Regents of the university when retired. This was important since the bonds could then offer a three percent interest rate instead of a higher amount, leading to marked savings for the athletic department over time. Yost was convinced, though, that the primary attraction to bondholders would be preferential seating in the new stadium, not the investment potential of the offering.

The athletic files of May 1926 are filled with letters from Yost about the approved stadium project. He wanted no further time wasted and was eager to have ground broken in the summer of 1926, with an official stadium dedication in 1927. A letter dated May 3, 1926, written to Bernard Green of Osborn Engineering, covered in great detail the required depth of the excavation, the drainage that would be necessary, the final elevation of the seating, and even the possibility of temporary seats for major games. Yost clearly had a great command of the construction demands.

The Board in Control of Athletics named Professor Aigler of the law school, Professor Johnston of the engineering school, and Yost to the Stadium Building Committee. These three men would have the authority to select the engineering company for the building of the stadium and to let all contracts. This approach greatly streamlined the decision-making process. By mid-July, this trio had selected the primary builder: Osborn Engineering of Cleveland, Ohio. No amount of research will change this fact for Wolverine adherents. Michigan Stadium was indeed built by a company from Ohio, albeit with Bernard Green, a Michigan graduate, as chief executive officer.

Sometime in late June 1926, test borings were drilled at the site to determine the soil content and check for water. Two sites were chosen where the south end of the field would lay, two at the north end, and one in the center. The soil was mostly clay, sand and gravel, and three of these probes were completely dry. One found "very little water," and another found enough water to "fill up about 10 feet of the hole."[409] Yost considered these "excellent results. Practically no water and principally sand and gravel were found in these pits."[410] This would prove to be unwarranted optimism.

An old Ann Arbor alderman urged caution. He said he knew there was much ground water in that vicinity. He asserted that years earlier the university had taken all of their water from a spring in the area and had pumped it to a water tower that stood near central campus.

The general plan for stadium construction submitted by Osborn Engineering would follow that of the Los Angeles Coliseum. The site would be excavated down to the field level, and dirt would be piled up around the sides and then compacted around cement piers to support a concrete superstructure for seating. Yost, looking to the future, insisted that these piers have the strength to support a second deck someday.

By late June, newspapers were running pictures of Michigan's

---

[409] Board in Control, Box 8, folder July 1926 (2)
[410] Board in Control, Box 8, folder July 1926 (1)

proposed oval showing that spectators would enter over the top on the north, west, and south sides and through portals only on the east side. Most newspapers showed a small cut in the middle of the east stand, which would be the "players' entrance."[411]

The first printed mention of Michigan Stadium's famous tunnel in the athletic files is contained in a letter dated June 29, 1926, from Osborn Engineering. "While our plans are not as yet developed for the stadium structure, it is our conception that some form of tunnel or field entrance will be used…extending eastward for a short distance."[412]

This idea was confirmed in a letter from Yost to Osborn Engineering dated July 20, 1926. "The size of the tunnel to the stadium should be on an average 12 feet high, 16 feet wide, and approximately 260 feet long, and was to be located approximately in the center of the east side of the stadium."[413] Where did this concept originate? Of course, the players had to enter somewhere, and the east side, the open side of the hill, was the one area where much of the excavated earth would be piled. From a construction standpoint, it was no doubt quite logical to locate an entry tunnel in this location. At the University's Bentley Historical Library, the Board in Control's Box #46 contains the actual notebook that Yost used to compile information on other stadiums. It boasts beautiful black and white photographs of stadiums at numerous schools including Illinois, California, Pittsburgh, Pennsylvania, and Yale, but in the center portion of the notebook are several pictures of ancient Roman coliseums.

The oldest existing amphitheater in the world is the 20,000 seat arena excavated at Pompeii in Italy. Built in 80 B.C., it is a microcosm of Michigan Stadium with seats resting on the ground, and a tunnel that extends from the outside to the floor of the arena. The tunnel lies in the short axis of the stadium, not the long, but it was no doubt used for processions that would line up outside and enter

---

[410] *Cleveland News*, 6/24/26, p 12
[412] Board in Control, Box 8, June 1926 (2)
[413] Board in Control, Box 8, July 1926 (3)

the arena through the portal, much as the Michigan Band enters Michigan Stadium today. Surviving Roman coliseums in other cities often contain the same kind of entrance. Could Michigan's tunnel have originated from this concept? There is no definite confirmation, but sources do state, and his notebook confirms, that Yost studied ancient arenas when he proposed the design for Michigan's stadium.

By late July 1926, Yost was ready to accept bids and award a contract for excavation. However, there were some unhappy contractors in the state of Michigan. A sharp letter was addressed to the Board in Control of Athletics in late August 1926, from the Builders and Traders Exchange of Detroit.

*The tunnel in the stadium at Pompeii, Italy*

The Detroit group was not happy that an Ohio company had been selected for construction of the stadium. Even more disconcerting, the group couldn't obtain any information from Osborn Engineering about the project and were concerned they weren't being fairly considered in the bidding process. Their desire to be involved,

> most graciously offered due to the great number of worthy alumni engaged in the building industry, has been abruptly and discourteously disregarded by the Osborn Engineering Company of Cleveland, Ohio...We not

only cannot get your plans and specifications, but we can get no information whatever from this Organization, apparently in complete control of the construction of your operation. We regret this situation exceedingly and trust that it may be remedied to the extent of giving the building industry of Detroit at least an equal show with the wishes and opinions of an Engineering Organization unrelated in any way to the principles and precepts established by the builders of the State of Michigan.

We desire to place this information before you, believing that you are exceedingly anxious to avoid the appearance of a slight to a community of men sincerely engaged in furthering the welfare of the Athletic Association of the University of Michigan.[414]

No doubt this letter was not happily received by Yost. He had already obtained estimates for the excavation of the stadium site and a company from Cleveland put forth the low bid at $175,600. Some Michigan contractors wanted as much as $275,000 for the job, but R. A. Mercier of Detroit bid $185,000. Undoubtedly, some politics were involved here. Overnight, Mercier's company adjusted its bid $10,000 so that it came in $600 less than the Cleveland outfit. The athletic department then announced on August 25, shortly after receiving the letter from the disgruntled Detroit builders, that Mercier of Detroit had won the contract. Mercier would live to regret it.

Excavation began immediately, but no official groundbreaking ceremony was announced. Yost, just happy to have finally won his stadium for Michigan, would initially proceed with little fanfare. By August 27, Mercier had several smoking steam shovels on the job. On September 2, the *Ann Arbor News* ominously reported that an "abundantly flowing spring"[415] had been found. On October 20, the *News* published a photograph of the excavation showing

[414] Board in Control, Box 8, August 1926 (2)
[415] *Ann Arbor News*, 9/2/26, p 1

five of the ten steam shovels hard at work. The dirt piled on the east side of the excavation already made quite a dike with a cut in the center where the tunnel would be.

However, early November presented a serious problem. Water was everywhere. As the excavation deepened, more and more flow occurred. Engineers estimated that 1,000,000 gallons a day were pouring over the construction site. At one point, a flood of water broke through the sides of a ditch and nearly drowned several workers. The main drainage ditch for the stadium, which was to run east and west under the 50-yard line and out of the stadium under the tunnel, caved in again and again from the water pressure. For that reason, it was impossible to lay the necessary drainage tile. Work came to a halt.

Osborn Engineering wrote a letter to Mercier indicating that the excavation was much behind schedule and that they felt he was "operating with considerable lack of system."[416] Since the main drain could not be laid, water poured all over the excavation site. Osborn

*Stadium excavation with earthen dike on the east side. Note the cut in the dike where the tunnel lies*

Photo courtesy of Bentley Historical Library

---

[416] Board in Control, Box 8, October 1926 (3)

wrote Mercier that they knew he had encountered quicksand and that it had greatly delayed his progress, but they emphasized that Mercier should focus all resources on laying the main drain to solve the water problem before attempting further excavation. By this time, Mercier had so many water pumps running that he couldn't find any more in the private market. Ultimately, he borrowed some from the Ann Arbor Fire Department.

By early December, the whole project was a mess. Quicksand was preventing the placement of some of the concrete support pillars, and the main drainage tile had still not been laid. A letter from Osborn Engineering to Yost indicated that they had recommended more borings of the site the previous summer, but that Yost had opposed the suggestion. They were "now faced with a condition which indicates water underlying the stadium site over at least a considerable portion of it and standing at a level approximately 9 feet higher than the proposed level of the playing field." Further studies have shown "a large volume of water at lower levels in the ground and under a sufficient head to cause it, when released, to rise to levels higher than the proposed level of the playing field… We may have a very serious problem before us if we are going to maintain the Stadium at the levels planned."[417] If water indeed was pouring out from under the stadium site, the whole project might have to be abandoned.

One can only imagine the anxiety Yost must have experienced at this juncture. Keep in mind that all this concern about water at the site occurred in November, when the coach's Michigan squad was defeating Wisconsin, Ohio State and Minnesota to bring another Big Ten football title to Ann Arbor. Each day that passed brought Yost more bad news from the construction site and it must have distracted from his game preparation. All through November, engineers studied the site and tried to decide how to proceed. Finally, in early December, it was agreed to try to sink several wells through the floor of the stadium. If the water was coming primarily from

---

[417] Board in Control, Box 9, December 1926 (3)

above the area already excavated, it would be caught in the wells from which it could be pumped and the stadium floor would dry. If the water was coming from underneath the site, the wells would fill, drainage would be hopeless, and the effort might have to be abandoned. No doubt a very worried Yost awaited the verdict.

A dry site was chosen, and a well was dug 30 feet below the surface of the proposed field. Water on the floor of the excavation was directed into the well from which it could be pumped outside. To the relief of many people, not the least of whom was Fielding H. Yost, the stadium floor slowly started drying. Finally, the trench could be dug for the four-foot drainage tile that would lead from the stadium site, connect with city of Ann Arbor drainage, and eventually empty into the Huron River. The water problem had been resolved. (When the floor of Michigan Stadium was lowered several feet in 1991, water again became a problem. In fact, the water table around Michigan Stadium today lies about 18 inches above the level of the field. Pumps are in place and in regular use to keep the flooding at bay).

The Detroit excavator, Mercier, would face a very serious financial constraint because of all the delays and the extra work required. It would lead to a conflict with the athletic department that would

Photo courtesy of Bentley Historical Library

*Excavation of Michigan Stadium*

last for a long time after the stadium was completed. Mercier claimed that the borings from the summer of 1926 "in no way indicate the true soil conditions which I have encountered"[418] and, for that reason, his compensation should be significantly increased. (Mercier's losses were considerable, but there is no confirmation to be found in the contemporary newspapers or the athletic files of the often repeated Ann Arbor legend that the quicksand under Michigan Stadium swallowed a whole steam shovel.)

The *Michigan Daily* had much fun with Yost's miserable predicament. In late November, an editorial was entitled, "Drowning Out Football."

> Digging Michigan's new stadium is just one lake after another in the opinion of the contractors. Before they had gone a dozen feet they struck water and every time they sink a shaft now it turns into a well. The new stadium will be built in the center of this beautiful expanse of water, it has been decided. Finding it impossible to drain the lake, the contractors will put in floating goal posts and build the stands on rafts.
>
> A new style of football will be necessary next year…The team will wear water wings instead of shoulder pads…The officials will go around in row boats…Varsity football men are to train under the direction of the swimming coach next fall.[419]

Two days later, the editors jokingly announced that the whole project was a misunderstanding. The new stadium was for hockey, not football. No attempt would be made to drain off the water and a perfect frozen lake would exist all winter. Stadium bondholders might find their prime seats a bit chilly in January, but the athletic department could promise a competitive hockey team. In the spring and summer, the new arena would be used by Michigan's racing crew.

Finally, on December 4, a day set aside for visits by prospective

[418] Board in Control, Box 9, December 1926 (2)
[419] *Michigan Daily*, 11/27/26, p 4

students, the *Daily* advised, "You must really see our new football stadium. There's nothing like it this side of Venice."[420] It is hard to imagine Coach Yost finding much humor in these remarks.

In early August, the prospectus for the bond offering was mailed. It reviewed the tremendous growth in demand for Michigan football tickets, included a description of the stadium site and the type of construction, and predicted athletic department earnings to exceed $400,000 per year. The proposal indicated that the income from the sale would be used to purchase more land for athletic purposes and for the new stadium, but also for the creation of a new intramural building on campus. The athletic department would guarantee redemption of one-twentieth of the bonds each year so that the whole issue would be paid off in 20 years. Owners of the bonds would be permitted to make application each year for 10 years, from 1927 to 1936, at regular prices, for a "specially reserved section of the stadium."

> This privilege means that any Alumnus, former student, or citizen of the State of Michigan, may make a perfectly safe investment, exempt from taxation in Michigan, at a satisfactory yield, and at the same time be sure of seats at all football games played by the University team in Ann Arbor for the next 10 years.[421]

Only two bonds could be purchased by any one person, but the prospectus stated the bonds would go quickly.

> While $1,500,000 is to be raised through the sale of Stadium Bonds, there are only 3000 bonds to be purchased and these are reasonably certain to be taken within a very short time. You are one of 63,000 Alumni and former students to receive a Subscription Blank and an opportunity, not only to help your University, but also to secure advantages and privileges for yourself. If only 10 per cent of Alumni and former students alone,

[420] *Michigan Daily*, 12/4/26, p 4
[421] Board in Control, Box 46, folder: Osborn

to say nothing of other citizens of the State of Michigan, subscribe, there will still be more than twice as many applicants for Bonds as can possibly be accommodated. This means that you should not delay in subscribing…

Michigan is counting on the aid of her Alumni and friends throughout the country. Michigan is not asking for gifts, but merely for small loans for which a substantial return is assured. Other Universities, most of them, in fact, have built stadia through Alumni gifts—ours will be made to pay for itself out of the increased earnings made possible by the additional seats, provided you help us first with your loans to build the new stadium.[422]

In early August 1926, initial mailing of the prospectus went to 65,000 alumni addresses. Yost's dear friend, and the man who hired him at Michigan, Charles Baird of Kansas City, wanted bond number one; Yost duly reserved it for him.

Shortly after the mailing, Yost left Ann Arbor, but asked his assistants to keep him informed about bond sales. The athletic files contain a handwritten note dated August 17, 1926, from Yost to one of his assistants. Yost stated he had sold four bonds himself on the train the previous evening to a group from Holland, Michigan. It would have been interesting to sit in on that conversation and listen to Yost promote his bonds and watch his rapt audience.

Bond sales trickled in to the athletic department. By September 1, 170 bonds had been sold. By September 6, another 90. The census then showed 40 bought in Ann Arbor, 106 in Detroit, 90 in other Michigan cities, and 24 in other states. However, the great demand Yost had anticipated was not coming to fruition. In fact, bond sales were disappointingly slow, and by September 25, only 559 had sold for a total of $279,500, an amount that was not even 20% of the ultimate goal, $1,500,000 (the equivalent of $16,570,000 today). By October, as the great hole enlarged at the

---

[422] Board in Control, Box 46, folder: Osborn

corner of Stadium and Main Street, real concern ran through the halls of the athletic department.

Charles DuCharme, one of the alumni representatives on the Board in Control, wrote Yost in late September.

> Since last Saturday I have been giving the bond situation considerable thought and while, of course, the slowness with which they have been subscribed for is a disappointment to all concerned, I do not believe it is by any means hopeless and am sure that with some modification the greater part of the issue can be sold.
>
> In the first place, I think we made a serious mistake in limiting the preferred seat privilege to ten years. My vote was cast for the twenty year privilege which I thought every bond purchaser is entitled to…
>
> I am also of the opinion that we fooled ourselves in regard to the rate of interest on the bonds. Naturally, the possibility of securing a million and a half dollars at 3% was one which appealed to all members of the Board, but I do not think it was high enough to induce the individual to subscribe when the proposition was considered in the light of an investment.
>
> I have no doubt that if the interest rate was raised to 5%, many would be inclined to favorably consider the purchase of the bonds from an investment standpoint.
>
> The real reason for the present situation, as I see it, is that we did not offer the prospective purchaser sufficient inducement to buy a bond.[423]

Indeed, the offered interest rate seemed to be a major problem. Yost had very confidently felt that the seating privilege would sell the bonds and that the interest rate was almost immaterial. This assumption now seemed false. In mid-October, Yost wrote a letter

---

[423] Board in Control, Box 8, September 1926 (3)

to sympathetic newspaper editors asking for their help and admitting the sales were not going well. "Confidentially, we have sold less than $400,000 worth of the stadium bonds and we are just now starting a general publicity campaign…Naturally, we do not want the public to know that the bonds have been going disappointingly slow."[424] An editor responded,

> I am sorry to note that the stadium bonds are not going so rapidly as we all might wish, but I presume the difficulty is mainly in the low rate of interest…I talked with a man this morning…who talked as if he would like one of the bonds if the interest rate were high enough in justifying him in borrowing the money to pay for it. I mention this personally, because I think that is the rub with a great many people. They don't like to pay 6 or 7% to borrow the money to buy a bond for $500.00 and then have to pay at least 3% or $15.00 a year interest out of their own pocket. Obviously, this makes two football tickets come pretty high for the average fellow.[425]

As the football season started in earnest, Yost sat down with his staff to re-consider the bond campaign. Several decisions were quickly made. First, Yost lifted the restriction on one person being able to buy only two bonds. Second, a decision was made to more actively target the general public as opposed to focusing on the alumni. Lastly, a decision was made to allow buyers to purchase the bond in installments, so long as the final payment was made before September 1, 1927. Despite the obvious concern, Yost held firm on the three percent interest rate, since to change that number would not only increase the athletic department's long term financial obligation, it would also clearly signal that the bond issue was not going well.

However, Yost was not one to sit back and wring his hands. If the bonds would not sell themselves, then Yost would go out

---

[424] Board in Control, Box 8, October 1926 (1)
[425] Board in Control, Box 8, October 1926 (3)

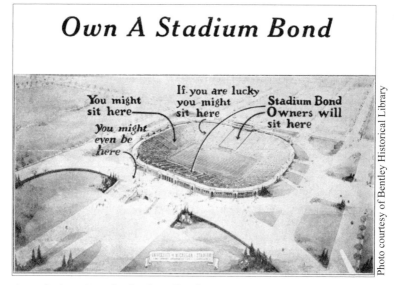

# Own A Stadium Bond

You might sit here

You might even be here

If you are lucky you might sit here

Stadium Bond Owners will sit here

*A marketing piece for Stadium Bonds*

and sell them. Immediately, the athletic department mailed a letter and prospectus to all editors in the state, all bank presidents, all secretaries of service clubs, all chambers of commerce, and all members of the Detroit Athletic Club. Stories about the stadium with pictures were sent to all daily newspapers in the Midwest with follow-up stories twice a week. Since the first mailing had gone almost exclusively to alumni, Yost now sent the prospectus to all people who had ever purchased game tickets. In addition, a list of all Detroit residents with incomes in excess of $10,000 was attained, along with another list of everybody in Michigan with an income over $5,000. They all received letters.

While the alumni response had been disappointing, Yost would not give up on Michigan graduates. He sent a second mailing and made a personal appeal to all Michigan alumni clubs to help with the sale. Bond solicitation cards were developed and distributed at all home football games. A huge banner hung in the center of the desirable south stands of Ferry Field; in bold letters, it proclaimed that this was where bondholders would sit in the new stadium. A sign parade was initiated by students around the Ferry Field track before each game and again at halftime. The first sign said, "Own a Stadium Bond;" the second, "Stadium Bonds Assure Good Tickets;" the third, "Stadium Bonds Provide Good Seats;" and the last, "Interest on Stadium Bonds Pays for Your Tickets." This final sign referred to the fact that three percent interest on a $500 dollar bond would yield $15, which would buy six tickets to Michigan games at $2.50 each. A bondholder could buy his tickets for the season with the interest earned.

To Yost's great relief, the bond sales began to increase significantly, and by early 1927, the whole initial issue, 2000 bonds, was sold. (The athletic department subsequently issued and sold another 1000 bonds before the end of 1927 for a total of 3000). December was a particularly good month. Yost was convinced that many a Wolverine adherent found a Michigan Stadium Bond under the Christmas tree. Yost's decision to seek a broader audience than the alumni community was crucial. The final analysis showed that 60 percent of the bonds were sold to people who had never attended the university. Yost wrote a friend in January 1927 to confirm that "the bonds have all been sold."[426] His friend responded warmly, "I will have to congratulate you upon being some financier. When a man can put out a 3% bond as successfully as you have, he should be moved to Wall Street."[427]

Yost's decision to allow a person to buy more than two bonds created what must have been heartwarming events for the old coach. Charles Baird, a man who perhaps loved only Yost more than he loved the University of Michigan, originally offered to buy two bonds, but told Yost that he really only wanted one. If the sale went well, he would gladly relinquish the second. After all, he lived in Kansas City, and it wasn't likely he would be in Michigan Stadium often. However, when Baird heard that the sale was faltering and that a person could now buy more than two bonds, he promptly bought 38, the most Michigan Stadium bonds to be owned by a

[426] Board in Control, Box 9, January 1927 (2)
[427] Board in Control, Box 9, January 1927 (2)

single person. Ralph Aigler, law professor and Chairman of the Board in Control of Athletics, bought 10, but what must have been the most endearing purchase for Yost were the bonds accumulated by the Redden family. Curtis G. Redden, as previously described, was captain of the Michigan football team of 1903 and died in World War I. Yost committed $500 to dedicate the column to him at Illinois' Memorial Stadium. The Redden family, the soldier's surviving widow and children, stepped up and bought 22 Michigan Stadium bonds. One can only imagine the wave of emotion that must have swept over Yost when that check arrived.

The *Michigan Daily* took a grim view of the bond sales. Students always sat in the poorest seats on Ferry Field, usually in the endzone and far from the action. Since bondholders would get preferential seating, the student body assumed it would have the worst seating in the new stadium. After all, $500 was an immense sum in 1926 (the equivalent of $5,336 today). A semester's tuition, room and board could be had for about $400. Clearly, students would occupy a much less desirable place than fat cat alumni in Michigan's new arena.

In mid-October, a columnist for the *Daily* proclaimed that a new game day program would be developed for students. "In this program it would be useless to list the players with their numbers. You students couldn't see the numbers anyway."[428] The program would only be sold in the endzones, "the finest student stands in the country. But, remember, students, you are only here because we couldn't sell all the tickets to alumni—especially the seats you occupy. So keep the proper attitude at all times."[429]

In late October, a columnist announced a tongue-in-cheek drive to buy a bond in the name of the student body. Since Michigan had 10,000 students, a contribution of five cents each would make the goal possible. Then, according to the *Daily*, two students would be chosen by lottery to sit in prime seats at each game in the new

[428] *Michigan Daily*, 10/23/26, p 4
[429] *Michigan Daily*, 10/23/26, p 4

stadium. Those students would be obligated to write a story about the game that could be published in the *Daily*. That way, all the students on campus would find out what happened at the game since the rest of the student body would be so far from the action they wouldn't have a clue as to what occurred. The columnist committed the first five cents and announced a need for $495.95. He was sure the biggest argument among the student body would be how to spend the $15 interest they would receive each year.

The *Daily* carried on this column for several weeks. Proclaiming that 16 cents had been received by November 2, the writer exhorted, "You must feel that this cause is so magnificent that it is a privilege to work for it. Think of the joy in raising some poor student from the lower levels of the endzone and placing him in the seats of the mighty alumni!!"[430]

On November 7, the columnist brought attention to a picture of the proposed stadium exhibited in one of the stores on State Street. Study it carefully, he said, for if you don't contribute to the student bond fund your seats will be somewhere outside the boundaries of the photograph. In another edition, a blank photo was entitled, "Student View of a Game."[431]

An imaginary interview was then conducted with the manager of the athletic department's ticket office. How, exactly, asked the *Daily*, are student seats determined? "All there is to it is that I collect all the tickets that are returned by alumni because of the seats not being in view of the playing field, and pass them out to students."[432]

Finally, at the conclusion of the football season, the *Daily* announced the failure of their fund drive. However, in a column entitled, "Did You See a Game?" a columnist wrote, "If you saw a game this year, write in…describing it briefly. We are offering a prize for the best student eyewitness account of a game on Ferry Field."[433] The *Daily* would be putting together a special edition

---

[430] *Michigan Daily*, 11/2/26, p 4
[431] *Michigan Daily*, 11/23/26, p 4
[432] *Michigan Daily*, 11/20/26, p 4
[433] *Michigan Daily*, 11/17/26, p 4

called, "Football From Afar," wherein students could describe their experiences.

All this student sarcasm and skepticism directed at the new stadium culminated in a letter to the editor published on November 18, 1926.

> Four score and nine years ago our fathers brought forth upon the left meander of the Huron River a new university, conceived in a moment of ecstasy, and dedicated to the proposition that all men must study or play football.
>
> Now we're engaged in a great stadium drive, testing whether that university or any university so conceived and so dedicated, can long endure, within thirty yards from either goal post...
>
> It is altogether necessary and proper that we do this, but in a financial sense we cannot build, we cannot dedicate, we cannot pay for this ground. The big buggymen of Detroit, graduated and expelled, who have left here have raised the price far above our power to pay.
>
> The world will little note or long remember that we studied here, but it can never forget what they paid here.
>
> It is for us, the students, rather to be here resigned to the money making proposition that they have thus far so loyally perpetrated. It is for us, rather, to be here dedicated to the great task remaining before us, that for these ex-students we take seats in sections X, Y, and Z, that they may sit on the 50-yard line, for which they have paid $500, interest at three per cent, and redeemable in 10 years; that we here highly resolve that the money shall not have been paid in vain, and that this University under the Regents shall have a new stadium; and this stadium of the "alums," by the "alums," and for the "alums," shall not perish from the state of Michigan.[434]

---

[434] *Michigan Daily*, 11/18/26, p 4

Nonetheless, by January 1927, Yost had survived a particularly harrowing six months. Since July, his football team had won another Big Ten championship. Frightening and surprising water problems had developed at the stadium excavation site, but had been solved. The bond sale, which no doubt produced some sleepless nights, had finally proved a success. The money was in the coffers, the hole had been dug and the dirt was piled high about the perimeter. With the coming of warm weather, the cement could be poured. The old coach had much to celebrate with the advent of the new year.

With the arrival of spring weather, Yost spent virtually every day at the construction site. He wasn't the only one. The *Ann Arbor News* reported that up to 1000 spectators a day watched the progress of construction, and on Sundays the onlookers routinely swelled to 3000. Michigan Stadium was attracting crowds even before the first seat was placed.

Yost indicated great concern about the quality of the cement to be used. The south stands of Ferry Field had been poured in 1914, but the athletic department had already been forced to do much repair work. When Yost visited other stadium projects, one of his primary goals was to examine the quality of the cement work. He insisted on the best cement he could find and wanted a successful mix that had been in use for at least two years. In early 1927, there was much discussion about this concern in the athletic files. Osborn Engineering assured Yost that they would insist upon

> unusual rigidity of specifications for concrete in all of the deck structure which is to be exposed to the elements and desire to especially impress upon you that all of these requirements are to be rigidly observed to the end that concrete of an unusual impervious character will be produced capable of enduring thru various changes in temperature, frost, moisture, etc.[435]

Yost was finally satisfied with these assurances, and sealed bids were accepted for the cement work in March 1927. Two Detroit

---

[435] Board in Control, Box 9, February 1927 (1)

firms submitted estimates for the job, but the lowest bid, $75,000 under what Yost and Osborn had estimated, came from the James Leck Company of Minneapolis. Yost was quite pleased, because this was the same company that had poured the cement for Minnesota's new stadium, and he was impressed with the quality of that work. Huron Cement Company won the contract for the cement itself and announced that it would be of the finest quality and would come from their new plant in Wyandotte, Michigan.

In early April, Yost wrote to Bernard Green, the president of Osborn Engineering, to make sure there would be electrical conduits within the cement large enough to accommodate any future needs. This important request would be much appreciated when Michigan Stadium would be expanded in later decades.

By May, the frames were in place for the pouring of the first cement for the giant stadium deck that was to fill the excavation. The cement would be poured in sections, beginning on the east side and gradually moving clockwise around the stadium over the spring and summer until the final unit was finished. Yost was personally present for every bit of this work. The first pour was not very satisfactory and Yost was not happy, but he immediately communicated his concern and soon Osborn Engineering could write to the cement contractors:

> Referring to our letter of May 9th regarding the first concrete poured in the deck for the University of Michigan Stadium, we wish to compliment you on the change made in the next two pours. The handling and the placing of the concrete was much better organized. The cement finishers with new edging tools were on their toes and kept right up behind the placing of the concrete so that they were able to do a very satisfactory piece of work.
>
> Everyone was pleased with this…It looks as though we are going to have a bully good piece of concrete in the deck of this Stadium.[436]

---

[436] Board in Control, Box 9, May 1927 (1)

By early June, the subsoil for the football field itself was in place, one foot of clay loam on sand and gravel. Carefully selected sod was transported from a farm 10 miles outside of Ann Arbor. Weather conditions for the grass were so perfect it seemed every blade took root. Within 10 days, the groundskeeper even found he had to mow the grass. As the summer progressed and the cement workers rotated around the stadium, a beautiful carpet of green already awaited the victories to be won.

Yost kept a very close eye on every budgetary item. He knew there were disgruntled opponents to the stadium project who would exploit any financial shortfalls. He was also very aware that the Regents of the University had placed great trust in his ability to manage this project, and he was determined not to betray their confidence. The guideline put in place by the Regents, that the stadium project should not "overdo it," was foremost in Yost's mind. He insisted on very careful financial management as the stadium project unfolded and did not hesitate to cut proposals that appeared superfluous. Engineers had originally proposed a walkway over the railroad tracks between the new stadium site and campus, but Yost eventually rejected the idea. Fifteen iron gates that were to be placed around the field were eliminated, and even the size of the press box was somewhat diminished. Yost had seen an electric scoreboard for the first time at the Army-Navy game on Soldier Field in Chicago in 1926, but he wasn't convinced of the need for one in the new stadium. He instructed the ground crews to dismantle the manual scoreboards on Ferry Field and haul them over to the new arena (Yost would eventually change his mind and install electric scoreboards in Michigan Stadium in 1930).

The only flourish Yost allowed was the design for the east side of the stadium. Here the entrance to the great facility would be through portals rather than over the top of the concourse. Yost accepted the donated services of an alumnus architect who designed the brick work and placed eight unassuming Doric columns flanking the entrance to section one.

*Stadium excavation: note the huge drainage ditch that circles the field.*

By the end of August, the great stadium had taken shape. As bleacher seats made of California redwood were put in place, Yost and the Board in Control pondered the width to be allowed each patron. The original plan called for 18 inches, but 3000 more seats could be created by making the spacing 17¼ inches. Yost surveyed several schools and convinced the Board that the smaller size should be quite acceptable while also providing the athletic department with more income.

Tom Hammond, an alumnus member of the Board in Control and a former football letterman from the point-a-minute years, lived near Chicago. He made a special trip to Ann Arbor as the summer waned to view the great project. He walked all over the structure, up and down, completely around. He checked out the sight lines and couldn't find a bad seat. His words were not only very gratifying to Yost, but they speak for generations of Wolverines: "Your stadium is certainly a masterpiece."[437]

Yost had accomplished his great goal of building a new stadium in Ann Arbor, a proper edifice for the great Michigan football tradition he had created and to which he had devoted his life. But

[437] Board in Control, Box 9, August 1927 (2)

Yost was not finished building for Michigan. While many of his critics had been dubious of his commitment to "athletics for all," Yost now fulfilled that great dream for Michigan's student body. Few realize that the bond sale that built Michigan Stadium also built the facilities on Palmer Field for women, the great intramural building that stretches so magnificently, even today, along Hoover Street, and the award-winning university golf course that lies south of the stadium. Part of the reason Yost was so conscious of cost as the great stadium took shape in 1927 was that he had a commitment to intramural sports that he was determined to fulfill.

Before the summer of 1927 was over, Yost was already taking action. There were 3000 women studying at Michigan, but virtually no athletic facilities for them. Palmer Field, in neglected condition, was the only place for co-eds to play. Yost had it completely refurbished and extended to include four hockey fields, 18 tennis courts, special fields for archery, and some putting greens. A new field house for women was built adjacent to the field at a cost of $250,000. When completed, Michigan had the finest athletic plant for women in America. Athletic facilities for co-eds were widely ignored by American education at that time, but Yost was pleased to use athletic department money, football money, to build a modern

*Photo courtesy of Bentley Historical Library*

*Stadium construction: pouring cement.*

plant. To Yost, even in 1927, "athletics for all" included women. When he received a letter sharply critical of this expenditure for women, Yost replied,

> I want to say that I am convinced that no better use has ever been made of athletic incomes at this or any other institution than the development and equipment of a suitable place to carry on the physical education activities of this group of students who have, to some extent, been heretofore neglected. It is fully as urgent that the women have these essential facilities as it is that men have them.[438]

The *Ann Arbor News* could only celebrate:

> The activities on Palmer Field remind us of football for the very good reason that football is paying the shot. The state of Michigan isn't spending a nickel for the improvements. Yet it is an improvement that might very well be financed from the state treasury as indeed it would in almost any place but Michigan.
>
> The news story concerning the letting of these contracts ought to be considered seriously by any man who opposes intercollegiate football on the ground that it "benefits a few." For here is an instance of football benefiting every woman student at the University of Michigan. Eleven boys playing on Ferry Field have provided more than 3000 girls with the facilities for beneficial physical culture…
>
> Yes, we have commercialized athletics at Michigan. There is no denying that statement. And we regard the situation as extremely gratifying. There should be more of this kind of commercialized football…Ferry Field has been one of Michigan's very best investments.[439]

---

[438] Board in Control, Box 9, April 1927 (3)
[439] *Ann Arbor News*, 3/7/27, p 4

Yost was not finished. As the old wooden north stands on Ferry Field disappeared in the summer of 1927, the athletic department announced that contracts were being let for a new intramural building along Hoover Street. At a cost of $750,000, it would be an immense structure with outside dimensions a little longer and narrower than a football field. The architecture would resemble Yost Field House. Inside, for the use of students, not varsity athletes, would be 4000 lockers, 10 squash courts, 24 handball courts, four basketball courts, four indoor tennis courts, an auxiliary gymnasium, and fencing, boxing and wrestling rooms. A swimming pool was also part of the project and would be used by the varsity team, but at other times it would be available to the student body. The nation had never seen such a project, all of it a gift from the athletic department to the university and to the student body.

Finally, Yost would use the remaining money from the bond sale to construct a university golf course south of the stadium site. It would be only the fourth such course in the country to be university owned, and as recently as 2004, it would be acclaimed as one of the 10 best in the nation. While varsity teams would use the course, it would also be open to Michigan students. Yost, the legendary football coach, the builder of Michigan Stadium, would make the ultimate commitment to Michigan's student body, leaving behind an intramural plant matched nowhere in the world. "Athletics for all" would be a reality in Ann Arbor thanks to Fielding H. Yost.

*Newly completed stadium, Fall 1927*

# Chapter 12

# "The Greatest of Great Games"

Fielding H. Yost was consumed by the details necessary to ready the new stadium for the first game on October 1 against Ohio Wesleyan. Seats had to be numbered, the scoreboards erected, the press box completed, the peripheral fencing placed, the walkways finished, and the locker rooms painted. The demands were endless. However, as September progressed, another football season loomed. After much contemplation, Yost finally decided that he could no longer lead his beloved Michigan Wolverines. For 1927, at least, he would have to relinquish the reins. Yost first confirmed his decision in a letter to Michigan's Governor on September 7, 1927:

> On the evening of September 15th I will announce that I will not find it possible to coach this year. We are undertaking the development of the Women's Athletic Building and Athletic Field, a new Intramural Sports Building, and the new football stadium. This, with my work in the Physical Education Program, makes it necessary for me to make the above announcement. I have no idea, of course, of giving up my work as coach permanently.[440]

Yost still could not quite imagine that he would never coach again, but this decision would be a permanent one. He wrote his

---

[440] Board in Control, Box 10, September 1927 (1)

dear friend, Dan McGugin, "I will not have charge of the team this year as I have entirely too much work to do. I am already eating sodamint tablets without the burden of the whole football season."[441] Heartburn and nervous indigestion were common complaints of Yost's whenever he commanded the Wolverine football squad.

His family, too, saw the strain. Yost's wife received this communication from her brother: "I have thought a whole lot about Fielding since I was in Ann Arbor last and hope he has not worked and worried himself to death with the stadium and other factors he is contending with in Ann Arbor."[442]

Football practice for the 1927 season opened on September 15, and Yost kept his secret until then. He showed up in uniform to welcome the players back to Ferry Field, but that evening he made his announcement to the assembled Michigan team.

> At the first meeting of the football squad held Thursday night, in a low voice, filled with emotion, Yost announced that "I do not find it possible to coach football this year." The 60 athletes, who Thursday reported for the first practice of the season, were stunned by the brief announcement of the "Old Man," as he is affectionately known by those who have learned the game under his tutelage.[443]

The *Ann Arbor News* published a glowing editorial.

> Announcement that Prof. Fielding H. Yost does not "find it possible" to coach football this year comes as a somewhat startling piece of information upon the eve of the 1927 season, with a fine new stadium opening its gates for the first time…It is almost like taking the sun out of the sky or extinguishing the stars, for Yost and football have seemed as inseparable at Michigan as bread and butter on the family table.

[441] Board in Control, Box 10, September 1927 (2)
[442] Board in Control, Box 10, September 1927 (2)
[443] *Ann Arbor News*, 9/16/27, p 1

However, the Yost plan calls for something above and beyond football. His dream for Michigan consists of a physical training plant that will lead the way to a new era in athletics at American colleges. Intercollegiate athletics has been Yost's specialty…but he has been thinking of athletics for all as an ultimate goal of his endeavors. His dream is being realized now, with the expansion of physical development facilities, including the two new field houses, which football income has made possible. But it has been one of those dreams that could not be translated into reality without an immense amount of physical and mental labor.

While he has been thinking of forward passes and line defense, he likewise has been obliged to think of blueprints and drainage systems. He is a big man, physically as well as figuratively, but there is a limit to individual energy…

Yost has earned relief from direct responsibility of building a football machine. His countless friends and admirers all over the country—with the exception, perhaps, of those at Columbus, Urbana, Minneapolis and a few other places—will regret exceedingly to see him "retire," but there are few who will not recognize the fact that he is more nearly indispensable as an athletic director than as a coach…[444]

It was the end of a most remarkable era. Yost had coached at Michigan for a quarter of a century, and in that time, he had taken the program from obscurity to the top of the collegiate football world. While the phenomenal success of Yost's point-a-minute teams at the turn of the century are often recognized, the achievements made on the football field in his last five years were as extraordinary. Yost, in retrospect, preferred to ascribe the 1924

---

[444] *Ann Arbor News*, 9/16/27, p 4

season to George Little. By doing so, he could avoid responsibility for the losses to Illinois and Iowa that year. Thus, Yost claimed 1921, 1922, 1923, 1925, and 1926 as his last five years as Michigan head coach. During this span, Michigan won 33 games, lost 3, and tied 2. The Wolverines averaged 24.7 points per game to the opponents 2.3. The squads won four Big Ten championships, produced five All-Americans, and would have been national champions in 1925 and 1926 if not for single losses to Northwestern and Navy, respectively.

However, there is an even more admirable aspect to this most distinguished record. When Yost was appointed athletic director at Michigan in July 1921, at a salary of $8500 (which didn't change through 1927), he refused to accept any further compensation for coaching the football team. The average yearly wage for a head football coach at a comparable school was around six to ten thousand dollars, but Yost coached with no contract and for no salary. There was no income from corporate endorsements, no radio or television show that rewarded him for his post-game wisdom, and no bonuses promised for beating Ohio State or winning a Big Ten championship. He coached for his love of the game, his love of his players, and his love of the great university to which he was so devoted. There is no parallel example to be found in the annals of American college football. Yost won 33 of 38 games, brought home four Big Ten titles in five years, and provided this performance for free to the university community he felt so privileged to serve.

Elton E. "Tad" Wieman would be Michigan's new head coach. Wieman arrived at Michigan in 1915 and immediately went out for the football team. He played fullback and was elected to captain the 1917 team, but he gave up that opportunity in order to enlist when war broke out. He didn't return to Michigan until 1920, when Yost made him captain again and placed him at one of the tackle slots. When Wieman's playing eligibility expired at the end of that year, Yost named him line coach. Over the next six years, Wieman developed four All-Americans on Michigan's lines: Vick,

Blott, Slaughter and Oosterbaan. Yost assured the Michigan alumni community that the team would be in good hands.

Unlike the confusion with George Little in 1924, there would be no confusion about Yost's role this time. When Wieman announced the first scrimmage of the year, 5000 spectators showed up to watch the event. Yost was not on the sidelines, but was identified in the stands with the rest of the crowd. Shortly thereafter, an *Ann Arbor News* reporter spotted him watching a practice:

> With hat pulled down well over his eyes, standing silently among the spectators who lined the practice gridiron at Ferry Field Monday night, Fielding H. Yost watched his first practice session in 30 years, without issuing one command or handing out instruction to a single blue jersied athlete…
>
> Silently, Yost watched the practice. When Wieman blew a whistle to assemble the squad, as Yost had always done when he wished the group to gather around him, the veteran coach half started, but he is only athletic director now and he remained stationary while the blue hosts led by Wieman trotted under the stands…
>
> The crowd followed, but Yost remained—as if in a trance and he remained there until everyone had departed…For a long time Yost remained on the deserted gridiron —probably thinking over the 30 years of his endeavors in the coaching game. Suddenly he came out of his trance, looked quickly around to see if he had been noticed, and walked slowly into Yost Field House…
>
> It was a pathetic picture as "Hurry-Up" slowly walked off the deserted field Monday night and one cannot help but feel that he will return some day because his heart and soul are wrapped up in the coaching game.[445]

---

[445] *Ann Arbor News*, 9/20/27, p 12

There was only one change in the football rules for 1927, but it would be a lasting one. Ohio State had lost to Michigan in Columbus the previous year when the Buckeye kicker missed a point after touchdown in the closing minutes of the contest. Ohio State's coach, Jack Wilce, launched a personal campaign to eliminate the point after touchdown from the game. He garnered no significant support at the Big Ten meetings at the end of the season, but the argument was carried on to the national coaches meeting. The rules committee listened to all the testimony and decided to move the goal posts from the goal line to the end of the endzone. Such a move would make the point after more difficult to convert. Yost, however, thought the change made no sense at all. If the original idea was to prevent one point victories, moving the goal posts back would only make for more of them. Good kickers would still not be challenged by the point after, said Yost, but poor kickers would surely miss more of them. Even more objectionable to Yost, field goals would now be more difficult for everyone. If the rules committee thought more of a challenge was needed for the point after, Yost would have preferred them to move the scrimmage line back 10 yards for only that play. In any case, the rule was changed and the goal posts in the new stadium were set at the endzone line, providing a novel change for the season of 1927.

Coach Wieman claimed the new location of the goal posts was a nightmare for his backfield candidates. In the initial practices, they were all throwing the ball beyond the posts because that was where the endzone used to be. Now such catches were out of bounds and his players were having some difficulty adjusting their passing attack accordingly.

While the much anticipated dedication game with Ohio State was scheduled for October 22, Michigan would play its first game in the new stadium on October 1. To celebrate the event, the University had issued an invitation to the game to all high school students in the state. Those who came would be hosted by the university and admitted to the game for free. The plan was warmly received by Michigan high schools and a contingent of 30,000 was expected. University President Clarence Little agreed to address the assembled students on the "outstanding merits of the University"[446] at Yost Field House before the game. The Michigan Marching Band would then lead the whole crowd to the new stadium.

The *Michigan Daily* editors wanted to know what the new arena would be called. The athletic department informed them that it would be known as Michigan Stadium.

The opponent for the first game was Ohio Wesleyan. The choice of this school for the very first game in Michigan Stadium was no accident. Fielding Yost had started his coaching career at Wesleyan exactly 30 years earlier, in 1897. Yost had completed law school at West Virginia in the spring of 1897, where he played football for the Mountaineers and had fallen in love with the game. He soon learned that a coach was needed at Ohio Wesleyan, and so he had traveled west to look over the situation. The team at Wesleyan had never even had a coach before, but they had promised to scrape together $300 to pay Yost. Upon arrival, Yost was not impressed with the recruits and had described the football field as a "cowpatch."[447] Nonetheless, he agreed to stay, and his legendary coaching career was launched. Michigan was on the Wesleyan schedule that year, but when Yost arrived in Ann Arbor with his team, he only had 10 players. To complete a contingent of 11, he inserted himself in the game. In a radio address the night before this first game in Michigan Stadium, Yost reminisced:

> Thirty years ago I began my coaching experience at Ohio Wesleyan University and that year brought the team from that institution to Ann Arbor for a game against Michigan. I played with the permission of the Michigan coach at left tackle with the Ohio Wesleyan team, the score resulting in a tie, nothing to nothing.

Tomorrow Ohio Wesleyan and the University of

---

[446] *Michigan Daily*, 10/1/27, p 1
[447] *Ann Arbor News*, 2/23/27, p 10

Michigan play again. This game will open the 1927 schedule and will be the first to be played in the new Michigan Stadium. At the game 30 years ago there were not more than 1000 spectators present and most of these were students. Indications are that there will be some 50,000 to 60,000 spectators present at the game tomorrow.[448]

*The first game in Michigan Stadium, October 1, 1927 (note the manual scoreboard at the south end).*

In fact, the 1897 Wesleyan team, which included Yost's younger brother, Ellis, held a 30-year reunion in Ann Arbor for this game. Yost enjoyed the company of his former players, who enthusiastically reminded him of the huge holes he had personally created in the Michigan line in that 1897 encounter.

Unfortunately, the weather refused to cooperate for this initial game. It rained all week. Wieman allowed his team only one warm-

[448] *Michigan Daily,* 10/1/27, p 1

up practice within Michigan Stadium for fear of harming the field. The team spent the week tearing up the sod on abandoned Ferry Field instead. Yost decided late in the week to have cinders poured over the walkways around the stadium because the rain had reduced them to soggy muck. Unhappily, the rain continued into Saturday, and it greatly reduced the crowd expected for the game.

While prior to the rain, it was predicted that 50,000 would attend this opening day in Michigan Stadium, only about 40,000 braved the wet weather to witness this historic contest. Reserved seating was in place only for the bondholders and for visiting guests from Ohio Wesleyan. Otherwise, the stadium filled on a first-come basis. Spectators congregated in the highest rows first, and marveled over the view of the field.

The Wolverines poured out of their tunnel for the first time in "bright new jerseys of blue with block numbers of flaming yellow."[449] Within five minutes of the opening kick-off, the Wolverines scored their first touchdown in their new home. Halfback Louis Gilbert threw a perfect strike to Ann Arbor's own Laverne "Kip" Taylor, the latter playing his first game for Michigan as a sophomore end. As a harbinger of much to come, Michigan easily won this game, 33-0.

An editor at the *Daily* would speak for generations of visitors as he expressed his awe of Michigan's great new home.

> It was Michigan's vast new stadium! But it was wet; awfully wet; dripping wet; wet in the sky and wet on the field; and wettest of all in the stands. It was also the first game in the new stadium; and it was a crowd of more than 40,000 intrepid souls who made their way through the bogs to the great new edifice.
>
> But there was color in the stands—yellow, green, blue, red, all colors. It was all so new and shiny; so vast and impressive; so bright and so wet that no one could

---

[449] *Michigan Daily*, 10/1/27, p 6

keep his eyes on the game. There was a new press box, new goal posts, a new crowd, new rules, new referees, everything new; and it was not a Michigan football game at all, but merely a great spectacle—a new and gigantic spectacle...

Michigan's new traditions; Michigan's great new field; Michigan's powerful teams to be all belong to Michigan's vast new bowl. But after the game is over and the next day has come, it doesn't seem real at all; it seems like a dream rather than a Michigan institution; it fails to ring true—but it was the first game.[450]

There was only one bad omen the *Daily* could chronicle. The Michigan drum major missed catching his baton toss over the goal post.

Michigan's next game would again be in the new stadium, this time against Michigan State College. The athletic department had ordered new flags to fly over the stadium in appropriate colors for all the Big Ten schools, but someone realized in late September that no such pennant had been ordered for MSC. An urgent order was sent asking for "white letters on a green background"[451] in time for the October 8 contest.

A crowd of about 30,000 showed up for this traditional meeting. The highlight of the affair seemed to be that the two marching bands were directed by brothers, Leonard Fanconi for Michigan State and Nicholas Fanconi for Michigan. Before the game started, the two bands intermixed and played a most inspiring rendition of the national anthem. The game itself was rather uninspiring, but Michigan won its second victory in its new home, 21-0.

The Wolverines now had a road game in Madison, but the attention of the whole university community was already focused on the game to be played in Ann Arbor the following week, the stadium dedication encounter against Ohio State. The *Daily* tried

[450] *Michigan Daily*, 10/2/27, p 1
[451] Board in Control, Box 10, September 1927 (1)

to remind students of the game against the Badgers, but it was a sparse contingent that showed up at the train station to send off the team.

At Wisconsin, George Little had hired Glenn Thistlewaite from Northwestern to be the new Badger head football coach. As a result, neither Little nor Yost would walk the sidelines for this game. In what must have been a novelty for both men, they sat together in the stands to watch this contest.

Michigan won the game, 14-0, and the only remarkable event was an injury to sophomore Kip Taylor. Taylor came out of the game with an injured neck and tried, to no avail, to limber it up along the sidelines. After the game, he climbed on board the train and rode all the way back to Ann Arbor, wincing from discomfort. It wasn't until late Sunday night that he finally made it to the health service where x-rays showed a fracture in one of his cervical vertebrae. He had, essentially, broken his neck, but he was a fortunate young man in that there had been no bone displacement. His season, however, was over.

With the exception of the injury to Taylor, Michigan's new coach was very pleased with this victory in Madison. The pressure on him to win, of course, was intense:

> For Wieman it was his first conference game as head Michigan coach. Had Michigan been defeated, it is not hard to imagine that the Wolverine alumni would have risen en masse and demanded the return of Yost. They would have put up a howl without ever looking into the situation…The entire fault would be laid at Wieman's door.[452]

Now the Michigan community could focus completely on the dedication of their great new stadium. Over 88,000 tickets for the game had been sold on September 1, 1927, the first day sales occurred. Ohio State had been given 17,500 tickets that were gone in

---

[452] *Ann Arbor News*, 10/17/27, p 10

a flash, and the school clamored for more, but Yost indicated there were none to be had. The *Ann Arbor News* reported that even Yost couldn't get extra tickets for some dear friends. Harry Tillotson, Michigan's ticket manager, had "heard so many hard luck stories that they claim around the athletic office that it's just like pouring water on a duck's back. Harry listens intently, graciously but firmly explains for the thousandth time that he is sorry, but there are no more tickets available…Hard-hearted Harry."[453]

Yost had skirmished through May and June with the new members on the Board in Control of Athletics about the ticket policy. His nemesis, Robert Angell of the sociology department, felt strongly that alumni should get ticket preferences for the games. Yost was adamantly opposed to the idea. In one of the very first meetings of the new Board in Control, Angell moved that alumni should get ticket priority. This suggestion was defeated by a 6-4 vote, with Yost leading the opposition. However, Angell then moved that members of Michigan Alumni Clubs be given ticket preference. This would, essentially, establish the same principle except that alumni clubs were all male, and women would not be included in the preferential group. Yost put up another fight, but this time he lost. However, Yost did offer an amendment that women graduates should receive the same priority as men in alumni clubs, and that proposal passed. Yost won another key victory on the Board in Control, however, by insisting that any such change in ticket policy be approved by the Regents.

Since President Little seemed to be undecided about this issue, Yost wrote a strongly worded letter to him.

> In considering plans for the allotment and distribution of football tickets at the University of Michigan, it must be kept in mind that this is a tax supported University, not a privately endowed one as are Harvard (Little graduated from Harvard), Yale, Princeton and Chicago.
>
> The titles to all University properties are held in trust

by the Board of Regents for the citizens of the State of Michigan whose taxes have built and supported the University.

Among the citizens of Michigan there are many thousands of college graduates of institutions other than the University of Michigan. Among these are those charged with the responsibility of conducting the educational program of the state. We at the University expect the cooperation and hearty support of these people—the superintendents, principals, teachers, coaches and other officers of high schools and colleges of the state—and of all the citizens as well. But cooperation is two sided —it doesn't work one way alone. If we want the good will of the people of the state of Michigan, we must do everything possible to build up a fine spirit and morale for the University and not do anything to destroy it.

Whether it should be true or not, it remains a fact that at present there is no better way to develop and maintain an active interest in the University on the part of our citizens than through our intercollegiate contests. It is at the same times of these contests that a great number of our people want to come to Ann Arbor. Why should we deny them this right?

The resolution creating an alumni preference makes no provision for women graduates of the University and former women students. It creates a preference for alumni who are members of some local University of Michigan club…

Personally, I think it would be a great mistake to create alumni preference.[454]

This was one battle for Yost that just never seemed to go away. He was fighting this pitched contest with faculty members in the

---

summer of 1927, after the bond campaign of the previous autumn. While it hadn't been made public knowledge, Yost knew that the campaign had faltered among alumni groups and had only become a success when rescued by purchasers who were not alumni. This experience only confirmed Yost's strongly held belief that the University of Michigan, as a tax-supported institution, should not provide a ticket preference for alumni over citizens.

Yost once more directed all his energies toward the university Regents, since they would make the final decision. At the June 1927 meeting, the Regents finally put the issue to rest by voting to support Yost. All citizens of the state of Michigan would have the same ticket preference as alumni. The *Ann Arbor News* welcomed the decision in an editorial entitled, "It's All Settled."

> The coach would be delighted if he could provide everyone who wants to see the games with a ticket, but it is absolutely impossible…Whereas the era of disappointment formerly has come principally from citizens, a wail will now be heard from the great army of alumni. That the regents adopted a wise course in considering the citizens who support the state University cannot be disputed. It had to be. The public no longer can be ignored in the matter of University activities.[455]

There would be a scramble for tickets. Yost now had a stadium that would seat 75,000, but on September 1, 88,000 tickets had been sold for the dedication game. Yost immediately proposed building 10,000 temporary seats around the stadium concourse that would duplicate, to some degree, the way Michigan Stadium looks today. Yost calculated it would cost $12,000 to put them up, but they would bring in $30,000 for each of the three sold-out games, which also included the home contests against Navy and Minnesota.

This proposal was opposed by faculty members led by Angell, but Yost prevailed when he agreed that the seats would only be

---

[455] *Ann Arbor News*, 6/30/27, p 4

temporary and in no way represented any intention to permanently enlarge the stadium. Yost had kept all the timber from the north stands on Ferry Field that had already been torn down to make way for the new intramural building. He saved funds by having the builders use that wood for some of the bleacher seats around the new stadium concourse.

So now the new Michigan Stadium could seat 85,000 spectators for the dedication game against the Buckeyes. Even so, the athletic department returned 3000 ticket applications to unhappy fans. Of course, when the faculty initially approved the stadium project in 1926, it advised that a stadium of 60,000 would be appropriate. The Regents were persuaded to raise that number to 70,000. Yost, however, now had 85,000 seats in Michigan Stadium.

Reserved seats had not been used for the Ohio Wesleyan and Michigan State games except for the bondholders and visiting guests, but everyone would have to find their assigned spot in Michigan Stadium for the Ohio State game. Where would the athletic department place the students? Would they end up in the endzone as the *Daily* had speculated so cynically the year before?

It was a generous tradition throughout the Big Ten at this time that the supporters of the visiting team have prime seats. Yost put Ohio State's 17,500-person contingent on the east side of the stadium, starting at the 50-yard line and running north as far as necessary. Stadium bondholders were placed next to them on the east side, beginning at the 50-yard line and running south to the 30-yard line. The remaining bondholders were placed at the north 45-yard line on the west side, running south to the 30. The athletic department had agreed to give 1000 male students a special cheering section centered on the 50-yard line on the west side of the stadium. Having done all that, Yost placed the rest of the students in the west stand, starting at the 30-yard line on the north side and running north as far as needed. (Essentially, this placement is where the students are today, except that over the decades they have lost a few yards. The student section now begins at about the

22-yard line and extends into the endzone. Of course, in 1927, Michigan's student body was much smaller so there was very little need for endzone seats). Michigan's students of 1927 were happily surprised with their place in Michigan Stadium.

Both teams held secret practices all week. The *Daily* warned that the Buckeyes would be "fighting mad to avenge five years of successive defeats."[456] The first pep rally of the year was held in Hill Auditorium the night before the game. The place was packed with the marching band, cheerleaders and rabid Wolverine students. Tad Wieman spoke first, and then Judge William Day of Cleveland, a renowned Michigan alumnus who lived and died by the fortunes or misfortunes of the Wolverine football team. The judge finished his wildly applauded speech by proclaiming, "Men and women of Michigan, when the sun sets tomorrow night on that glorious stadium that we are dedicating, it sets on a stadium that has seen a victory over Ohio State!"[457] The *Daily* proclaimed that the game to be played in Ann Arbor on the morrow would be "the greatest of great games."[458]

The athletic department had prepared the largest game program ever to be sold at a Michigan football game. It contained a beautiful lithograph of the stadium from the air on the front cover, and contained 160 pages. Significantly, it contained several speeches from various notables. The Governor of Michigan, the Governor of Ohio, and the two university presidents were all invited to submit a proclamation, but Yost had decided months before that there would be no oral speeches to celebrate the stadium. The stadium would appropriately be celebrated by the football game.

The day dawned beautifully, sunny and crystal clear. The colorful crowd flowed into Michigan Stadium long before the opening kick-off. At 2:00 P.M., the ceremonies began with the Ohio State Marching Band emerging first from the tunnel, followed by the Michigan Marching Band, the two Governors, the Presidents of

[456] *Michigan Daily*, 10/19/27, p 6
[457] *Michigan Daily*, 10/22/27, p 1
[458] *Michigan Daily*, 10/21/27 p 8

the two universities, the Board of Regents, the Board in Control of Athletics, the two teams, and then all the former "M" lettermen accompanied by Fred Lawton, the composer of "Varsity." The whole ensemble swung to the north, passed through the goal posts, and then crossed the field to the south where the two bands played the Star Spangled Banner for the flag raising. Fred Lawton had arranged for two live wolverines to be brought from the Detroit Zoo for this occasion. They were hauled around the field in a specially constructed wire cage by several attendants who kept a respectful distance.

After the coin toss, two co-eds provided mums to the captains, a golden bundle for the Wolverines and a crimson collection for the Buckeyes. The great contest was about to begin. It was almost five years to the day, October 21, 1922, that Michigan had dedicated the great horseshoe in Columbus.

Bennie Oosterbaan, Michigan's captain and celebrated end,

*The team captains receive bouquets prior to the Michigan Stadium Dedication Game—Bennie Oosterbaan on the left; Ted Meyer, OSU, on the right.*

would own this day in Michigan Stadium, but not for catching the ball. Rather, Oosterbaan would throw the pigskin for three touchdowns. With the game scoreless in the second quarter and Michigan on the OSU 41-yard line, Oosterbaan dropped back from his end position, took the ball, and threw it to halfback Louis Gilbert who made a great catch at the 15 and took it in for the score. In the third period, from almost the same place on the field, Oosterbaan threw again to Gilbert who caught it at the two and stumbled into the endzone. In the fourth, Michigan faked a field goal attempt from the OSU 38-yard line, the holder scampering loose to the nine. From there, Oosterbaan threw again to Gilbert who crossed the goal for the final score of 21-0. Louis Gilbert, Michigan's 160-pound halfback, scored all of the Wolverine points by catching all three of Oosterbaan's touchdown passes and kicking all three points after.

While 85,000 tickets had been sold, Yost claimed 87,000 in attendance by the time he counted all the players, referees, sportscasters, newspapermen, and the 1000 Boy Scouts who ushered. It was not only the largest crowd to ever see a game in Ann Arbor, Michigan. It was the largest crowd to watch a game anywhere in America that day.

*Dedication Game*
*October 22, 1927*

*Note the wood superstructre at the bottom corners. This was built by Yost to boost capacity to 87,000.*

Michigan adherents didn't know what to celebrate more, the game or the stadium. Coach Wieman had not only handed Ohio State their sixth straight loss to the Wolverines, but he also had a team that had not yet been scored upon. Michigan had won their stadium dedication game and that event in itself thrilled many a Wolverine.

But, oh, my, the stadium. What could be said about the stadium? The Michigan crowd loved the place. The *Daily* did its best to put the celebration into words.

> The University of Michigan, nor the whole state of Michigan, has never seen a crowd so vast. Endless files of human beings, piled nearly a hundred rows high, encircled the smiling green area in which was enacted the business of the afternoon. It took one's breath away, this multitude, upon first entering that immense bowl; but after one took his infinitesimal place in the scheme of the thing, and cheered and shouted and sang with the 86,000, it finally becomes so natural that the whole affair seemed quite in the scheme of things.[459]

> In the many years to come, whenever the stadium— something of a Yost symbol—is spoken of or referred to, his name will be remembered.

> It has often been said, and it is now more than ever before coming true, that "Michigan will never forget Yost."[460]

After the game, letters poured into the athletic department congratulating Yost on his great creation. One missive typified the feelings of the ebullient Wolverines: "I wish you could have mingled with the crowd as I did during the game, after it and since I have been home. Everyone who had seen it was amazed with the stadium and was singing the praises of the man who made it possible."[461]

---

[459] *Michigan Daily*, 10/23/27, p 1
[460] *Michigan Daily*, 10/22/27, p 4
[461] Board in Control, Box 10, October 1927 (2)

Fans loved the simplicity of the stadium, the ease with which people could access their seats, the overall capacity, and especially the nearness of the seats to the field. Michigan Stadium's great innovation is taken for granted today, but at the time the idea was Yost's original concept. He insisted on building this stadium only for football. There was no track circling the field and there was no elliptical shape to the stands curving fans away from the action. Yost's rectangular creation was a great success, and was much appreciated by those who sat in the stands on that opening day.

However, not everything was perfect. There were some misunderstandings. The tunnel attracted spectators like filings to a magnet. Everyone wanted to leave the stadium through the great tunnel. After the dedication game, spectators flooded the field and tried to exit through that beckoning portal. Afterwards, several fans sent letters of complaint because they were crushed against the sides when the band came pouring through. Yost was forced to issue a statement that the tunnel was for the team and the band, not for spectators. Fans should leave by the same route they used to enter.

The Michigan Band, celebrating this wonderful victory, seemed to have swung right out of the tunnel, circled the south end of the stadium, and marched jauntily down Main Street to Hoover. Chagrined motorists, stuck in unending traffic, were not pleased. The athletic department would have to ask the band to change its route of egress.

Some complaints would find sympathy with the modern fan.

There was one feature to the football game Saturday which was quite unnecessary and which occasioned considerable adverse comment on the part of the people who witnessed it. The undesirable feature was the reckless flying over the field of three aeroplanes. At the best, flying is a hazardous undertaking which frequently results in the death of the aviator and occasionally results in the death of some innocent person on the land…it will require no stretch of imagination to visualize a terrible disaster that could easily occur if one of these planes should drop into the stadium and possibly catch fire.[462]

This concern greatly bothered Yost, too, and he asked the Ann Arbor police to track down the flyers.

A second complaint was written by a woman who stated in no uncertain terms that the toilet facilities were "pitifully inadequate and great crowds are lined up for an hour before each game."[463] Yost was meticulous in his planning for Michigan Stadium, but he sorely underestimated the demand for women's restrooms.

Yost, the man, was not forgotten by the Michigan community during this historic weekend. The University Press Club honored the revered coach Friday night before the game at a banquet at the Union. Several hundred alumni donors purchased for the "Grand Old Man" a specially built eight-cylinder Packard automobile. Yost, however, was most moved by a gift of 26 silver goblets, each one presented by a member of the 26 Michigan teams he coached. A local editor described the scene:

> Saturday was a glorious day. Glorious in its natural splendor as only comes in the charm of a Michigan October. It was glorious in another sense—a milestone in the athletic history of the University of Michigan; an historical day for the city of Ann Arbor and the peak in the brilliantly successful career of Fielding Harris Yost, the Michigan coach for the past twenty-seven years. The dinner of the University Press Club at the Michigan Union at which Coach and Mrs. Yost were guests of Michigan editors, was at times dramatic. The "old man," as Coach Yost is affectionately called by his years of football players, had just been presented with gifts from the Alumni, Ann Arbor City, and the Press Club, totaling beyond $10,000 in material values. Bending slightly, he touched the set

[462] Board in Control, Box 10, October 1927 (2)
[463] Board in Control, Box 10, November 1927 (3)

of silver goblets and remarked how much more the gifts meant to him in sentiment than value. He spoke slowly and at times hardly above a whisper as he mentioned the names, for example, of "Boss" Weeks, Capt. Redden, Neil Snow and other Michigan stars. It was the heart of the old coach speaking rather than the lips. We have many times felt the thrill of the spoken word but never more than by this homely bit, first of philosophy and then of tribute and appreciation. It was a classic in its simplicity of language and delivery. Here was a great personality bowed down by the love of friends.[464]

Yost sent a response to every one of the donors.

After two days use I have a greater appreciation of the very fine Packard car and all it means to me and Mrs. Yost. Many memories of my twenty-seven years at Michigan and the fine Michigan men I have known and learned to love have come to me as I have driven over the beautiful hills around Ann Arbor. Words cannot express to you and others how much I value all these associations. Forever for Michigan.[465]

And so this man was fortunate enough to realize the great culmination of his work and to know the love and respect for him that permeated every fiber of the Michigan community. He left a legacy in construction that is enjoyed by Michigan students, alumni and friends every day, but from this man originated also the Michigan aura that glows around Ann Arbor, that lives within every graduate, that motivates the standard of athletic excellence symbolic of the University of Michigan. Very few universities can claim a man so prophetic, so influential, so benevolent.

---

[464] Board in Control, Box 10, October 1927 (2)
[465] Board in Control, Box 10, October 1927 (2)

# Chapter 13

# The Epilogue

In 1927, Fielding H. Yost achieved his most ambitious goal. Michigan shattered all collegiate home attendance records by packing 330,000 people into the new stadium over the course of five games. Counting the fans that watched them at Wisconsin, Illinois and Chicago, the Wolverines played before almost 500,000 spectators, a resounding new national record.

However, Michigan Stadium might well have never been realized if Fielding H. Yost had been less articulate, less insistent, or less devoted. Two short years after the dedication game, almost to the day, the stock market crashed, and America entered its darkest economic experience. While Yost had proclaimed that one-twentieth of the bonds could be paid off each year for 20 years, this goal soon became untenable. In the midst of pervading financial crises, the crowds failed to appear at stadiums across the devastated nation.

Michigan Stadium was filled to capacity on October 19, 1929, for Ohio State, and again on November 9, 1929, to host Harvard, but it wouldn't happen again for at least a decade. In 1930, Michigan averaged 35,000 fans at home games, 26,000 in 1931. Michigan claimed a national championship in 1932, as Coach Harry Kipke's team was undefeated. Nonetheless, attendance at five home games in 1932 averaged only 28,000 fans. Athletic department income peaked in 1927 at $540,000. Yost claimed it would exceed $400,000 annually in the stadium prospectus, but it averaged only $175,000 a year from 1932 to 1936. No one would have proposed a new stadium in Ann Arbor during those years. The Ferry Field facility would have been quite adequate.

In fact, while the Michigan athletic department continued paying interest on all the bonds throughout the Great Depression, no stadium bonds were paid off at all during the years 1931 through 1936. Only in 1937 did the department begin retiring bonds again, but that year only 75 were reimbursed. Yost had confidently predicted in 1926 that the athletic department could pay off 150 bonds per year and in 20 years refund all subscribers. Obviously, the department had fallen woefully short of that goal. By the end of 1937, only 700 of the 3000 bonds had been paid back when the goal after 10 years was 1500.

Of the $1,500,000 raised by the bonds, the athletic department still owed $1,000,000 in 1940. Yost was athletic director until 1941, and he worked prodigiously to keep the bond commitment, but between 1927 and 1940, Michigan Stadium averaged only 40,000 patrons per game. Yost was quick to point out that the department never faltered on paying the interest on the bonds. To the credit of the Michigan community, many bondholders donated their holdings to the athletic department and relinquished their claim to reimbursement. The final bonds were not paid off until the years following World War II, when economic prosperity returned and the great teams of the late 1940s brought overflow crowds back to the stadium.

Needless to say, no new stadium would have been built in Ann Arbor if the proposal had been made in the few years following the 1929 season. If Yost had been less of an advocate, if faculty resistance had been more pronounced, if the Regents had been less convinced, this great stadium wouldn't have been.

The success of Yost's vision of a stadium only for football speaks for itself. Minnesota's stadium, the one dedicated by Michigan in

1924, was torn down years ago. A parking structure now stands in its place. The University of Pittsburgh stadium, the one Yost studied but didn't like because of its elliptical form, has also been abandoned. Both Ohio State and Illinois have removed the tracks around their field in recent years to provide more seating and better viewing. Michigan Stadium has not only withstood the test of time, but the concept that led to its realization has been copied again and again.

What happened to Yost's commitment to "athletics for all?" Yost insisted again and again that education required training for the body as much as for the mind. His advocacy convinced the Michigan faculty to require physical education as an integral part of the undergraduate experience. Many universities followed suit. However, all such requirements have been discontinued at most schools today. The University of Michigan hasn't required course hours in physical education for graduation since 1969, but in recent years many have come to recognize the poor physical conditioning that exists among the American public. The state of Michigan itself has some of the poorest public health statistics in the nation. Michiganians are too fat, smoke too much, exercise too little. Should there be a place in education for mandatory physical education? Yost thought so, but his influence has somehow been lost over the decades. However, few would argue today that he was wrong.

Wolverine fans like to say that the Michigan football program recruits not only the state of Michigan and not only the Midwest, but the entire nation. If one travels out of the Midwest in any direction, Michigan seems to be the Big Ten school that garners the most attention. Michigan athletic paraphernalia can be found in sports stores anywhere in the country, even overseas. Yost pointed out in 1923 that 40 percent of the undergraduates at the University of Michigan came from out of state. That number remains true today and is far higher than for any other Big Ten school. Why is this? Part of the reason is the legacy of Fielding H. Yost.

In 1925, an enterprising journalist asked Yost if he would list the places he had given speeches in the previous four years. Yost replied,

> It would be hard to give you complete information regarding the places I have talked the past four years.
>
> Boston, New York, Princeton, Lawrenceville, Philadelphia, Washington, Syracuse, Buffalo, Lawrence University, Pittsburgh, Morgantown, Fairmont, Clarksburg, Cincinnati, Columbus, Cleveland, Lima, Toledo, Nashville, Atlanta, St. Louis, Des Moines, Chicago, Milwaukee, Madison, St. Paul, Minneapolis, Cedar Rapids, Omaha, Lincoln, Kansas City, Denver, Salt Lake City, Los Angeles, San Francisco, Portland, Eugene, Corvallis, Seattle, Spokane, University of Montana.
>
> The National Education Association, Indianapolis, Culver Military, Howe Military Academy and almost every town with a high school in Michigan.
>
> In many of these places I have spoken several times.[466]

During his trip to the west coast in the spring of 1923, Yost estimated that he gave nearly 40 talks to 23,000 high school and university men as well as alumni. The coach was a very sought-after speaker, and witness after witness testified to the rapt attention he held from his audiences. Almost always, he focused on young people in high school and college. His message was one of the importance of sportsmanship, citizenship, duty, honor, commitment, and the need for physical education. Everywhere he went he promoted the University of Michigan. To many people in the United States, Yost and the University of Michigan were one and the same. He was a great roving ambassador for the university, and that legacy still percolates across this country.

Yost's selfless devotion to the University of Michigan, a personal commitment he maintained as either coach or athletic director

[466] Board in Control, Box 7, August 1925

for 40 years, from 1901 to 1941, is duplicated at no other school. In the years from 1921 to 1928, Yost built the nation's first field house, the nation's largest intramural facility for men, one of the few intramural facilities anywhere for women, and the nation's greatest football stadium. He purchased the ice coliseum for the hockey team and the land necessary for one of the first college-owned golf courses. He achieved all that while the athletic coffers were bulging with football income, but in all that time and with all that effort, he never requested a raise in salary. He took home a paltry $8500 per year. In the fall of 1927, the president of the Detroit alumni club appealed to his colleagues for contributions for an automobile to present to Yost the night before the dedication game. The president wrote,

> You know how much abuse and unjust criticism the coach has suffered…The coach has made a tremendous financial sacrifice in staying at Michigan at a salary with

Photo courtesy of Bentley Historical Library

*Yost and the Packard given to him by alumni the night before the dedication game. Photo taken in front of the original Michigan Stadium press box.*

which he could hardly pay his living expenses. Recently he was offered $50,000 a year to act as vice-president of a New York bank. He refused the offer.[467]

On his birthday in 1927, Yost told a reporter about a very touching letter he had received from his aged mother. Yost was born in a log cabin, the oldest of five children. His mother wrote that, "there have been many ups and downs, joys and sorrows, since we lived in the old log cabin. Most of my children are too far away to come often to visit me, but I can say they never gave me trouble. I am really proud of them. My son, don't worry about me. I want the Lord to so deal with your soul that you may always do your duty."[468] Yost related the contents of this letter and then said, "I hope that I can always say to her that I have always done my duty toward Michigan."[469]

*Yost on the stadium construction site*

---

[467] Board in Control, Box 10, October 1927 (1)
[468] Yost papers, Box 7, Scrapbook, 40 Years at Michigan
[469] Yost papers, Box 7, Scrapbook, 40 Years at Michigan

In a speech to alumni many years later, Yost verbalized his deeply felt credo.

> What you remember as the Michigan Spirit is still throbbingly alive. This spirit is based upon a *deathless loyalty* to Michigan and all her ways; an *enthusiasm* that makes it second nature for Michigan men to spread the gospel of their university to the far corners of the earth; and a *conviction* that no where is there a better university than this Michigan of ours.[470]

One needs only to walk the athletic campus at the University of Michigan today to recognize the duty Yost performed for Michigan. The next time there is a home game at Michigan Stadium, walk through any portal and gaze upon the immense celebration that is maize and blue football. Is there an outstanding debt of gratitude owed Fielding H. Yost that generations of Wolverines can never repay? Unquestionably. But no doubt it would be reward enough for him to see the joy expressed by countless fans as they enter the great stadium on any given football Saturday. It is always the largest crowd to watch a game anywhere in America. This is Yost's house, The Big House.

---

[470] Yost papers, B0x #7, Scrapbook, 40 Years at Michigan